D1241923

Productivity Gains Through Worklife Improvement

Productivity Gains Through Worklife Improvements

Edward M. Glaser

HARCOURT BRACE JOVANOVICH
New York and London

HF
5549.5
.J63
G57

Library of Congress Cataloging in Publication Data
Glaser, Edward M
  Productivity gains through worklife improvement.
  Bibliography: p.
  Includes index.
  1. Job satisfaction. 2. Labor productivity—United States. 3. Labor productivity. I. Title.
HF5549.5.J63G57   658.31'42   76-2044
ISBN 0-15-800095-1

First edition

B C D E

Contents

v

411032

III. Problems 195

Preface

In the United States today, and in other countries around the world, there is a growing concern about the overall quality of people's lives. One of the strongest currents of this concern is the new interest in improving the quality of life at work.

Some research coupled with case-report evidence suggests that improvements in the work climate and structure—such as increasing career opportunities and inviting employees to have a significant degree of influence in decisions made about the design, organization, and rewards of their work—frequently lead to greater productivity as well as to greater job satisfaction. People perform better when the work situation encourages ego-involvement in shaping the tasks they are asked to perform, and manifests facilitative interest in the advancement aspirations of individual employees.

Economists are in general agreement that increasing productivity in the United States is one of the more effective ways to fight inflation and to keep our products competitive in the world market because if output efficiency can be increased without concomitant increase in labor or other resources utilized, the price of the product or service can be reduced. There is evidence that redesign of work systems to improve the quality of life at work can—at least under certain conditions—yield greater productivity, greater job satisfaction, and enhance organizational effectiveness. Thus, there are important reasons why information about such systemic programs should be carefully examined and analyzed. "Examine carefully" is what this state-of-the-art report attempts to do. It will present evidence from the reality of experience, as well as from research studies, with regard to the conditions seemingly necessary for success. It will also discuss the challenges, criticisms, and possible negative aspects that should be considered before venturing to undertake such a program.

This report does not in itself pretend to constitute basic research, but it does present and attempt to integrate a good deal of relevant research. Most of the case-study material drawn together here has been published elsewhere, but in scattered places and varied forms. The commentaries on most of the cases are original, as are the Edward Glaser & Associates guidelines for introducing a systemic job redesign or quality of worklife improvement program.

In the foreword to *Work in America*,[1] a special HEW Task Force Report on the health, education, and welfare problems involved in the workday world, Elliot L. Richardson, then Secretary of HEW, summed up the wide scope of any study of worklife:

Most of the people in the United States will work, or have worked, forty or more years. To be concerned about the worker is to be concerned about the aged, who, through their labors, brought this Nation to its present level of affluence and well-being; about the youth, who have yet to choose from among a thousand occupations; . . . about the new role of women in our society; and about the rest of us who depart from our homes and return and who seek to fill the time in between with meaningful and well-recompensed activities.

It should be added that concern with the quality of life at work also involves the companies that hire the workers, the unions that often represent them, and the customers they serve. And, as the

[1] Cambridge, Mass.: The MIT Press, 1972.

participants of the Forty-third American Assembly ("The Changing World of Work") at Arden House in November 1973 concluded in their final report, "improving the place, the organization, and the nature of work can lead to better work performance and a better quality of life in the society."[2]

[2] J. M. Rosow (Ed.), *The Worker and the Job: Coping with Change* (Englewood Cliffs, N.J.: Prentice-Hall, 1974).

ACKNOWLEDGMENTS

This manuscript has been intensively revised and expanded from a study carried out in 1973–74 under a grant from the Office of Manpower Research and Development, U.S. Department of Labor, entitled "Improving the Quality of Worklife . . . And in the Process, Improving Productivity." I am indebted to the Department for support and for helpful critiques from Judah Drob, chief, Division of Research and Development Utilization, and Dr. Robert Foster, acting chief, Social Psychology Research Group.

I am also indebted to Dr. Thomas Backer, Dr. David Berger, and Ms. Molly Lewin, Human Interaction Research Institute colleagues, for their valuable criticisms and suggestions.

Mrs. Elsa Porter, director of Clearinghouse on Productivity, Bureau of Policies and Standards, U.S. Civil Service Commission; Mr. Terence Jackson, assistant to the executive director, National Commission on Productivity and Work Quality; Ms. Lynne Lipsitz, work environment improvement coordinator, Social Security Administration, and Mr. Ted Mills, director, National Quality of Work Center, have provided useful information regarding recent innovative programs initiated by government agencies to improve productivity through various types of job enrichment or other quality of worklife programs.

Professors Louis Davis and James Taylor, Graduate School of Management, University of California, Los Angeles, provided some of the case material reported herein.

To all of these and to persons from a number of companies whose quality of worklife efforts are summarized in this report, I make grateful acknowledgment for cooperation and help. My thanks also go to Ms. Arden Sinclair and Ms. Nancy Gordon for their infinite patience and perspicacious suggestions as they shepherded this manuscript through its many retypings.

EDWARD M. GLASER

Orientation

Background

Contemporary human society, especially in modern industrialized countries, consists of many interlocking environments. The traditional agricultural way of life, arguably one interlocking environment, had the kind of productive and consumptive coherence mirrored in its major unit, the extended family. Although there are few if any pure examples left of the traditional agricultural society, there are many countries in the world today that are in the process of modifying and extending previously traditional agricultural communities into social orders in which mechanization not only changes the way farming is done but also introduces the challenge and benefits of industrialization.

One of the things historians report about the Industrial Revolution in nineteenth-century Europe and America is that the men and women who left the farms and went into the mills were often disoriented by the experience and found the change of roles that factory work imposed difficult and distasteful. The routine of agriculture, of course, was a tyranny of its own, but it was a different, a more familiar and familial tyranny from that imposed by the factory. Between the beginnings of industrialization in the Western world and its present conditions lie nearly two centuries of complex and astonishing development. The worklife of the American farmer or French peasant 150 years ago was a fairly independent one. The farmer and his family understood what they had to do; their work roles were clear. For them, training was absorbed from the environment from childhood on. The skills were diverse and every adult had a large repertory of them. Tasks like sowing, harvesting, storage, and butchering were often cooperative. Decisions were participatory, in that the elements of the decisions were clear to everyone, though final authority often rested with the head of the family.

The world of work in a modern industrial setting is utterly different. For most men and women working within it, the old preindustrial world has left no trace. People's worklives today are spent in an environment of complex interdependence characterized by productive processes in which for efficiency's sake the tasks are usually broken down into single operations repeated over and over throughout the workday. This is not always the case; a single employee may sometimes perform several steps in a larger productive process. What does characterize most modern work situations is that employees do not see both the beginning and end of what they do. It is difficult for them to feel that they have *made* anything tangible or completed a total process as a result of what they are engaged in. Thus, modern industry characteristically creates a situation in which the morale of the employee is threatened by the impersonality of the work situation itself. Management and organized labor have been aware of this condition for years. So have the behavioral sciences. It is from this conjunction of awareness that the contemporary interest in improving the quality of worklife derives.

What Constitutes a Quality of Worklife (QWL) Program?

The term "quality of worklife" recently has come to mean more than job security, good working conditions, adequate and fair compensation—more even than equal employment opportunity or "job enlargement." A working definition of QWL suggested by Wood, Rasmussen and Lawler is: "Quality of working life research is concerned with how the relationship between individuals and features of their physical, social and economic work environment affects those on-and-off the job attitudes and behaviors that society considers to be important."* The absolutely *essential* component of any QWL program is real and ever-present opportunity for individuals or task groups at any level to influence their working environments, to have some say over what goes on in connection with their work. This, in turn, requires organizational climate and structure that really encourage, facilitate, and reward questions, challenges, or suggestions related to improving the existing *modus operandi* in any way. It also requires expeditious, respectful, and appropriate responses to such inputs.

Thus, a style of management that invites participation or consultation from members of the workforce on matters that affect them and with regard to which they might have some pertinent ideas, is an essential condition for a QWL program. It is this style that tends to increase the psychological meaningfulness of work. At the same time it provides a springboard from which a large variety of other improvements in the design, structure, and organization of work can be developed.

Systematic feedback regarding progress toward agreed-upon objectives is another very important ingredient. So is a work setup, if feasible, that provides opportunity for employees to coordinate around their jobs in small, naturally cohesive groups.

Some of the subsidiary elements involved in programs designed to enhance QWL are:

• Achieving sustained commitment from management to an open, nondefensive style of operation which includes sincerely inviting employees to speak up regarding problems or opportunities. A related element is provision of a practicable means for having

---

* M. Wood, J. E. Rasmussen, and E. E. Lawler, *Federally Sponsored Research on the Quality of Working Life: Planning, Support, and Products.* (Seattle: Battelle Memorial Institute, Human Affairs Research Centers, 1975), 23.

members of the workforce participate in the refinement and implementation of promising suggestions.

- Establishing a work environment that encourages continuous learning, training, and active interest regarding both the job and the product or service to which the job contributes. Such an environment enables an employee to use and develop his personal skills and knowledge, which in turn affects his involvement, his self-esteem, and the challenge obtained from the work itself.

- Making the job itself more challenging by structuring it so that an individual (or small work team) can "self-manage" and feel responsible for a significant, identifiable output if that kind of responsibility is desired.

- Affording opportunities for continued growth; that is, opportunities to advance in organizational or career terms.

- Training of supervisors to equip them to function effectively in this less directive, more collaborative style.

- Breaking down the traditional status barriers between management and production or support personnel—achieving an atmosphere of open communication and trust between management and the workforce.

- Providing not only feedback with regard to results achieved, and recognition for good results, but also providing financial incentives such as cost-savings–sharing where feasible.

- Seeking to select personnel who can be motivated, under appropriate conditions, to "give a damn" about striving for excellence in task performance.

- Evaluating and analyzing results, including failures, leading to revised efforts toward continual improvement.

Harvard professor Richard E. Walton[1] offers eight conceptual categories as a framework for describing the salient features of

[1] R. E. Walton, "Improving the Quality of Worklife," *Harvard Business Review,* May–June 1974, 12ff. Used with permission.

quality of worklife; these categories overlap to some extent with those noted above. UCLA Professor James C. Taylor proposes eleven quality of worklife criteria, chiefly from the perspective of the individual.[2] Most of these criteria are similar to Walton's categories but are stated as outcome variables that could also function in behavioral terms, such as alienation, self-esteem, control, and influence exercised on the job. Such outcome variables make cause-and-effect case studies or experimental settings more susceptible to evaluation. Taylor draws a useful distinction between work-system restructuring, which begins with a technical whole or task process from which human assignments are made, and job enrichment, which starts with an individual job and then proceeds to redesign that job.

Not all relevant categories or factors need be present to constitute the beginning of a meaningful QWL improvement program. If management did nothing more than start by sincerely inviting the people involved in a particular task to suggest ways to improve their operation and overall work situation; if these ideas were received and considered in a spirit of appreciation; if the employees then were asked to participate in studying the feasibility of each suggestion and recommending appropriate means of implementing those that survive such consideration, the quality of life at work probably would be enhanced. Further, there is evidence that productivity often would increase in the process. And still further, a style of management practice that manifests concern about basic factors such as job security, good working conditions, good pay, financial incentives, career opportunities, and job enrichment— a style which gives employees an opportunity to have a voice in matters that affect them—is entirely consistent with meticulously controlled operations. Controlled, that is, in the interest of efficiency, effectiveness, quality assurance, customer service, profitability, and high employee morale.

Such an approach is not to be confused with some abstract sociopolitical concept of "democratic management." Managers who

[2] "Concepts and Problems in Studies of the Quality of Working Life," Graduate School of Management, UCLA, December 1973.

evince concern with QWL considerations continue to be accountable for carrying out their other responsibilities effectively. If they learn that inviting consultation or "collective wisdom" in appropriate kinds of problem solving or decision making from the persons they supervise is likely to lead to better quality and acceptance of those decisions, then they simply better become managers.

A QWL program is not proposed as a panacea for the various problems encountered in managing the human organization—or for any other multifaceted, complex set of problems. There *are* no known, sustained panaceas. But there do seem to be better and poorer arrangements of work. The kinds of QWL efforts to be described in this book, pitfalls notwithstanding, seem to offer evidence of some *relatively* more effective and satisfying ways of integrating human effort toward the accomplishment of given tasks —if certain important conditions are present.

The experience of the Kaiser Steel Company offers a case in point. In early 1973, three months after management gave employees at the Kaiser steel mill in Fontana, California, responsibility for saving the plant, which was operating at a loss and was threatened with shutdown because of inability to compete with Japanese imports, there was an astonishing 32.1 percent increase in productivity. The *Los Angeles Times* quoted one worker's observations on reasons for this jump:

Look, before, nobody paid any attention to a guy and so he figures why in hell should he pay any attention to the pipe. . . . People finally paid attention to the men, the boss started listening, the man on the next machine started looking around, and pretty soon everybody got into the swing of things.[3]

A Complementary Federal Government Program

In late 1972, the U.S. Department of Commerce's National Commission on Productivity launched the Quality of Work Pro-

[3] A full report on the Kaiser/Fontana situation begins on page 42.

gram (QOWP).[4] The program's purpose was to stimulate and evaluate management-union-employee collaboration in experiments to improve the workplace and thereby better utilize human —along with technological—resources. It was hoped that productivity would increase as well.

QOWP was set up to fund a limited number of demonstration projects in companies and municipalities. The government limits itself to the bringing in and initial financing of consultant teams that are expert in the fields of motivation, work structure, and organizational change. If, after six months, the participating managements and unions wish to continue the project, they must match QOWP funds for the ensuing 12 months as proof of their commitment to the project's success. At the end of 18 months, the full demonstration period, all government-supported QOWP funding is terminated. If the experiment is continued thereafter, the decision—and financial support for it—is that of the participants.

Each QOWP project belongs equally to the management and to union and worker participants, since the expectation is that all concerned will benefit. Each demonstration will be evaluated to document the results and the conditions that seem to make for project success or failure. Upon completion of this first series of experiments, outcome data will be made available.

Changing Orientations toward Worklife

In the United States and other technologically developed countries, objectives and values seem to be in the process of change. During the nineteenth century, the goal of economic

---

[4] On March 18, 1974, the author was notified that QOWP, authorized for continuation by the Senate, had failed to pass the House. It is dead, therefore, insofar as *government* participation is concerned. Its *work,* however, is continuing under the name National Quality of Work Center (NQWC), Washington, D.C., with funding from other sources, and under the same director, namely, Mr. Ted Mills. NQWC is affiliated with the Institute for Social Research/University of Michigan.

emancipation gradually was superseded by that of political liberty. Next came the quest for a higher standard of living, coupled in recent years with a growing concern for social justice. Now added to this list of goals is the demand to enhance the quality of life at work, which has recently manifested itself with greater sharpness.

Studs Terkel, writing on "Work without Meaning," describes the plight of the jobholder in these terms:

[To write] about work is, by the very nature of the subject, [to write] about violence—to the spirit as well as to the body. It is about ulcers as well as accidents, about shouting matches as well as fistfights, about nervous breakdowns as well as kicking the dog around. It is, above all (or beneath all), about daily humiliations. To survive the day is triumph enough for the walking wounded among the great many of us. . . .

There are, of course, the happy few who find a savor in their daily job: the Indiana stonemason, who looks upon his work and sees that it is good; the Chicago piano tuner, who seeks and finds the sound that delights; the bookbinder, who saves a piece of history; the Brooklyn fireman, who saves a piece of life. But don't these satisfactions, like Jude's hunger for knowledge, tell us more about the person than about his task? Perhaps. Nonetheless, there is a common attribute here: *a meaning to their work well over and beyond the reward of the paycheck.*

For the many, there is a hardly concealed discontent. The blue-collar blues is no more bitterly sung than the white-collar moan. "I'm a machine," says the spot-welder. "I'm caged," says the bank teller, and echoes the hotel clerk. "I'm a mule," says the steelworker. "A monkey can do what I do," says the receptionist. "I'm less than a farm implement," says the migrant worker. "I'm an object," says the high-fashion model. Blue collar and white call upon the identical phrase: "I'm a robot." "There is nothing to talk about," the young accountant despairingly enunciates. . . .

As the automated pace of our jobs wipes out name and face—and, in many instances, feeling—there is a sacrilegious question being asked these days. To earn one's bread by the sweat of one's brow has always been the lot of mankind. At least, ever since Eden's slothful couple was served with an eviction notice. The scriptural precept was never doubted, not out loud. No matter how demeaning the task, no matter how it dulls the senses and breaks the spirit, one must work. Or else.

Lately there has been a *questioning of this "work ethic," especially by the young.* Strangely enough, it has touched off profound grievances in others, hitherto devout, silent, and anonymous. Unexpected precincts are being heard from in a show of discontent. Communiqués from the assembly line are frequent and alarming: absenteeism. On the evening bus, the tense, pinched faces of young file clerks and elderly secretaries tell us more than we care to know. On the expressways, middle management men pose without grace behind their wheels as they flee city and job.

There are other means of showing their attitude, too. Inchoately, sullenly, it appears in slovenly work, in the put-down of craftsmanship. A farm equipment worker in Moline complains that the careless worker who turns out more that is bad is better regarded than the careful craftsman who turns out less that is good.[5]

Concern with life on the job is not new. The increased ferment of union activities in the 1930s and 1940s as a result of labor legislation and collective bargaining led to improved conditions. Even before that, labor was vigorously protesting management attempts to change the work environment. In a 1915 study[6] requested by Congress, University of Chicago professor Robert F. Hoxie reported how the unions, particularly the machinists, were fighting scientific management techniques. So-called scientific management, labor complained, condemned the workers to a monotonous routine, destroyed their creativity, and drove them to the brink of nervous exhaustion.

Today's aspirations for an improved worklife, however, go well beyond continuing efforts to improve benefits and working conditions. Workers are now questioning traditional managerial prerogatives. They seek, as UAW vice president Irving Bluestone puts it, "more meaningful ways and means to participate in the

---

[5] S. Terkel, *Working: People Talk About What They Do All Day and How They Feel About What They Do.* Copyright © 1972, 1974 by Studs Terkel (New York: Pantheon Books, 1974), xi–xii. Reprinted by permission of Pantheon Books, a division of Random House, Inc.

[6] R. F. Hoxie, *Scientific Management and Labor* (New York: Appleton, 1920).

decision-making process that directly or indirectly affects their welfare."

This new questioning is not limited to workers. Cornell professor Jaroslav Vanek writes: "The quest of men to participate in the determination and decision making of activities in which they are actively involved is one of the most important sociopolitical phenomena of our times."[7]

Emerging countries, for example, once dominated by stronger nations, have demanded independence, hoping in part to fulfill aspirations for improved standards of living and greater social justice. College students have won a greater degree of self-determination in the administration of the education system—sometimes even taking part in policy formulation. Minority groups have fought for equal opportunities. Youth has gained a greater degree of freedom from parents and other adult authorities. Citizen groups and environmentalists have called for more corporate responsibility, at the expense of profits if necessary. Many companies are responding with thoughtful plans and tangible actions.

Over a large part of the world, the style of behavioral response to personal or group feelings of frustration has changed discernibly from a fatalistic acceptance of one's lot in life to a thrust for change through confrontation politics. Ever since Adam bit into that apple, people have experienced discontent and dissatisfaction. Now an increasing percentage want to express this, often militantly. At the same time, the dominant powers-that-be seem reluctant to risk direct confrontation. Negotiate, bargain, and—if necessary—accommodate tends to be the order of the day.

Another force to be reckoned with is a rising level of expectations for a higher standard of living, especially among American workers and consumers, coupled with a rising educational level of the workforce. (The percentage of the labor force with some college experience will double between 1960 and 1985.) In earlier times a worker felt lucky just to have a job, since others were waiting at the gate ready and eager to take his place. Nowadays people demand more.

[7] From *The Participatory Economy: An Evolutionary Hypothesis and a Developmental Strategy.* Unpublished study, Cornell University, 1972.

At one major auto company, for example, 4,000 newly hired workers did not stay through the first day on the job.[8] And this was in a recent year (1969) when local unemployment rates were between 8 and 9 percent. This would not have happened in the thirties, no matter what was wrong with working conditions. As Eli Ginzberg has observed, "the combination of more education, less fear of unemployment and higher family income is loosening the monolithic relationship that existed for so long between people and work. In an earlier day men had to work in order to eat. That is less true today."[9]

The Organization of Work and What Employees Want

As the organization of human effort at work becomes more specialized and compartmentalized, the worker grows even more remote from the end result of production. Only a few individuals— artists, writers, craftsmen—can turn out a complete product or service without a good deal of dependence upon the contributions of others.

Usually only an integrated pattern of component activities provides finished goods or services. And the task of integrating a complex pattern requires management. That, in turn, calls for the assumption of managerial responsibility, which traditionally has taken the form of more or less continuous supervision and control, thereby minimizing the independence of workers.

Specialization is almost unavoidable in a technological society. And it must be remembered that specialization has enabled us to obtain many things that most of us value and otherwise could not have. But, as Aristotle observed, "Vice may be defined as the excess or deficiency of that which in adequate amounts would constitute virtue." In the pursuit of mass-production techniques, our society also has generated simplified jobs that so fragment tasks

---

[8] C. R. Price, *New Directions in the World of Work.* A Conference Report. Kalamazoo, Mich.: W. E. Upjohn Institute for Employment Research, 1971, 9.

[9] J. M. Rosow (Ed.), *The Worker and the Job: Coping with Change* (Englewood Cliffs, N.J.: Prentice-Hall, Inc., 1974), 70.

that many employees find their work unfit for either the human spirit or the human body.[10]

Added to the trend toward restrictive, repetitive specialization is the fact that many managers understandably see the individual employee as nothing more than a replaceable production component in the impersonal system. Obviously, such a depersonalized view of the individual does not tap his potential for ego-involved commitment on the job.

Thus we have the ingredients for deterioration of satisfaction: boredom, alienation, and hostility on the part of many workers who want to do a good job and want to feel ego-involved. These are factors related to low productivity, poor workmanship, increasing absenteeism and sometimes sabotage on the part of a growing number of workers. Some economists, however, would argue: "not proven."[11]

As already noted, in today's world there is a growing number of alternatives to unsatisfying employment: living on welfare or unemployment benefits, parental largesse, or that street tactic called hustling. Still, American youth has not altogether rejected the work ethic. In a 1971 survey of college students conducted by Daniel Yankelovich,[12] 61 percent expressed interest in a practical

[10] It is important to note at this point, however, that some individuals prefer routine tasks which they feel they can handle with no strain and little pressure of responsibility. As M. G. Wolf points out ("The Relationship of Content and Context Factors to Attitudes toward Company and Job," *Personnel Psychology,* 1967, 20, 121–132), whether a person perceives a job situation as an opportunity for gratification of his psychological needs would depend in part on the level of need that the individual is seeking to satisfy. Thus, for an individual who is trying to satisfy his safety and belongingness needs, the additional complexities and responsibilities inherent in working under certain kinds of job enrichment programs may create an increase in emotional stress rather than constitute reward; whereas individuals who are seeking self-esteem through achievement and independence, or self-actualization, may thrive and blossom under job enrichment conditions.

[11] R. J. Flanagan, G. Strauss, and L. Ulman, *Worker Discontent and Work Place Behavior* (Reprint No. 388). Berkeley: University of California Institute of Industrial Relations, 1974.

[12] D. Yankelovich, *The Changing Values on Campus* (New York: Washington Square Press, March 1972).

career orientation, and 75 percent believed collecting welfare would be immoral for a person who could work. Only 30 percent said they would welcome less emphasis in the United States on hard work. The work ethic does appear to be changing, however. Among *non-college* youth—the majority—Yankelovich interprets his study data as indicating that:

Today's young people are less fearful of economic insecurity than in the past. They want interesting and challenging work, but they assume that their employers cannot—or will not—provide it. By their own say-so, they are inclined to take "less crap" than older workers. They are not as automatically loyal to the organization as their fathers, and they are far more aware of their own needs and rights. Nor are they as awed by organizational and hierarchical authority. Being less fearful of "discipline" and the threat of losing their jobs, they feel free to express their discontent in myriad ways, from fooling around on the job to sabotage. They are better educated than their parents, even without a college degree. They want more freedom and will bargain hard to keep their options open. A bitter fight over the right to refuse mandatory overtime, for example, does not mean that young workers will not work overtime. It does mean that the freedom to say "no" assumes symbolic significance as an expression of freedom and autonomy. Moreover, if the work itself is not meaningful to them, they will opt for "thirty and out" forms of retirement, shorter work weeks, frequent absenteeism, more leisure, and other methods for cutting back and cutting down on their job commitment.[13]

Further evidence that people now want more satisfaction from the job and better resources to get the job done can be derived from a 1971 survey of working conditions.[14] The survey, carried

[13] D. Yankelovich, "The Meaning of Work." In J. M. Rosow (Ed.), *The Worker and the Job: Coping with Change.* © 1974 The American Assembly, Columbia University (Englewood Cliffs, N.J.: Prentice-Hall, Inc., 1974). Used by permission of the publisher.

[14] Survey Research Center, University of Michigan, *Survey of Working Conditions* (Washington, D.C.: U.S. Department of Labor, Employment Standards Administration, August 1971). Obtainable from the Superintendent of Documents, U.S. Government Printing Office, Washington, D.C. 20402. Stock no.: 2916-0001. Price: $3.50.

out by the University of Michigan, asked a representative 1,533 American workers at all occupational levels to weigh various facets of their jobs and report whether each item was: (a) very important, (b) somewhat important, (c) not too important, or (d) not at all important. The findings are shown in Table 1.[15]

If work conditions are growing in importance, it does not follow that income is irrelevant. In a study of what elements of work needed improvement most, union leaders ranked pay first and job content aspects lower.[16] As Dr. Edward Lawler noted in a paper presented at a symposium in Chicago in November 1974:

. . . Over the last fifty years a great deal of research has been done that supports the view that pay is an important influence on behavior. As suggested by the Western Electric studies (a series of famous studies in the 1930s conducted at the Hawthorne plant of Western Electric Company) and described in Roethlisberger and Dickson, *Management and the Worker* [New York: Wiley Science Editions, 1964 (originally published 1939)], *perceptions* (by employees) of the relationship between

[15] While these survey data are interesting, the importance ratings shown in Table 1 are unrealistic in that the "typical worker" is a statistical composite of many workers with distinct demographic and occupational characteristics. These different characteristics are in turn associated with differences in importance ratings—and it is possible to exaggerate these differences. The fact that blue-collar workers assign greater importance to "financial rewards" and less importance to "challenge" than white-collar workers does *not* mean that blue-collar workers are exclusively motivated by pay and white-collar workers by interesting work. Such an inference would be patronizing, and contradicted by available data, in its assumption that workers are incapable of motivational complexities or of being attracted to work for more than a single reason.

Also, as Dr. Edward Lawler suggests ("What Do Employees Really Want?" paper presented at APA Convention, Montreal, 1973), "it is not possible to learn how important job factors are to employees by asking them to rate the importance of some set of job factors. The evidence clearly shows that the importance ratings . . . are subject to so many biasing effects that they are useless for this purpose. . . . However, . . . ratings . . . can be used to determine if (say) pay is more important to person A than to person B or to group A than to group B."

[16] H. L. Sheppard and N. Q. Herrick, *Where Have All the Robots Gone?* (New York: Free Press, 1972).

TABLE 1

Percentage of Workers Rating Job Facets as "Very Important" to Them

JOB FACET	ALL WORKERS (N = 1,500)[a]		WHITE-COLLAR WORKERS (N = 730)[a]		BLUE-COLLAR WORKERS (N = 685)[a, b]	
	%	Rank Order	%	Rank Order	%	Rank Order
Resources						
I receive enough help and equipment to get the job done.	68	2	64	4	72	1
I have enough information to get the job done.	68	2	67	3	68	2
My responsibilities are clearly defined.	61	7	58	7	65	4
My supervisor is competent in doing his job.	61	7	60	6	63	6
Financial Rewards						
The pay is good.	64	4	57	8	72	1
The job security is good.	62	6	54	10	72	1
My fringe benefits are good.	51	10	40	14	62	7
Challenge						
The work is interesting.	73	1	78	1	68	2
I have enough authority to do my job.	65	3	67	3	64	5

Table 1 (*continued*)

JOB FACET	ALL WORKERS ($N = 1,500$)[a]		WHITE-COLLAR WORKERS ($N = 730$)[a]		BLUE-COLLAR WORKERS ($N = 685$)[a, b]	
	%	Rank Order	%	Rank Order	%	Rank Order
I have an opportunity to develop my special abilities.	64	4	69	2	57	9
I can see the results of my work.	62	6	60	6	64	5
I am given a chance to do the things I do best.	54	8	54	10	55	10
I am given a lot of freedom to decide how I do my work.	53	9	56	9	50	11
The problems I am asked to solve are hard enough.	30	16	31	17	29	17
Relations with Co-workers						
My co-workers are friendly and helpful.	63	5	61	5	67	3
I am given a lot of chances to make friends.	44	12	39	15	49	12
Comfort						
I have enough time to get the job done.	54	8	48	11	60	8
The hours are good.	51	10	41	13	62	7
Travel to and from work is convenient.	46	11	42	12	50	11

Physical surroundings are pleasant.	40	13	32	16	48	13
I am free from conflicting demands that other people make of me.	33	14	26	19	40	14
I can forget about my personal problems.	31	15	26	18	35	15
I am not asked to do excessive amounts of work.	23	17	16	20	30	16

[a] Base *N*'s vary slightly from row to row because of missing data.
[b] Farm workers have been excluded.
Source: Robert P. Quinn, the survey senior author, Survey Research Center, University of Michigan.

pay and performance are crucial in determining motivation, and feelings of satisfaction are crucial in determining absenteeism and turnover.

There is no inconsistency between the finding that employees' motivation is influenced by their perception of "pay fairness" for given types of work and given levels of task performance, and the observation that many workers also are finding it important to be allowed to have some control over their job environment, to feel that they and their work are important—the twin ingredients of self-esteem.

Worker Motivation, Satisfaction, and Effectiveness

Three decades ago, Harvard professor Gordon Allport, in what is now regarded as a classic paper, nicely expressed a key psychological consideration bearing upon the quality of worklife.

When the work situation in which the individual finds himself realistically engages the status-seeking motive—when the individual is busily engaged in using his talents, understanding his work and having pleasant social relations with foreman and fellow worker—then he is, as the saying goes, "identified" with his job. He likes his work; he is absorbed in it; he is productive. In McGregor's term, he is industrially *active*. That is to say, he is participant.

When on the other hand, the situation is such that the status-motive has no chance of gearing itself into the external cycles of events, when the individual goes through motions that he does not find meaningful, when he does not really participate—then comes rebellion against authority, complaints, griping, gossip, rumor, scapegoating and disaffection of all sorts. The job satisfaction is low. In McGregor's term, under such circumstances the individual is not active; he is industrially *reactive*.

. . . The problem before us is whether the immense amount of reactivity shown in business offices and factories, in federal bureaus and schools, can be reduced. . . . We are learning some of the conditions in which reactivity does decline. . . . Patronizing handouts and wage-incentive systems alone do not succeed. Opportunities for consultation on personal problems are . . . found to be important; and group decision, open discussion and the retraining of leaders in accordance with democratic standards yield remarkable results. . . . In other words, a person ceases to be reactive and contrary in respect to a desirable course of conduct only when he himself has had a hand in declaring that course of conduct to be desirable. Such findings add up to the simple proposition that people must have a hand in saving themselves; they cannot and will not be saved from the outside.[17]

The question is how to translate Allport's insights into practice in the world of work. How, in other words, do we best utilize and facilitate the development of human resources?

Looking at the matter of human motivation from a different perspective, Dr. Richard Shore of the U.S. Department of Labor, in an unpublished (1972) paper called "Worker Motivation, Satisfaction and Effectiveness: A Rationale and Strategy," asks:

[17] G. W. Allport, "The Psychology of Participation," *Psychological Review,* 1945, *52,* 117–132. Copyright 1945 by the American Psychological Association. Reprinted by permission.

"(1) How prevalent is discontent within the society, what varied consequences does it have for the functioning of economic and social institutions, and (2) is it becoming more prevalent, and is it likely to have more profound consequences in the future?"

One piece of evidence comes from the answers to a recurring question in the periodic Gallup Poll: "On the whole, would you say you are satisfied or dissatisfied with the work you do?" On the basis of nationwide interviews with 1,520 adults 18 and older, the questions produced the following results:

	Satisfied	Dissatisfied	"Don't Know"
July 1963	85%	11%	4%
September 1965	82	13	5
November 1966	86	8	6
April 1969	87	7	6
December 1971	84	9	7
January 1973	77	11	12

Note that between April 1969 and January 1973 there was a 10 percent drop in respondents' assertions regarding their satisfaction (whatever they meant by "satisfied" at the times they answered the question). Gallup's analysis of the survey findings shows that although the recent drop in job satisfaction (or it may be the increase in articulating dissatisfaction) has been greatest among blacks and young persons, some decline has been recorded for all major groups since 1969. As noted by Quinn, Staines, and McCullough (Survey Research Center, University of Michigan), however, a major limitation of the Gallup data is that

. . . The satisfaction question was asked of all people sampled, not only those who worked for pay, but the unemployed, housewives, retired people, and students as well—in other words, all people willing to comment on any "work" they did. Some adjustment is therefore required in the Gallup data if they are to be used to document any longitudinal trends in *job* satisfaction or to be compared with data obtained from the Research Center surveys. Because the Gallup surveys did not identify subjects according to pay status, the data could not be re-analyzed to yield descriptive statistics on those who work for pay. To get data on this group, the Gallup survey results were reanalyzed using a restricted sample—males, aged 21 through 65—a large portion of whom work for pay.[18] [See Figure 1, which gives the re-analyzed data as presented by the Quinn-Staines-McCullough monograph.]

Complex issues such as what may be involved in attitudes toward work and life cannot, of course, be fathomed by simplistic survey-poll questions that do not probe the full flavor of reasons behind a response. (The downtrend in job satisfaction since 1969 reported in Gallup's overall figures, for example, is paralleled by dissatisfaction in three other areas: housing, income, and education. Between 1949 and 1969, satisfaction with housing, income, and education was on the increase—a period when job satisfaction showed a comparable uptrend.) However, the Gallup figures—showing at least an *allegation* of decreased job satisfaction—are reinforced by other evidence gathered in limited surveys of worker attitudes, manpower program reports, and documented instances of increasing rates of turnover and absenteeism, as well as by deteriorating product and service quality plus growing evidence of industrial sabotage and theft.

In some cases there have been dramatic breakdowns of organizational functioning, such as the celebrated 1972 GM Lordstown, Ohio, case that shut down the Vega production line, or the less well-known strike at Chevrolet's Norwood plant that year, where auto workers walked out, not for higher wages, but (according to the union chairman at Lordstown) from frustration at not having a chance to participate in work decisions, particularly concerning the management of the speed of their assembly line. Another, less well-known reason for these two walkouts was the reorganization by the corporation of its assembly operations into the General Motors Assembly Department, which called for the union to merge seniority lists of separate locals that hitherto had been

[18] R. P. Quinn, G. L. Staines & M. R. McCullough, *Job Satisfaction: Is There a Trend?* (Research Monograph No. 30), Washington, D.C.: U.S. Department of Labor, Manpower Administration, 1974.

Figure 1

Percentage of "Satisfied" Workers, 1963–1973, Based on Eight Gallup Polls (men only, ages 21 through 65)

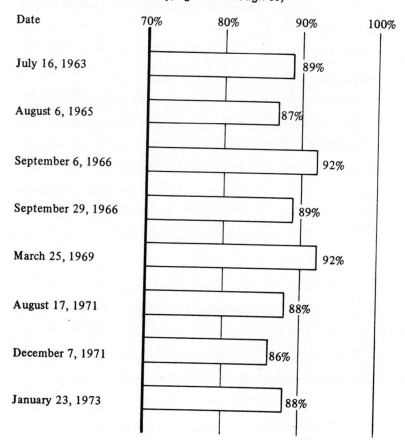

Note: This figure is based on the eight Gallup polls. The dates correspond to those printed on Gallup's questionnaires and are reportedly field dates of the polls. "Don't know" answers were excluded from the percentage bases.

autonomous. Clashes in "property rights" over seniority have frequently led to acute conflicts, resulting in a strike.[19]

In April 1973, Gallup released another poll bearing upon productivity. Gallup interviewed a representative sample of U.S. wage earners and found that:

- Half of all wage earners say they could accomplish more each day if they tried, with three in five of this group indicating they could increase their output by 20 percent or more.

- The percentage who say they could get more work done is highest (61 percent) among young adults in the workforce—those between the ages of 18 and 29. Men are more likely to state they could accomplish more than are female earners.

Here are the questions asked of wage earners and the results:

Some persons claim that American workers are not turning out as much work each day as they should. Do you agree or disagree with this?

Workers Could Produce More

Agree 56%
Disagree 33
No opinion 11

In your case, could you accomplish more each day if you tried?

Yes 50%
No 47
No opinion 3

How much more could you accomplish each day if you tried?

Ten percent 15%
Twenty percent 15
Thirty percent 7
Forty percent 2
Fifty percent 5
Over fifty percent 3
Don't know/No answer 3

                                 50%

[19] William Gomberg, Professor of Management and Industrial Relations, The Wharton School, University of Pennsylvania, personal correspondence, August 1973.

Gallup comments: "A key factor affecting productivity is job satisfaction. The worker who hates his job or is bored with it is not likely to be as productive as he could be. . . . A cross-tabulation of survey findings is most revealing on this point. Among those in the survey who say they are 'very satisfied' with their jobs, less than one quarter say they could do 30% or more additional work per day. In sharp contrast, among those in the survey who say they are 'very dissatisfied' with their jobs, about four in ten (two-fifths) say they could do 30% or more additional work per day."[20]

One more input on the subject of job satisfaction may be cited from the Quinn-Staines-McCullough interpretation of published studies on the subject:

1. In spite of public speculation to the contrary, there is no conclusive evidence of a widespread, dramatic decline in job satisfaction. Re-analysis of 15 national surveys conducted since 1958 indicates that there has not been any significant decrease in overall levels of job satisfaction over the last decade.

2. Job satisfaction among blacks and other minority groups has been consistently lower than that of whites, but has fluctuated as much as 13 percent in the past 11 years. These changes do not correspond to any consistent pattern and are most probably due to sampling error.

3. Younger workers are less satisfied with their jobs than older workers, but this has been true for the past 15 years. Therefore, the much-discussed large recent decline in job satisfaction of younger workers has not been substantiated.

4. Among occupational categories, professional-technical workers, managers, officials, and proprietors register the highest levels of job satisfaction, while operatives and nonfarm laborers register the lowest. Nondomestic service workers and clerical workers are also among the relatively dissatisfied, a factor of potential importance since these workers represent a growing sector of the labor force.

5. Women workers, by and large, are about as contented with their jobs as are men. But it appears that women workers with one or more children under 6 years of age in their households are signifi-

[20] Used by permission of The Gallup Poll.

cantly less satisfied than are either women without preschoolers in the household or male workers in general.

6. Among workers without a college degree, there is little relationship between educational level and job satisfaction. Those with college degrees, however, have high levels of job satisfaction. Surprisingly low levels of satisfaction are registered by workers with some college education but no degree.

7. When asked to identify the individual facets of the job which were of greatest importance to them, most workers in a national sample gave high ratings to the availability of the resources needed to perform well and to the challenge of their jobs and lower ratings to financial rewards and "comfort" factors. Blue-collar workers, however, tended to consider pay more significant than the challenge of the job, while women workers were somewhat more interested in "comfort" than were men.

   Because the "average" American worker appears to seek many things simultaneously (e.g., good pay, interesting work) from each job, there may be no *one* way to increase job satisfaction.

8. A long list of job-related stresses have been implicated in various types of physical and mental illnesses, indicating that expressions of job dissatisfaction may be viewed as an important early warning system to both employees and employers.

9. There is no convincing evidence of the existence of a direct cause-effect relationship between job satisfaction and productivity. In reality, the contribution of job satisfaction to productivity is probably indirect and more likely to be reflected in reductions on the "cost" side of the corporate ledger than in increases on the output side. These indirect benefits are associated with reductions in turnover, absenteeism, alcohol and drug abuse, sabotage, and theft—all of which have been linked to some degree with job satisfaction.[21]

Aside from job satisfaction studies and considerations, there is a preponderance of evidence suggesting a societal need to be concerned with factors that might alienate or motivate people at work. These factors do have a direct bearing on costs, productivity, craftsmanship, and loss of product sales to foreign competitors who can produce for less—sometimes with better quality.

It seems fruitless to argue over the degree of discontent among

[21] Quinn, Staines & McCullough, op. cit.

workers. Variables such as the age of the worker, the expectations he or she brings to the job, and the differing economic and psychological satisfactions that people seek from their work are among the factors that bear upon degree of job satisfaction. *The important point on which many people—managers as well as workers and union leaders—can agree is that a pragmatic effort to improve the American workplace for the benefit of all concerned (customers, the company, task groups, individual workers, labor unions, and stockholders) is a valid, worthwhile objective.*

Productivity: Definition, Concept, and Ramifications

To many an employee, the word "productivity" connotes some sort of exploitative management pressure to speed up output per man-hour. It suggests efficiency experts, workforce reductions, and even layoffs. This has been true in some cases in which efforts to improve productivity have focused only on cost reduction. Perhaps because of this, some labor union leaders see efforts to improve productivity and broader attempts to enhance the quality of work as tricks on the part of management to circumvent collective bargaining and thereby weaken unions.

It is interesting to note in this context that instances of union cooperation with management to improve productivity can be found. Bruce Thrasher, assistant to the president of the United Steelworkers of America, strongly disagrees (or at least so stated in 1973) with the social scientists, pollsters, and journalists who have talked of the American labor force's growing alienation from work. Like a number of other union leaders, Thrasher sees attempts to counter this alienation by job enrichment outside collective bargaining as an effort to attenuate the role of labor unions. And yet, during a discussion period at the March 1973 "Changing Work Ethic" conference in New York, when Thrasher was asked what objection he as a union leader had to the splendid results (a reported 32 percent improvement in productivity) achieved through union-management joint effort at the Kaiser/Fontana pipe plant,[22] he replied (according to the author's notes): "None. I

[22] The Kaiser/Fontana case is discussed on pages 42–47.

have been part of the Steelworkers committee that developed the Fontana plan. That was accomplished in collaboration with the union, with no violation of contract provisions and no speedup. Now, if you want to focus on how to improve productivity without manipulating or trying to take advantage of labor, and experiment in sincere partnership with the union, we're for that." The author agrees with Thrasher's sentiment. In work situations that are unionized, labor-management cooperation is essential.

As already stated, labor productivity is only one among many factors involved in overall productivity. But in many cases it is a crucial one. Management people who can easily grasp the techniques of improved technology often find it less easy to understand the mechanics and psychological dynamics of labor productivity.

The real meaning of productivity is to produce more (or rather, optimally, if the baseline level was suboptimal) with the same amount of human effort. To oversimplify a little, labor productivity is the efficiency with which output is produced by the resources utilized. It refers to either man-hours worked or total hours paid for measurable labor output.

This concept is illustrated by a clause in the 1950 management-labor agreement between General Motors and the UAW:

The improvement factor provided herein recognizes that a continuing improvement in the standard of living of employees depends upon technological progress, better tools, methods, processes, [and] equipment, and a cooperative attitude on the part of all parties in such progress. It further recognizes the principle that to produce more with the same amount of human effort is a sound economic and social objective.

As General Motors board chairman Richard Gerstenberg pointed out in his speech before the American Newspaper Publishers Association in April 1972:

Productivity is not a matter of making employees work longer or harder. Increased productivity results mostly from sound planning, from wise investment, from new technology, from better techniques, from greater efficiency—in short, from the better exercise of the functions of management. . . . Beyond this, productivity depends upon the conscientious effort of every employee, a willingness to do a fair day's work for a fair day's wage. If America is to improve its productivity—and we must—then productivity must be everybody's job.

The focus of this book will be on *how* to elicit that "conscientious effort of every employee" to which Mr. Gerstenberg refers. The author agrees with his conclusion that:

Only if we increase productivity will America be able to:

- Arrest the spiral of inflation.

- Create jobs for the 15 million Americans who will enter our workforce in this decade.

- Compete in the markets of the world and prevent American jobs from being exported overseas.

- Earn enough profits to provide and attract capital investment for further growth.

- Finance the ambitious social and environmental goals our people have set for themselves.

The author further agrees with the following policy statement from the National Quality of Work Center:

NQWC stresses that it is the *total work environment*—the total three-in-one workplace of individuals, machines, and organization—within which any effective Quality of Work effort takes place.

A Quality of Work effort is not concerned *merely* with better human motivation and attitudes.

It is not concerned *merely* with more efficient machines, systems, and men.

It is not concerned *merely* with design and structure of organizations.

It is not a purely psychological effort, nor a purely engineering effort, nor a purely organizational effort.

To be effective, any change effort must be concerned with the combination and interaction of worker psychology, machine and system design, and organizational structure. All three areas of concern must be subject to integrated restructure if a more effective, productive, motivated, and efficient workplace is to be created.

It is a three-in-one effort. When successful, the result is a better quality of work by and for people, machines, and organizations.

In conjunction with this book, two documents well worth reading are *The Worker and the Job: Coping with Change*[23] and *Work in America*,[24] a 1972 special task force report to the Secretary of Health, Education and Welfare. The latter states:

The redesign of jobs is the keystone of this report. Not only does it hold out some promise to decrease mental and physical health costs, increase productivity, and improve the quality of life for millions of Americans at all occupational levels [but also] it would give, for the first time, a voice to many workers in an important decision-making process.

Redesign of jobs, when undertaken as part of a program to improve quality of worklife, usually involves the elements stated earlier in this chapter under "What Constitutes a Quality of Worklife (QWL) Program?"

While improvement in our nation's economy is obviously affected by many factors besides labor productivity, improvement in the latter may hold the key to our national ability to compete in the world's markets. In this book the focus is on how the structure, design, and organization of work relate to the problem of quality of worklife—a problem which bears directly on our national productivity.

[23] Rosow, op. cit.

[24] U.S. Department of Health, Education, and Welfare task force, *Work in America* (Cambridge, Mass.: The MIT Press, 1972).

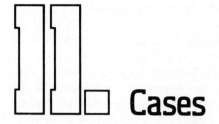

Cases

The cases selected here deal with a broad spectrum of situations: 15 pertain to varied types and sizes of American companies; there are several federal agency programs; one case deals with a city police department; two are British; one has headquarters in the Netherlands; one is Norwegian; two are Swedish (there is also a good deal of supplementary material on joint efforts of the Swedish government and labor industry); various Japanese experiments are presented; and there is a summary of Yugoslavian efforts.

Some of the principles involved in quality of worklife improvement, such as inviting the workforce to participate or become ego-involved in problem or opportunity identification and problem solving, are common to all situations. In some cases the restructuring and reorganization of work seems a key ingredient. In still others, such as Shell UK Ltd., the program seemed highly successful for a few years, then faltered badly when top management changed and the needed commitment no longer was present. A commentary and an analysis, focused on principles or lessons to be learned, are appended to some cases, such as Medical Specialties and Gaines

Pet Food, but not to those in which the results or implications seem clear as presented.

The cases and related material from England, Italy, Japan, Norway, Sweden, and Yugoslavia, plus references (the Ginzberg–Ford Foundation tour) to experiments in France, Germany, and Israel, give some idea of current international developments. The differing national roles of labor unions and governments come through most clearly in the material concerning Japan, Sweden, and Yugoslavia, along with the Shell UK Ltd. case. The role of unions in France, Great Britain, Italy, Sweden, and West Germany in relation to job-restructuring efforts is described more specifically in an article by Joseph Mire.[1]

Most of the case illustrations are from highly successful companies. But all human organizations have problems—and opportunities. It is likely to be the more successful companies that have the will and skill to seek renewal as part of their standard operating procedure, and in that process to recognize both their problems and their opportunities. Such organizations are likely to be among those especially interested in trying out promising new concepts or procedures.

City of Redondo Beach, California

On September 1, 1972, Louis J. Sunyich, chief of police of Redondo Beach, California, issued the memorandum shown here.

Chief Sunyich's invitation yielded 18 thoughtful responses from the Redondo Beach officers. One was a proposal for team policing. Another called for a police-sponsored program (jobs, education, counseling, and recreation) as an antidote to juvenile crime. The department gave serious consideration to the feasibility and potential costs of the ideas submitted, and a few were tried. Although most of them were not, an explanation of the reasons why proved useful.

[1] "Improving Working Life—The Role of European Unions," *Monthly Labor Review,* September 1974.

INTER-OFFICE MEMORANDUM   City of Redondo Beach, Calif.

TO: All PD Personnel

FROM: Louis J. Sunyich, Chief of Police   DATE Sept. 1, 1972

SUBJECT: Invitation for New Crime-Prevention Ideas

Enclosed is a copy of *Life's* (June 27, 1972) survey of readers on their personal opinions regarding crime. The findings are informative and sobering. 70% expressed willingness to pay higher taxes if that expenditure really would result in better protection.

Neither we in Redondo nor any other police organization is batting anywhere near 1,000 in prevention of crime, apprehension of suspects, and citizen support. But some cities, for various reasons, seem to have appreciably higher batting averages on these and other relevant counts than others.

We would like our city to have the best police department we have the potential to develop. To progress further and faster toward that goal, I would like to invite and urge each and every member of the force to put on his creative thinking hat and ask himself the following questions.

Suppose you were running the department and had the authority and resources to do anything you seriously thought might be likely to prevent, control, or reduce crime in Redondo to a significant degree.

1. What would you do or try out experimentally that we are not now doing? And how would you implement it—whatever "it" is?

2. What, if anything, would you stop doing, that we are now doing?

3. Now, if you were limited by approximately the present financial resources, where or how would you change our emphasis—or change anything else in our present programs or practices related to crime prevention and control?

Your written responses would be desirable, and be assured that *every response* will receive careful attention and thoughtful discussion. If you don't wish to write but would prefer to talk, make an appointment with any of the three Captains or with me to discuss your ideas.

Louis J. Sunyich, Chief of Police

LJS/ae

Enc.: A *Life* dialogue on "A Plan to Cut Crime," June 27, 1972.

Used by permission.

Comment

The police chief's memo had a more important result than the possible merit of the ideas it elicited: It helped to open up communications within the department, at least for a time. For some lower-ranking officers, the spirit of the memo and the follow-up review program gave hope of a better chance to influence department policy and receive top-level consideration of their suggestions. However, the general situation was not propitious for the realization of such a hope over the long term. Not all the high-ranking officers in the departmental hierarchy were supportive of and psychologically "ready" for the somewhat unusual approach of inviting those at the lower levels to have an influential voice in what was perceived as top management's prerogatives. Further, in a case like this, the kind and degree of support from the city manager can have a major bearing on the development of such a modus operandi. At Redondo, a new city manager was appointed a few months after the chief invited participatory suggestions. The new city manager's style was to give appreciably less latitude to department heads than his predecessor had. Thus, the new "smoke signals from on high" discouraged the development of an openly consultative style of management. Another factor in the situation was that this particular chief had only a few years left to serve because of age (he retired in July 1975). These factors served to reduce the thrust toward change.

A police department cannot alter its work patterns as easily as private industry. There are strongly entrenched organizational traditions plus political factors and the influence of internal and external pressure groups to be considered. A memo like the one reproduced here, inviting suggestions from all members of a given task group, is only a single element among many which go to influence a department's operation. It is included here to illustrate how a decision at the top of a given organization or division to encourage bottom-up communication can stimulate ego-involved, even creative response, yet to be largely ineffective over the long term unless there has been adequate preparation to assure understanding and support from middle management and *sustained* support from superiors in the chain of command.

Medical Specialties Company[2]

This case illustrates, among other things, what can be accomplished when a company announces that part of its operation must become profitable or be discontinued. As in the Redondo Beach case, the program started with the top man in a given department inviting his subordinates to participate in identifying and solving problems. In this case, the followup was far more comprehensive and systematic than at Redondo.

Medical Specialties Company manufactures and distributes some 800 products and has an annual sales volume of more than $80 million. The top management structure is conventional: a president who also is chief executive officer; an executive vice president; and vice presidents for marketing, manufacturing, finance, and research. There are also some wholly-owned subsidiaries, each with its own president.

Management can be described as conservative, somewhat paternalistic, and interested in sound development and expansion. The company prides itself on being fair and considerate toward its employees, who are fully unionized.

In 1965, the vice president in charge of manufacturing called in one of the psychologists who had been doing consulting work for the company since 1950, to work with a department that had been losing money steadily on an item produced in 20 variations. Among his concerns were low productivity, high operating costs, and too many labor grievances proceeding to the third stage.[3]

The consultant first met with the department head, who had his

[2] This report is an updating of a paper by Edward M. Glaser published in the *Newsletter* of the Division of Consulting Psychology, American Psychological Association, Spring 1969. The name of the actual company is disguised.

[3] At this plant, a first-stage labor grievance is the filing of the grievance by the aggrieved with the supervisor concerned, who must answer by the second day. If the grievance is not answered or if the answer is unsatisfactory, the second stage is that of appealing the grievance to higher company officials. If the result still is unsatisfactory, the third stage consists of both parties (union and management) agreeing to arbitration by an impartial arbitrator.

own reasons for complaining: The sales department turned in too many small orders on variations of the product; the engineering department demanded tolerance standards that were too close for economical mass production; the suppliers delivered poor raw materials; and so on. When the consultant then talked to the heads of the sales, engineering, and quality control departments, each passed the buck back to the others involved.

The first psychological objective was to change the nature of the game—and the reward system—from survival by taking no blame, to frankly admitting problems and solving them. The lesson was to be made plain: either a cooperative problem-solving approach or discontinuance.

The consultant, with the concurrence of the manufacturing vice president, suggested that the president decide what percentage of the market his company reasonably could expect to capture if design, price, quality, and service were first-rate. After making his estimate, the president advised the appropriate people in manufacturing, engineering, and sales that unless they could come up with a surefire plan to capture the agreed-on share of the market, the company would discontinue that set of products and lay off some 60 hourly-rate workers.

This ultimatum from the president supplied a very powerful motivating force. Those concerned met and decided they did not want to go out of business. In short order, a number of plans were evolved. Among them were the redesign of the product set and the addition of a technical service man in each region to help the users with any problems they might have.

Implementing the new plans, however, would cost considerable money. The president agreed to provide the additional funds only if those who recommended the plan guaranteed it would bring the desired results. Their necks were on the line, so to speak. With some gulping, they agreed to the plan.

With the ultimatum in force, those concerned were glad to have a consultant available to them. The consultant first made psychological evaluations of the head of that particular department in the manufacturing division and the two supervisors who reported to him. The evaluations were designed to enhance the development of personal insight. The consultant then discussed his report with each man in a private counseling session. When the consultant felt that the leadership in the department was sufficiently nondefensive, the department head invited the five subsupervisors—who were union members as well as a part of management—to a meeting with him and their two supervisors. (The union had been consulted and had expressed no objection.) The consultant, the department head, and the seven supervisory personnel joined in a frank and honest attempt to define problems, opportunities, goals, and means of goal-attainment. The department manager set the climate nicely. He explained that the consultant was there to help solve problems and to facilitate communication within the group. He further reassured those present that any increase in productivity or improvement in quality which resulted from their proposals would be translated into efforts to expand sales. Management had already agreed that no worker would be laid off, no matter how great an increase in productivity might be achieved.

In the next 35 minutes, 27 work problems were identified and organized under appropriate headings. Two of the suggestions for change were simple enough to implement (one was protection for the workers against a hot afternoon sun coming into the windows of their work station). The department head said "yes" to these immediately. Two other proposed changes he knew could not be brought about (one, indeed, would have constituted a violation of the state labor law), and to these he said "no" immediately, giving clear and persuasive reasons.

The remaining 24 suggestions needed further investigation of some sort: fact-finding, cost analysis, feasibility study, the cooperation of other departments, or authorization from a higher level. Ad hoc volunteer committees were formed to look into those suggestions for which implementation authority resided in the department, and to develop a recommended plan of action.

Within three months, every suggestion was answered with either "We'll do it" or "Analysis reveals that it isn't advisable or feasible for the following reasons," or "We can do it in part, or in modified form." At the end of the same three-month period, productivity was up 32 percent, rejects had dropped from 12 to 9 percent, and there had not been a single labor grievance that advanced beyond the first stage. The entire group received periodic reports of improved productivity and reduction of labor grievances, machine downtime, absenteeism, turnover, and rejects.

The supervisors came to realize that under the new system positive reinforcement was given for openly admitting and solving problems. They held relaxed post-mortem reviews of the department's results, asking themselves and each other, "How can we do it better?" Communication became freer and more honest. The entire group felt the new spirit of open, problem-solving communication. They were actively participating in the goals of the department and in the organization of the work to achieve those goals. A sense of responsibility for their own destiny developed. Now there was an opportunity to try out creative innovations and encouragement to become *ego-involved.*

These supervisors, then, working collaboratively with their teams, became industrially active rather than industrially reactive people. As a result of *their* suggestions, work was restructured and jobs were enriched. They found new meaning in mass-producing products—the same products which had previously been produced with such travail. They found greater pleasure in their work now, and chose to invest more of themselves in trying to increase productivity and find greater job satisfaction for all involved.

After the first three months, the approximately 60 hourly-rate union employees were invited to participate. At the first meeting they were divided into subgroups of 12. These subgroups came up with 78 ideas. Again, some suggestions were settled on the spot. Others required study, and the employees were invited to volunteer for ad hoc committees to conduct such studies and recommend appropriate action. No pressure was exerted to get anyone to volunteer who did not spontaneously do so; the majority did volunteer.

In the following weeks and months, many of the employee ideas were adopted in whole or in part. Improvements were made in product design, work structure, and departmental organization, as well as in "comfort" items or working conditions.

Periodic reports were made to the hourly workers, either in department meetings or in writing. The people were shown that their efforts were not only appreciated but acted on by management. Their self-confidence was enhanced; they derived satisfaction from cooperative achievement. They truly were participating in the activities and decisions that affected them. No one needed to file a formal grievance to be heard without prejudice on any subject he might wish to bring up. And, although there was no guarantee that their ideas would find agreement, the implicit guarantee was that they would be treated with dignity and respect, and given explanations of why any suggestions were deemed inappropriate:

The results of the experiment were impressive:

1. Labor grievances dropped from an average of one a week in 1965 to only one third-stage grievance in three years (1966–1968).

2. Three months after the intervention, productivity rose 32 percent and the reject rate fell from 12 to 9 percent. Then, following the intervention of all members of the department, productivity continued to climb. In 1968 it was an almost unbelievable 190 percent greater than the 1965 baseline, and rejects fell to 3.2 percent.

3. Average labor turnover and absenteeism fell significantly.

4. Improvement continued *under the group's own motivation* through repeated application of the principles and procedures initially used in this program. The consultant tapered off his aid after one year, and, under the able leadership of the department head, the group continued to achieve fine results.

5. Department operations had increased substantially in both complexity and volume during this 1965–1969 period of time, and have continued to increase since then.

It should be emphasized that if any employee did not find a more responsible involvement in his work personally satisfying, no pressure was exerted on him to become more involved. He could leave problem solving and decision making to others, as long as his own performance was reasonably satisfactory.

Most important, all the improvements reported came from members of the department, including management and supervision, supported by help from the engineering staff on some items and reports from the sales department about customer acceptance or complaints. All the consultant did was to help develop a nondefensive climate that permitted constructive and creative challenge of standard practice, along with certain skills, such as listening skills, that facilitated the identification and solving of problems, and the implementation of progressive change.

This experiment in the manufacturing department was not adopted by other parts of Medical Specialties Company. The plant manager, whose sustained support of the experiment was clearly evident and *was crucial to its success,* was transferred to another of the company's plants where his talents were needed. His successor, who wanted to make his own mark, operated in the more conventional style of hierarchical authority, and did not support the program. The plant manager who had been transferred, however, invited adaptation of the consultation in his new situation.

There is a promising sequel to the foregoing: In late 1970, Medical Specialties decided to expand its manufacturing facilities for a certain important group of products by enlarging one of its conventional mass-production plants. At a meeting with the vice president for manufacturing and the several plant managers, the author of this report and an associate pointed out the kinds of productivity improvement that have been demonstrated in certain companies through sociotechnical approaches which recognize that there is a technical and a human contribution to every job, through small project work teams and other job enrichment ideas, sometimes coupled with the Scanlon Plan[4] of financial incentives. The

---

[4] Conceived in the late 1930s by United Steelworkers vice president Joseph Scanlon (later a professor at MIT) and his associates, the Scanlon Plan states that employee interest and contribution can best be stimulated by providing the employee (and the participating union, if the workforce is unionized) with all the information concerning company problems and successes that can safely be shared in a competitive society, and by soliciting the employee's ideas on how the job is best done. The concept included a system of rewards to stimulate employee interest in and acceptance of technological change by arranging an appropriate wage structure reflecting

consultants offered information on quality of work projects carried out by some other respected firms known to the managers, and also reminded the group of its own limited but successful experiment, reported above.

As a result of the meeting, Medical Specialties formed a committee to explore productivity, chaired by the man who had been the department head in the original small experiment. Key personnel from this committee contacted another company, with a technological stucture similar to their own, which was using job enrichment and participative management concepts with demonstrable, sustained success. The personnel from Medical Specialties who made a visit to the other company became excited by what they saw in operation there. A behavioral scientist's words could never have provided the living evidence of practicability and suitability that was supplied by a visit to a respected and successful business operation in a somewhat comparable industry.

As a result of the thinking stimulated by this visit, the managers abandoned the idea of expanding the conventional plant. Instead, they decided, in 1971, to build a new plant designed to accommodate small work teams and staffed from the top with persons receptive to the concept of participative or consultative management. The Human Interaction Research Institute received a research and demonstration grant from the U.S. Department of Labor to provide planning and start-up consultation to help the new plant organize and structure the operation along participative management lines. (The Department of Labor later made another grant to an independent evaluation team from a major university to see what could be learned and verified for possible application to other work situations.) Construction was started in October 1972, and actual production got under way in June 1974.

Beginning in the fall of 1973, the plant was staffed and organized

---

individual skills and additional rewards based on the success of the enterprise, to be shared by all employees and management. Companies usually implement the Scanlon Plan with a system of departmental production committees and an overall steering committee. (F. G. Lesieur and E. S. Puckett, "The Scanlon Plan Has Proved Itself," *Harvard Business Review,* September–October 1969, 109.)

to incorporate quality of worklife programs which the Medical Specialties group believed would be suitable to their highly technical biochemical manufacturing requirements. Some steps and guiding concepts have been:

- As soon as it was decided to construct the new plant, its manager moved to the site, where he became involved in engineering design and layout. The next two key people named were a personnel manager[5] with some experience in procedures for quality of worklife improvement and a production manager promoted from the parent plant.

- The technology, though exacting and precise, was worked out to match the concept of small (5–20 persons) task teams whenever feasible. The psychological consultants became available on a continuing basis of several days a month (or as needed) to the plant manager and his key people as they were added in preparation for the start of production.

- As personnel were added, they received orientation in the philosophy and practice of quality of worklife programming. A comprehensive three-week training program was developed, as well as much more extensive training in task technology. Employees at all levels were invited to participate in general planning for the production start-up. Although the exacting technical system design was outside the experience of most of the workforce and therefore had to be determined by engineering, safety, and quality control requirements, the production personnel not only were trained in the tasks to be performed and in the technology but were encouraged to raise questions, make suggestions, and have a voice in the planning and carrying out of the work structure. The managers and supervisors were accountable for carrying out their responsibilities, but the theory was that they could

[5] The General Foods plant in Topeka (described on pp. 52–63), which was another new operation, deliberately omitted a personnel manager from its organizational plan. The idea was that the workforce itself should develop its own personnel policies. Questions of this sort come down to matters of judgment, style, special circumstances such as the size of the workforce, and what might be termed "organizational readiness."

do so more effectively and efficiently if they invited the people they supervised to have a voice and an influence in matters within their concern and competency.

- Frequent evaluation of the start-up procedure and prompt reports to all concerned were planned. Tasks whose objectives could be defined were to be reviewed upon completion or at agreed-upon stages, in an effort to help employees learn nondefensively from each experience and thereby pursue excellence in flexibly responsive ways.

- Outcomes were to be evaluated partly by comparison on a number of measurable indices with the parent plant, which continued to manufacture some of the identical products. Further evaluation was to be achieved by measuring degree, kind, and speed of progress from the new plant's own start-up baseline.

Comment

It should be noted that the remarkable improvement achieved in the first experiment within the single department did not result in similar experiments in other parts of the company. In this case, sustained internal advocacy and the necessary support for further innovation from a key source, the new plant manager, were lacking.

Probably another and more subtle reason why the experiment did not spread within the plant is that part of the support for it had come from the president of the company, who died a few years thereafter. In his enthusiasm as an observer, and perhaps partly because of a notably cordial relationship with the consultant, he suggested that other departments might well seek the same kind of consulting help. This tended to give the impression that he felt the consultant was primarily responsible for the gains achieved, whereas in fact all the substantive ideas had been developed by the employees themselves, some of whom worked literally day and night to refine and implement them. What was perceived as giving too much credit to the consultant led to displeasure and resistance from others, who understandably felt that *they* should have received the major recognition. As Lao-tse once observed, "Of the best leader, when the job is done, the people will say, 'We did it ourselves; we did not really need him.' " Consultants should be alert to and take every precaution to avoid this potential pitfall.

With regard to the participative management style in this company's new plant, it should be noted that the concept has received support from a capable plant manager and his staff, a few persons at the corporate office headquarters, but not the new top management,[6] and two Department of Labor grants. It was predicted that when the outside supports were withdrawn after November–December 1975, the concept would not spread within the corporation unless there were a deeper, more powerful, and more sustained commitment to an objective appraisal of the result achieved through this more demanding style of management. At best, if the particular plant maintains its commitment to this nontraditional style of operation, it will be allowed to proceed in its own way *so long as the results seem clearly good* and *so long as the plant manager firmly espouses this style.* Otherwise, only vestiges of what has been developed here will survive.

Kaiser Steel Company (Pipe Mill), Fontana, California

The following is condensed from an account in the *Los Angeles Times* on January 26, 1973:

The tough corporate decision was finally made in October, and M. J. (Smitty) Smith sent the word down to the workers at Kaiser Steel Co.'s pipe mill at Fontana: "We're going to shut the place down."

"We just told the men the facts of life," plant manager Smith said last week, "and the facts were that the Japanese produce the same high-quality steel pipe we make, but they do it a hell of a lot cheaper. We're losing money and the mill had to go."

The decision came as a surprise even though the men in the mill had been hearing rumors of a shutdown for a year or more. They appealed to the company to let them try to save the mill.

Management, while retaining final authority, gave the workers the responsibility for saving the mill.

---

[6] Medical Specialties was bought out by a successor company early in 1973. This has led to many changes in staffing and management style.

Now, three months later, the company reports that there has been a 32.1% increase in productivity, an astonishing figure when it is remembered that a 4% to 5% annual increase is regarded as a good average.

"The situation at our CW (continuous weld) pipe mill is just part of the experiment we're trying throughout the whole plant here at Fontana. Nationally, the nine major steel companies are doing the same kind of experimenting in cooperation with the union," Smith said.

Past efforts to get mutual cooperation between workers and management in the industry have been unsuccessful, and the Fontana effort may not save the pipe mill. Japanese competition is still highly competitive, and the industry and unions say only government help can stem the tide of imported steel.

But everybody involved in the pipe mill's increase in productivity says it has exciting possibilities.

The basic problem is that the Japanese are delivering 2-inch galvanized steel pipe for $240 a ton, while U.S. steelmakers, including Kaiser, sell it for $300 a ton. Kaiser says it takes a loss on each ton.

One company official estimated that with the productivity gain, the company will save between $10 and $15 a ton, but the resulting profit is not close to the margin steelmen say they need to stay in business.

"The workers came to us and said they wanted to try to run the mill even though our statistics showed it just wasn't economically feasible," Smith said, "and they didn't want any reduction in crew sizes, either."

But "finally we told them, OK, see what you can do."

The spokesmen for the workers were Dino Papavero, president of the AFL-CIO United Steelworkers of America Local 2869, and Timon (Curley) Covert.

Papavero's role, in addition to handling problems of the entire plant, is to find new ways to sell steel.

Covert is the grievance committeeman for the union in Zone 14 at the plant, of which the CW pipe mill is a part.

Covert said that management has "got to start really listening to the men for a change.

"It was a lot of little things and a few big things, and a change in attitude, but it didn't take long before those damned production figures were leaping up."

One of the "little things" which was changed when the workers were given responsibility to run the mill was a pay raise for a key helper on the pipe-straightening machine.

"The helper felt he was a nothing. When he was raised up, it really had an impact," Covert said. A few other men received pay hikes to make their earnings comparable with fellow-workers.

Then the workers demanded a new saw.

Although skeptical of the request, the company agreed to spend $125,000 for a new saw.

"It doesn't sound like much, but the men were getting bad cuts with the old saw. Now the pipe ends are not smashed down when it comes through the hot mill, which means the tools don't get torn up as the pipe is put through facers and threaders," Covert said.

"All of a sudden, we started getting some results when we called on maintenance to get a job done. You didn't put in a request for a job and wait a week. Like right now it was done," he said.

Smith, who became the top man at Fontana four years ago, is impressed with the changed attitude of the men. Covert agrees that attitudes have changed.

"Look, before, nobody paid any attention to a guy and so he figured why in hell should he pay any attention to the pipe. Nobody cared," Covert contended.

"People finally paid attention to the men, the boss started listening, the man on the next machine started looking around, and pretty soon everybody got into the swing of things."

Covert, Papavero and other union men interviewed at Kaiser were quick to stress that, as Covert said, "We aren't letting the company get away with one, not even one, contract violation. We live by that contract."

Al Chavez, another steelworker, said, "Let's put it like this: We're not fishing buddies with them [management] but if they'll listen, we will, too."

Reese Johnson momentarily stopped his threading machine to talk with a visitor. "You just kind of watch things more. If the threads aren't being cut right on one piece, you shut it down and fix it right away. That means one pipe goes back for reprocessing. Guess a few more were going back before we started watching things more," Johnson said.

Now only 9% of the pipes have to be sent back through the system for reprocessing. Three months ago the rate was 29%.

Papavero guessed that "a way of working can become a way of life. So what if a few pipes do go by? Nobody cares. Management never asked anybody to participate, to involve themselves.

"Besides, when people tell us something is impossible, if we don't think they're out to screw us, then we say the hell it is, and we do it."

The men in the pipe mill all have seniority, so even if the mill closed, they would still be working at Kaiser.

Papavero made certain that almost every other sentence of explanation about the overall Union–Management Productivity Committee was a reiteration of the union's determination not to lose any of its rights.

"There is a lot of apprehension about a speedup. We're not giving up anything, but we're ready to see how to increase productivity without any speedup."

Papavero knows about former Steelworkers Union International President David J. McDonald and his hopes for a "mutual trusteeship" of union and management over the steel industry.

"But somehow it never got off the ground. At Kaiser, it worked for a while with our 'fruits of progress' plan where workers get to share in the savings made by increased productivity, but we never really sat down with management and talked about our problems," Papavero said.

Under the "fruits of progress" plan, workers share in savings made when production costs are reduced.

Kaiser workers make about $40 a month more than workers doing the same job in other steel plants around the nation, and, according to management and union officials, Kaiser's productivity is generally higher than in other steel plants.

Both sides are now convinced it takes more than just a higher wage to raise production, and that involves cooperation on a variety of ideas.

Plant productivity committees are being created in all steel companies under the 1971 basic steel industry–union contract.

I. W. Abel, president of the international union, recently joined R. Heath Larry of United States Steel Corp, to report "substantial progress" in reducing unnecessary absenteeism and achieving "a better understanding among both company and union representatives of the role of plant productivity committees to make the domestic steel industry more competitive against the imports of foreign steel."

Foreign imports last year meant 108,000 fewer U.S. workers were needed in the steel industry, and union members are aware of this.

Ten years ago, foreign steel made up only 5.6% of the amount consumed in this country. By last year imports made up 18% of the nation's steel consumption. And on the West Coast last year the imported steel was a whopping 38% of the amount bought by those in Kaiser's prime market area.

The experience of workers at Kaiser's pipe mill cannot be duplicated exactly in other mills at Kaiser, or in other plants around the country. But the steel union and industry leaders, and rank-and-file workers, are at least talking about ways of cooperating. And in Kaiser's CW pipe mill, they have astonished even themselves.[7]

Comment

The Kaiser pipe mill, like the particular product group in the Medical Specialties Company experiment, had to increase productivity or discontinue operations. At Fontana, however, changes were made without the help of outside consultants. Furthermore, Kaiser had the direct, active collaboration of the United Steelworkers. The Medical Specialties Company had only the non-interfering acceptance of a strong union.

The key ingredients in the Kaiser/Fontana case were: (1) The workers wanted to save their jobs. (2) Management retained final authority but gave the workers responsibility for saving the mill. (3) Union and management collaborated instead of pursuing their traditional adversary relationship. Management really listened to and—whenever possible—went along with the worker-union suggestions, developing a climate that was constructively motivational. Also, the union was involved in finding new ways to sell the steel

[7] Copyright, 1973, Los Angeles Times. Reprinted by permission.

produced at Fontana. (4) The work and the organization were restructured.

The long-term results of this management-labor collaboration at Kaiser/Fontana remain to be seen. If the cost savings are not sufficient to permit the company to compete successfully with the imported Japanese pipe, it may still be necessary to shut the plant down.

Donnelly Mirrors, Inc., Holland, Michigan

Donnelly Mirrors' principal product is rear-view mirrors for automobiles. It is a relatively small, family-controlled company that operates four plants in Holland, Michigan, and one near Dublin, Ireland. Approximately 500 persons are employed in the United States and 100 in Ireland. The company's U.S. sales volume is about $20 million a year.

In 1952 Donnelly adopted a group incentive pay arrangement (the Scanlon Plan) that provides for the setting of plantwide standards and improvement goals, coupled with the sharing of productivity gains on a plantwide basis. Underlying the cost-savings-sharing feature is a concept of participative management supported by related organizational development (OD) activities. The Scanlon Plan, particularly in the modified version adopted by Donnelly, encourages employee participation in establishing goals and in making work-related decisions. It involves collaboration and cooperation, and employees share in the gains made as a result of their efforts.

In its organizational development work, Donnelly has emphasized the redistribution of influence from a top power center to all levels of the organization, the goal being to tap the creativity and resources of all employees. Further emphasis has been placed on developing in upper management personnel those concepts and skills that will enable them to implement the company philosophy that humane managing, genuine respect for each individual, and collaborative, total team effort do not have to exclude realistic concern for quality, productivity, and profit. As Donnelly Mirrors' president has commented, "Concern for people, coupled with managerial expertise, is clearly the most effective means of achieving corporate goals." Also noteworthy is the fact that organizational development at Donnelly is data-based throughout, and each aspect of the OD effort is directed toward obtaining *observable and measurable results* in terms of productivity, worker satisfaction, and company profits, with systematic reports on these data to all concerned.

The company is organized into a series of overlapping work teams, each of which operates as an autonomous unit on the basis of job function. Employees bring up suggestions directly with their own work teams, which discuss and weigh them and plan for their implementation. When any member of a work team spots a problem, the team may stop and tackle it on the spot. In the case of a maintenance problem, any employee may make the repairs if he knows how, or he himself may contact a maintenance mechanic.

As supervisors themselves compose a work team, they also take part in selecting and training new supervisors. All job openings are posted throughout the plant, and employees are encouraged to apply for any that would entail a promotion. A selection board (the production manager, four supervisors, and two personnel specialists) makes the final choice of applicants for supervisors' jobs, and Donnelly has had excellent results with this method. Because of its good reception on both sides, the company plans an expansion of the work-team system.

In one instance, the company posted openings for three new supervisors. Seventeen employees applied; following psychological testing and a review of past performance, the personnel department found ten acceptable candidates, all of whom were then interviewed by the selection board. The selection board chose three people to fill the openings. Each candidate was then called in for a discussion about why he had or had not been selected, including an evaluation of his strengths and weaknesses. If an individual was a potentially good supervisor, he was apprised of the skills he would need to develop; if it seemed an unrealistic goal for him, he was given career counseling to aid him in choosing a likelier one. In this particular instance, after the three applicants were chosen, the production manager went to the work teams involved to get their evaluations. The team members were given the names of the top ten selected and asked to rank them; their choices coincided with those of the selection board.

The teams, which have an average membership of ten persons, overlap in two senses:

1. Each team has a "link pin." That is, the manager or supervisor of each work team is also a member of the next highest group. It is his membership in this higher team that integrates his own team with the rest of the organization. As a manager works with his peers in the planning process or decision making, he may hold a decision in abeyance if he feels the need for a greater contribution from the team he is responsible for. It is not uncommon for a management team, or any work team, to call in members from other teams to get better and first-hand information before making a decision. The interlocking team structure and group process described, with the link pin functioning as described, allow an amazing flow of ideas. The system further ensures that no single person or group can force its ideas on others, and it eliminates a great deal of misinformation and rumor.

2. Since the production of the company's commodities is the result of *integrated* efforts of many kinds, Donnelly has Employees' Committees which are composed of representatives from each work team, and foremen or superiors. Four hierarchical levels are represented on the Employees' Committees; this facilitates instant three-way communication. Thus, for example, factory workers who represent their work groups on the Employees' Committees not only belong to a four-level council, but they interact with their peers from other work groups, thereby helping to integrate the entire workforce and improve communications upward, downward, and laterally. The company also has Employees' Committees, composed of members of work teams at all levels. These are essentially "ombudsman" groups that seek to ensure fair treatment for all employees. In that sense they func-

tion much like a bargaining or grievance committee in a unionized company.

Each team member is encouraged to learn every job performed by the team. This allows for job rotation and job enlargement (a worker may choose to perform several related operations). It also helps the team to function autonomously. Team goals can be met even during periods of absenteeism, as others can fill the vacancy or double up.

Relevant data—production standards, price changes, inflation factors, projected sales, and so on—are posted throughout the plant. Work teams are given any other information regarding new or unexpected occurrences that may affect goal attainment, either company wide or within the team. Each team sets its own production goals in line with company objectives, and each worker sets his or her own production rate within the framework of the production goals. Also, work-team members may help in deciding what mechanical capabilities would enable them to do a better job. As an example, ideas for an easily movable, easily repairable glass-beveling machine to replace a cumbersome, more costly one—$290 versus $900—were developed by a maintenance man. He was later elected by his work team to accompany the Donnelly engineers to California to examine new glass machines and test them before the company decided to make a purchase.

In 1970, all Donnelly employees who formerly had been paid on an hourly basis were put on salary. All time clocks were removed. Under the new policy, pressure for good performance comes from other team members rather than from superiors. A year after all employees became salaried, absenteeism had dropped to one-fifth of what it was when employees were paid by the hour—from 5 percent to 1 percent.

Work teams also have no reservations about reducing the number of jobs, since workers profit from increased productivity. Employees who are eliminated from their jobs in the interests of improved efficiency are assured work elsewhere in the company. And, as production costs are reduced by job eliminations, bonuses go up.

Bonuses are based on productivity increases, cost reductions, and quality levels that exceed the current base. In 1970, and again in 1971, employees decided on a 10 percent base-salary increase. To achieve that increase in 1970, employees needed to reduce costs by $610,000; they reduced them by $643,000. In 1971, the target was $453,000, and the result achieved was $511,000. For 1972, because of several external factors but mainly the federal government's Phase II wage controls, the pay increase decided upon amounted to 5.5 percent.

The results achieved by Donnelly Mirrors since the institution of the Scanlon Plan can be summarized as follows:[8]

- Between 1972 and 1974, the company was able to reduce the price of its main product by 25 percent.
- Since it began using the Scanlon Plan, the company's compounded growth rate has averaged 14 percent, and the average return on investment has almost tripled.
- In 20 years, productivity per person has almost doubled.
- Employee bonuses have averaged 12 percent over base pay.
- Quality levels have climbed from 92 percent to 98.5 percent.
- Quality control personnel have dropped from 14 to 4.
- Absenteeism has dropped from 5 percent to 1 percent, tardiness from 6 percent to less than 1 percent. Worker turnover is so small that it is not worth recording.
- There has been a marked reduction in returned goods.
- Employee job satisfaction has climbed noticeably.

Comment

Donnelly Mirrors is one of the most successful examples in the United States of a long-term (23-year) commitment to improving the quality of worklife in an organization. It must be remembered,

[8] Taken from information supplied by the company and from a presentation by Richard N. Arthur, former executive vice president of Donnelly and since 1974 an independent management consultant.

of course, that Donnelly is a relatively small firm and a nonunion shop; these factors allow management more flexibility in introducing new ideas. Still, Donnelly's record is impressive. One of the key underpinnings of Donnelly's long-term success is participative management supported by comprehensive organizational development efforts and structural arrangements to facilitate communication upward, downward, and laterally. Small work teams play an active and far-reaching role in the company, participating in everything from goal setting to the selection of new supervisors. It is rare to see this degree of privilege and responsibility given to a nonsupervisory workforce.

In addition, Donnelly's modified Scanlon Plan allows employees to share in the financial fruits of cost savings. The results seem to be profitable in spirit and substance to all concerned.

Gaines Pet Food Plant (Post Division of General Foods), Topeka, Kansas[9]

In February 1971, General Foods opened a new pet food plant in Tokepa with a new work approach. Like Donnelly Mirrors, the Gaines Pet Food plant extended to employees such privileges and responsibilities as recruiting, hiring, disciplining, and firing—normally considered supervisory functions. According to Gaines management, "Humans will best respond (be productive) when there exists a high feeling of self-worth by the employee, and employee identification with the success of the total organization."

The goals for the new plant were to minimize static hierarchies of job classifications, abolish lockstep work assignments, and give all employees a voice in the running of the plant. It took a year and a half of planning to put the plant into operation. A four-man primary project team (including the leader, who would later become plant manager, and an engineer) began with a statement of its principles:

[9] Summarized from L. D. Ketchum, *Humanizing of Work*. Paper presented at the American Association for the Advancement of Science symposium, Philadelphia, December 1972.

1. People have ego needs. They want self-esteem, a sense of accomplishment, autonomy, increasing knowledge and skills, and data on their performance. People invest more in situations that allow them to meet these needs.

2. An individual has a need to be able to see himself as a significant part of the whole—be it his position in a human group or his role in a complex technological process.

3. People have social needs. They enjoy team membership and teamwork. At the same time, they enjoy friendly rivalry.

4. People want to be able to identify with the products they produce and the firms that employ them. People care especially about the quality of the things with which they identify.

5. People have certain security needs. They want a reasonable income and employment security, and they want to be protected against arbitrary and unfair treatment. They also want to be assured of due process.

To staff the new plant, the following advertisement was run in Topeka and Kansas City newspapers:

GENERAL FOODS NEEDS PRODUCTION SUPERVISORS

To take on a new plant and an exciting new management concept in Topeka, Kansas.

General Foods, a leading processor and distributor of nationally advertised grocery products, including such household names as Post cereals, Kool-Aid, Maxwell House coffee, and many others, is opening a new Post Division plant. In the General Foods tradition of progressive, forward-thinking management, a young, new-breed idea in management is being introduced in the new facility.

If you're looking for something different, a flexible management structure that emphasizes individual abilities, an imaginative program that will set the pace for our multi-billion-dollar industry, you may be the young-thinking leader we need.

You must have mechanical skill–potential with a background in production. Previous supervisory experience desirable. You will need an above-average flair for working with people and ideas—with the very minimum of supervision. Excellent salary, benefits, and relocation pay.

Thirty candidates applied for the jobs, and interviews eliminated 20 of these. The project team, advised by a consultant, then offered a weekend of problem solving, exercise, and game play designed to reveal the attributes an individual would need to be a team leader. Following the weekend, six of the ten candidates were chosen. One of the four rejected became a supervisor in the parent plant. Two requested jobs as team members, and one of these was hired.

The next step was to help the new supervisors develop interpersonal skills and a knowledge of group dynamics consistent with the new value system. As Lyman Ketchum, General Foods' manager of organization development operations, described it:

It was important that the team leaders' worklife from the very beginning should be consistent with this system. Other skill development: technology, where the parent plant was used; business methods such as cost accounting, quality control, personnel procedures, capital programs, profit planning, and so forth.

One important task this new group performed was job design. The jobs were designed on the basis of the system characteristics, our agreed-upon notions of people needs, our knowledge of the process, and an opportunity we had had to observe a similar process in the parent plant. Then began more specific work on the compensation system.

With the plant still under construction and start-up approaching, there was a need for team leaders. At this time, another transition in primary responsibility and control occurred. After the team leaders were chosen, the direct role of the four primary-project team members began to diminish. The team leaders began exercising more autonomy in the process of recruiting and selecting, just as the project team without the plant manager had done earlier in its recruiting and selection. This again was consistent with the value system and was made even more practical by the knowledge and experience the team leaders had gained in their own recruitment and selection process, aided by their having strongly "bought in" to the new value system. They thus, with outside help, established the criteria, designed advertising, worked out testing and selection processes, and, indeed, did their own hiring.

A newspaper want ad was again used to find workers:

GENERAL FOODS/TOPEKA PLANT NEEDS PRODUCTION PEOPLE

Work in a new, modern Gaines Pet Food plant with an exciting new organization concept which will allow you to participate in all phases of plant operations.

Qualifications:

- Mechanical aptitude
- Willing to accept greater responsibility
- Willing to work rotating shifts
- Desire to learn multiple jobs and new skills

Although 625 people applied, only 63 were needed. All but 98 were eliminated by various screening methods. The team leaders again designed a selection weekend that eliminated an additional 35, and the remaining 63 were offered jobs. Lyman Ketchum explained:

Anyone rejected was offered . . . the reasons for rejection. We felt this was only right with regard to the applicant, and also, it gave the team leader an early opportunity to deal openly and honestly with people.

It is our opinion that the team member selection process, managed in large part by the team leaders with outside consultant help, was a better process than the process first designed for selection of team leaders. This was one of our earliest reinforcements that we were on the right track in having high expectations of people when we provided them with the resources and the opportunity to work on their own.

Systematic orientation and training then took place. Committees for safety, disaster and fire protection, recreation, and spare parts were formed.

The startup, while not without problems, has gone satisfactorily. Learning is taking place at higher-than-expected rates. The plant is manned with about two-thirds the number we would expect with traditional methods.

We learned a lot. We are still learning. Our board of directors has just authorized a second plant for this site. All of the learning from our first experience will be incorporated into the second. We have the opportunity in the second plant to introduce the requirements of the social system to the physical design process at the preliminary engineering phase. We will thus jointly optimize the social and technical systems, an opportunity we partially missed in the first plant.

Highlights of the Topeka program include:

- Building production around team units rather than the individual worker. The three components at Topeka are teams for (1) processing, (2) packing and shipping, (3) office duties. Each worker is assigned to a team, but not to a fixed task within the team. Rather, the total team is given the assignment, and the workers who make up the team can rotate jobs. This is proving to increase worker versatility, stimulate continuing learning, and —of primary importance—relieve boredom and the sense of doing meaningless work.

- Allocating a team leader to each team—someone who is not a foreman, supervisor, watchdog, or boss but, more accurately, a coach and a resource person.

- Arriving at team decisions after open discussion. Among the matters subject to team decision are: individual job assignments, including how to fill in for an absent member; interviewing and hiring job applicants; establishing and changing work rules, operating decisions, and policies; evaluation of individual job performance to determine need for improvement; progression within the compensation system.

- Encouraging initiative. To cite an example, there are no separate maintenance or utility departments in the plant. If there is an emergency in processing or in the packing lines, it is handled by the person within the team who has the necessary skills for that specific task. While he is dealing with the emergency, his position is covered by other team members.

- Assigning all production teams to handle quality control. This means that the worker who makes the product passes judgment on its suitability; the result is a sense of having a personal stake in doing satisfactory work.
- Eliminating many of the physical manifestations of status. The office of the operations manager is completely open to view, and any employee can get in to see him readily. The conference room is open to all personnel. All employees enter and leave by the same doors. There is no time clock. There are no reserved positions in the parking lot. The carpeting in the manager's office is the same as the carpeting in the locker room of the production workers.

Management has reported a discernible improvement in employee morale and in the entire work climate, including greater job satisfaction, more sense of responsibility, and an increased level of cooperation.

One major benefit of the program at the Topeka plant has been an increase in safety. The heart of the program is the safety committee, composed of 11 people—three from each shift, one from the office staff, and the plant safety coordinator. All members are volunteers and meet every two weeks, usually from one to three hours. Members carry the results of committee decisions back to their teams. According to the Bureau of Labor Statistics (all work-related injuries and illnesses are considered), in 1973 the Topeka plant had 4.4 injuries and illnesses per 100 full-time workers. The comparable rate for the food products industry as a whole is 19.3, and for all General Foods plants in the United States it is 7.2. There have been only two lost-time accidents in the plant's history, and none between January 1972 and June 1975.[10]

Professor Richard E. Walton of the Harvard Business School has served as a consultant to General Foods at the Topeka plant. Walton's observations regarding problems encountered are important. The following summary of his main points has been taken,

[10] Summarized from an article by G. Clack, *Job Safety and Health,* U.S. Department of Labor, Occupational Safety and Health Administration, July 1974.

with permission, from his article entitled "How to Counter Alienation in the Plant" in the November–December 1972 issue of *Harvard Business Review*.

A major problem cited by Professor Walton was the matter of compensation. There are four basic pay rates: starting rate, single job rate for mastering the first assignment, team rate for mastering all jobs within the team's jurisdiction, and plant rate for mastering all jobs. Virtually all employees in the initial workforce were hired at the same time, and at the end of the first six weeks most of them had qualified for their single job rate. Five months later, however, about one-third of the members of each team had been awarded the team rate. The decisions concerning individual pay had for the most part been made by team leaders, and the entire issue was discussed openly, with operators participating. Despite this openness, there remained questions concerning the fairness of the compensations awarded the individual operators.

Another source of difficulty was the reluctance and general uneasiness on the part of headquarters management, which displayed a traditional resistance to innovation. It was paramount that this be overcome since, in Professor Walton's judgment, involvement of the management group and commitment of it to the innovation were indispensable to the success of such a project.

He also cited several team and operator problems encountered. They were:

1. The expectations of a small minority of employees did not coincide with the demands placed on them by the new plant community. This small group of employees was uncomfortable in group meetings and uneasy in participating in the spontaneous mutual-help patterns which pervaded.

2. Some team leaders manifested considerable difficulty in not behaving like traditional authority figures. This difficulty was reinforced by the employees themselves, who, in some instances, seemed actively to seek traditional supervisory responses.

3. The norms covering various aspects of work were evolved by the self-managing work teams themselves, and if an individual

failed to conform to these norms, he was subject to excessive peer-group pressure.

4. There were some problems that ensued from the shifting of roles that took place in the plant. Team members were given assignments that are usually limited to supervisors, managers, or professionals. This sometimes generated mixed feelings among outsiders who had occasion to deal with persons in the plant. For example, a vendor who customarily made his sales to persons at higher organizational levels registered disappointment when he found he was dealing with a worker.

Management had specific expectations concerning anticipated gains from the new plant system: a more reliable, more flexible, and lower-cost manufacturing plant; a healthier work climate; and learning that could be applied to other corporate units. In his judgment, these goals were met. He cites the following eight factors which facilitated success of the plant:

1. Because of the particular technology and manufacturing processes used in this business, it was possible by more fully utilizing the human potential of employees to both enhance the quality of worklife and reduce costs.

2. It was technically and economically feasible to eliminate some inherently boring work and some of the physically disagreeable tasks.

3. The project had the advantage of being introduced in a new plant staffed by a workforce which was hired all at the same time.

4. The physical isolation of the plant from other parts of the company facilitated the development of unique organizational patterns.

5. Because the workforce was relatively small, it was possible to achieve individual recognition and identification.

6. The plant started as a nonunion plant and thus was unencumbered by constraints that organized labor might have imposed.

7. The technology called for and permitted communication within the workforce.

8. Employees were able to form a positive attitude toward the product and the company.

William Gomberg, a Wharton professor of management and industrial relations, is sharply critical of the Gaines experiment and the attempts to compare productivity at Topeka with the company's more traditional plant at Kankakee:[11]

Basically, what is claimed is that it was an innovative experiment in rescuing and revamping a low-morale workforce. But it really was a matter of running away from the original problems, in an Illinois plant, and building an ideal work environment through a careful selection of new personnel and the advantages of new physical facilities in Kansas.

Gomberg then goes on to criticize Professor Walton's analysis of the situation, citing in part from an article by Mitchell Fein ("The Real Needs and Goals of Blue Collar Workers," *The Conference Board Record,* February 1973):

Walton did not reveal that the new Topeka employees were screened for special skills and profiles to match the organization criteria that had been established for the new plant. . . . In a normal employee market, screening one out of four applicants is considered fairly tight. Here only one out of 10 was selected.

Nowhere does Walton mention that the problem-ridden plant is located in Kankakee, Illinois, and employs 1,200. At a 10–1 ratio, in hiring for a 1,200 employee plant, they would have to screen over 12,000. Where would all the people come from?

Walton says: "Using standard principles industrial engineers originally estimated 110 employees should man the plant. Yet the team concept, coupled with the integration of support activities into team responsibilities, has resulted in a manpower level of slightly fewer than 70 people."

[11] W. Gomberg, "Job Satisfaction: Sorting Out the Nonsense," *AFL-CIO American Federationist,* June 1973, 14–19. Quotation from Fein used by permission.

The results obtained at Topeka are valid only for Topeka. This was a stacked experiment in a small plant, with conditions set up and controlled to achieve a desired result. These employees were not a cross-section of the population, or even of Topeka. The plant and its operations are not typical of those in industry today. What are the other managers to do? Screen one in 10 employees and only hire these? And what about the other nine?

The GF-Topeka case proves nothing of value for operation managers.[12] Had the behaviorists gone to work on the Kankakee plant and shown how they converted a rundown plant, bursting with labor problems, into a plant where management and employees told glowingly of their accomplishments, the behaviorists would have earned the gratitude of everyone. Instead, they turned their backs on a plant which typifies the problems of the big city plants. Worse, they tantalize management with the prospect that, in building a new plant, with new equipment, with carefully selected employees and no union, productivity will be higher. Many managers have dreamed of relocating their plants in the wheat fields or the hills to escape the big city syndrome. Is this Walton's message to managers in his article "How to Counter Alienation in the Plants"? And is this case the HEW task force's contribution to the solution of the problems of the big city plants?

In a March 1974 update report on the Topeka plant, the following tangible results were reported by Edward R. Dulworth, the original Topeka project leader and plant manager, in a speech at the UCLA program on "The Changing World of Work."

1. Costs savings are 20 to 40 percent greater than for other plants in the company. This amounts to savings of about $2 million a year.

2. Regarding quality, rejects are about 80 percent less than what is normal in the business.

3. There has been minimal theft and no sabotage or worker-caused shutdowns.

4. Absenteeism is about 1½ percent, and 80 percent of that is with the knowledge and approval of management.

[12] True, the results of any given case do not *prove* that the methods which led to such results are generalizable. But the principles behind the Topeka *modus operandi* seem to show promising results in over 50 cases, many of which are cited in this report.—*E. M. G.*

5. Turnover is about 10 percent. This compares with about 15 percent for the parent company as a whole. About half of these people (the 10 percent) have quit and about half have been fired.

6. Three times as many employees are taking advantage of outside-education opportunities, compared with employees in the company's other plants.

7. Workers say they like the system, the work, and the opportunities. They are very open about any negatives. They feel they own the plant.

Dulworth also presented the following summary of problems:

1. The organization of the plant demands openness, honesty, and willingness to deal with problems among team members. Many people didn't respond initially to this type of demand, and this is still a problem.

2. The only real performance problem is in getting the workers to keep the plant as clean as it should be.

3. Some persons turned out not to fit well into this type of organization and have left or been fired.

4. There have been some problems to be worked through with the parent company, General Foods. Parent company management is uneasy about "who's in control" at Topeka. Also, the organization of the Topeka plant necessitates demands for much data by the teams that heretofore had not been available even to the plant manager. This sometimes creates difficulties for the parent company.

5. There has been some trouble getting *managers* to learn to operate in the open type of system that has been established at the Topeka plant. Most workers love the system.

Comment

Professor Gomberg's critique raises some legitimate questions about what can be generalized from the Topeka case. Contrary to what he says, however, overall evidence shows that permitting employees greater participation in decision making is successful in many situations other than the small, special one typified by the Topeka plant. Other case histories in this book do report substantial improvements in the quality of worklife and productivity in companies both big and small, new and old, unionized and non-union, urban and nonurban, and in different parts of the country. The conditions necessary for success are discussed in Chapter IV.

Three of the current and continuing difficulties noted by Edward Dulworth seem basic and pervasive in many company situations, even when hard-data results from an experimental program are very promising. One difficulty is that if top-level managers do not characteristically operate in this open style of inviting and rewarding problem identification and the involvement of the workforce in problem solving, they *are* likely to feel uneasy about "who is in control." Another difficulty is that many companies do not have the kinds of management information, productivity, and human-resources accounting systems that are needed to measure refined types of improvements over measured baseline data. To supply such data to work teams may be perceived as a burdensome chore, even though it can be argued that such data are very valuable as management tools under any rational style of management. A third difficulty—unfortunately—is that many managers feel psychologically threatened by systematically having problems brought into the open by those below them in the organizational hierarchy. Some managers see this as a threat, as an implication that they haven't been managing competently; others are inclined to feel there shouldn't be so many unresolved problems. An open system style of management does indeed call for a nondefensive climate in which constructive and creative challenge of standard practice is regarded as an act of caring, and as one of the best means of pursuing excellence, renewal, and progress.

American Telephone and Telegraph Company (AT&T)

This experimental study was prompted by the fact that, in the 1960s, when the nation's unemployment rate was low, AT&T was experiencing an unusually high turnover in virtually all departments. Jobs were relatively easy to find at the time, and there was little to persuade employees to stay on a job they did not find interesting. College recruiters, after listening to the complaints of those leaving the company, told AT&T: "You don't deserve the people we send out."

A particularly large number of new employees left after less than six months, before the company could offset their initial training costs. There was, then, a strong cost motivation to correct this situation.

The initial job enrichment study began in 1965 in AT&T's treasury department. Robert N. Ford,[13] personnel director of work organization and environmental research, listed the objectives of the treasury department experiment as:

1. Improve the quality of service.
2. Maintain or perhaps improve productivity levels.
3. Improve the turnover situation.
4. Lower costs.
5. Improve employee satisfaction in job assignments.

(The project director assumed that if the last objective was accomplished, the preceding four would follow—an assumption not always validated in other studies.)

The initial study group involved 104 women who answered customer-complaint letters and 16 women who handled telephone complaints. The employees were divided into five small groups:

1. The experimental group or, as it was called, the "achieving group" (20 women). These women's assignments would be vertically loaded (that is, loaded with additional responsibilities).
2. The phone answerers (16 women). Their uncommitted supervisor decided to make changes similar to those in the experimental group.

---

[13] R. N. Ford, *Motivation Through the Work Itself* (New York: American Management Association, 1969).

3. The control group (20 women). The second-level supervisor was asked to ignore the study, while the first-level supervisor and the employees were told nothing.

4. An uncommitted group (19 women).

5. Another uncommitted group (20 women).[14]

It is important to note that none of the women—or the first-level supervisors—were informed of the study in which they were participating.

The project director suggested certain starting guidelines:

1. Remove the sources of job dissatisfaction—poor wages, poor working conditions, inadequate supervision.

2. But don't expect removing these to make up for boring jobs. If the job is boring, load it with true work motivators: achievement as perceived by the employee, recognition associated with an achievement, more responsibility, advancement to a higher order of task, and growth of employee competence.

The project director had warned management that there might be an initial drop in productivity and in employee attitudes, and he requested that in spite of this possibility they permit the experiment to run for the full six-month period. Although there was considerable managerial anxiety about the experiment, this support was granted.

In designing the project, the director was eager to differentiate between horizontal and vertical job loading.[15] Horizontal loading,

[14] Note that the sum of the five groups differs from the number originally involved in the study. Dr. Ford explains: "The volume of letters tapered off during the six-month study period, as expected, when a business problem was resolved. Therefore, some natural shrinkage in the size of the total group was allowed to occur: It decreased from 120 to 95. Of these women in the September analysis, 90 were the same individuals who started out in March."

[15] These concepts were first developed by Frederick Herzberg, now a professor at the University of Utah.

he explained to top-level supervisors, meant simply enlarging a job or rearranging its parts without making it more challenging. The following suggestions for horizontal loading for the department were proposed and rejected:

1. Setting firm quotas of letters to be answered each day.

2. Channeling all difficult, complex inquiries to a few women so that the remainder might attain high rates of output.

3. Rotating the women through the telephone units to units handling different customers and then back to their own units.

4. Letting the women type the letters themselves, as well as compose them, or take on other clerical functions such as reviewing the files or obtaining detailed information.

"Obviously this type of loading does not really improve the task, but it is unquestionably aimed at this end," observed Ford. "We often turn completely away from a bad job assignment and attempt to make the work tolerable by improving rest rooms, adding soft music, subtracting time worked via coffee breaks and so on. In effect, these moves say, 'This work is boring but it must be done. Please do it and we'll try to reduce the level of pain.' "

Focusing on what could be done to make the job itself more challenging (vertical loading), the project director and top-level supervisors for the achieving group made the following changes:

1. Subject-matter experts were appointed within each unit for other members of the unit to consult with before seeking supervisory help. (Later on it was found that the women had rearranged these assignments among themselves along lines they felt to be more meaningful. This was a real test of the climate of responsibility the company was trying to build, and it was accepted as such by management.)

2. Correspondents were told to sign their own names to letters from the very first day on the job after training. Previously the verifier or supervisor usually signed for many months.

3. The work of the more experienced correspondents was looked over less frequently by supervisors, and this was done at each correspondent's desk. Instead of verifying 100 percent of the letters, the supervisors reduced the proportion to 10 percent, a source of significant dollar savings.

4. Less rather than more pressure was placed upon the group for production.

5. Outgoing work went directly to the mailroom without crossing the supervisor's desk.

6. All correspondents were told that they would be held fully accountable for the quality of their work—a responsibility previously shared with verifiers and supervisors.

7. Correspondents were encouraged to answer letters in a more personalized way rather than adhering to a standard form letter.

Among the results reported for the first six-month trial period were:

1. All groups within the experiment showed improvements in the quality of customer service, as measured by an index already used in the company, but the experimental groups were well ahead of the others.

2. Turnover was greatly reduced for the two achieving groups, but continued at the former high level for the control group and the two uncommitted groups.

3. There was a reduction in absences of long duration among the experimental workers: from 2.0 to 1.4 percent. The control group showed a slight increase in this category of absences.

4. No great emphasis was placed on productivity in measuring results, since it was conceded that it could take from 20 minutes to two days to compose an appropriate letter. However, the experimental groups exceeded previous levels of productivity.

5. The great majority of promotions were being made out of groups 1 and 2, because of their better performance.

6. There was a substantial improvement in job attitude among the achieving group, a smaller improvement in the telephone group, and a deterioration of attitude in the control group and one of the uncommitted groups. The other uncommitted group showed a slight improvement.

At the time of the final survey, members of the achieving group reported that they now derived greater satisfaction from the job and felt their performance had improved because of this. Achieving-group supervisors found fewer crises, few necessities for repeat calls, and higher group morale (demonstrated by group enthusiasm toward work problems). Achieving-group supervisors find that more of their time is now available for actual supervisory work rather than having all their time absorbed by verifying outgoing letters, a responsibility which the women now accept themselves.

At the end of the six-month trial, top management in AT&T's treasury department set up a small manpower utilization group involving more than 1,150 employees, including several hundred supervisors. A year and a half later, the company estimated that the program had saved $558,000.

On the basis of its successes in the treasury department, AT&T then conducted 18 additional studies at various companies within the Bell System. A variety of departments were included: engineering, traffic, plant, controllers, and commercial (service representatives). Space does not allow a detailed description of the project, but it can be stated that good results were reported throughout the system. None of the projects had the impressive results found at the treasury department, but there were substantial improvements in the commercial departments and visible, consistent good results with the controllers.

Early in 1968, top management of the Bell System decided to take employee-motivation programs out of the category of "special trial projects" and include them as part of its ongoing program of development. As Ford notes: "This is, in a very real sense, the most substantial proof of the success of the projects to date."

In his book on the AT&T experiments, Ford points out the need to distinguish between corporate purpose and individual employee purpose and to concentrate on helping the employee meet his job needs. The worker is deeply committed to serving the customer only when he is simultaneously meeting his own needs. The employee will serve management well because he has his own little part of the business to run, not because of attempts to motivate him from outside his own frame of needs.

Ford concluded: "The data from these studies show that it is possible to get an order-of-magnitude change, not just a small increment. Modern employees are bright, healthy, well-fed and well-educated compared to those in the time-and-motion study days. They will not accept dull jobs unless the jobs are their very own. We must set the conditions of work so as to gradually maximize the responsibility thrust upon the worker. . . . To do this we must ask ourselves:

- What do I do for him that he could now do for himself?
- What thinking can he now do for himself?
- What goals could we now set *jointly?*
- What advanced training or skill could he now have?
- What job could he work toward now? How could I help him?
- Is there a way of combining this job with another one he would like? Is the module right?
- Is there anything he does that could be given to a lower-rated job?
- Could anything be automated out of the job?

We must learn to trade off engineering economies for human values and not to assume that this will be costly. . . . We will know that we are doing something right if we can change the conditions of the job so that employees will stay on and work productively. . . . The way to achieve this end, for new or old employees, is not to confront them with demands, but to confront them with demanding, meaningful work. And the employee will always have the last word as to whether the work is meaningful."

In a *Harvard Business Review* article, Robert Ford[16] summarizes the specific steps toward improving a work task as systematic changes in (1) the module of work, (2) control of the module, and

[16] R. N. Ford, "Job Enrichment Lessons from AT&T," *Harvard Business Review,* January–February 1973, 96–106. Used with permission.

(3) the feedback signaling whether something has been accomplished. Ford describes how a "slice" of work can be redesigned into a natural, functional unit and control of it then given to the employee with sufficient feedback so the worker knows how he is doing.

In later discussions of the AT&T program, Ford emphasized that the way in which change is brought about is more important than the specific details of job redesign. In general, he says, those involved in the work must arrive at their own decisions about the changes to be made, and take joint responsibility for putting those changes into effect. (The author of this book found that there are many instances where this is not true. Sometimes change is most effectively brought about by a legal or administrative ruling which requires local conformance.)

Comment

AT&T is one of the largest companies, if not the largest, in the United States. Job enrichment efforts have the support of the company president and are spreading slowly through the company. How well it works depends largely on the receptiveness of local managers and department heads.

In the Bell System the guiding philosophy has been to give the employee every part of the job that he or she is able to handle in the area bearing on the employee-customer relationship. At the moment the company believes job enrichment should be confined to this area. Charles V. Pfautz, staff supervisor at C&P Telephone in Washington, D.C., diagrams this concept as follows:

SUPERVISOR ⟶ EMPLOYEE ⟶ CUSTOMER

Hiring
Developing   The task
Training   (enrich this
Setting goals and standards   area only)
Performance appraisal

AT&T and many other companies adopt a more conservative attitude toward job enrichment than firms like Donnelly Mirrors or General Foods. Size may have something to do with this—although other large companies, such as Procter and Gamble, General Electric, and Imperial Chemical, have pursued job enrichment efforts in areas other than just employee-customer relations.

Each company that decides to experiment with quality of work-life programs needs to do its own planning and to take account of its own situation. Of major importance is how the program is introduced and carried out.

CRYOVAC Division, W. R. Grace & Company[17]

In 1968, the CRYOVAC Division of W. R. Grace & Company made a decision to open its first West Coast manufacturing facility, and after surveys for a plant site were conducted in several areas, selected Camarillo, California. Viewing itself as an innovator in employee relations, this leader in the manufacture of heat-shrink plastic packaging material conducted a study of possible effects of operating this sixth plant in the 2,000-employee CRYOVAC organization in accordance with the concepts of behavioral science. Initial interest centered on fostering a participative approach to management, which, it was hoped, would alleviate sources of employee dissatisfaction. Of special interest was a growing trend to place blue-collar workers on a salaried status as one way of fostering mutual trust and respect.

CRYOVAC interviewed a number of all-salaried firms as it developed the following criteria to govern management at the new Camarillo plant:

- A belief that the potential for innovative or creative contribution is widely distributed in the working population.

- A belief that most people want to do a good job and will if they are given the opportunity.

[17] This section is based on R. M. Frame, *Organizational Redesign: A Study in Transition.* Prepared for McGraw-Hill Book Company, April 1973.

- A belief that most people flourish and improve in value to the organization when given increased responsibility commensurate with their capabilities.

- A belief that a maximally effective organization is achievable only through the development of a comprehensive program of human resource management.

Translated into operational terms, these beliefs meant conversion to a unified system of compensation for all nonexempt (that is, hourly-paid) employees; elimination of time clocks and of job titles which might be perceived as demeaning; reduction of differences in philosophy and policy toward exempt (salaried) versus nonexempt personnel; development of personnel policies consistent with certain assumptions about human nature (primarily those of mutual respect and trust in key areas); and finally, acceptance of the need to develop and implement—"at the earliest practicable date consistent with plant startup"—a systematic program of job enrichment.

At that time, the phrase "job enrichment" was merely a popular catchword to the newly-formed management team, which included representatives of various divisions of W. R. Grace. The many pressures and problems of plant startup notwithstanding, the group did hold several weeks of regular discussion regarding the philosophy of management they intended to implement and the benefits they hoped to achieve.

The actual benefits of the new managerial criteria are summarized in Figure 2. Top management backed off and took a good look. It then began to dimly realize that the real potential in human resource maximization did not lie in dealing with the environment or *context* within which the basic jobs were performed. Rather, it lay in the *content* of those jobs. And while most of the operational plans outlined above had been worked at with some vigor, a key element was missing. That key element was the redesigning, rearranging, and restructuring of tasks so that they would become more interesting and challenging, thereby providing more opportunities for growth, achievement, responsibility, and self-control. With only moderate differences, the Camarillo jobs were

Figure 2 The CRYOVAC Program

Program Objective:

THESE VARIABLES SHOULD YIELD THESE VARIABLES, WHICH IN TURN SHOULD PRODUCE THESE VARIABLES

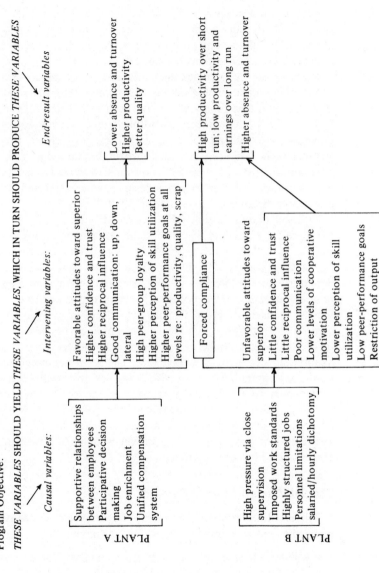

Causal variables:

PLANT A

Supportive relationships between employees
Participative decision making
Job enrichment
Unified compensation system

PLANT B

High pressure via close supervision
Imposed work standards
Highly structured jobs
Personnel limitations
salaried/hourly dichotomy

Intervening variables:

Favorable attitudes toward superior
Higher confidence and trust
Higher reciprocal influence
Good communication: up, down, lateral
High peer-group loyalty
Higher perception of skill utilization
Higher peer-performance goals at all levels re: productivity, quality, scrap

Forced compliance

Unfavorable attitudes toward superior
Little confidence and trust
Little reciprocal influence
Poor communication
Lower levels of cooperative motivation
Lower perception of skill utilization
Low peer-performance goals
Restriction of output

End-result variables

Lower absence and turnover
Higher productivity
Better quality

High productivity over short run; low productivity and earnings over long run
Higher absence and turnover

identical to those in the older company plants. Placing blue-collar employees on a salaried basis was not likely to have any of the desired results in motivation and productivity, nor was lip service to management philosophy, however sincere. Professional help was indicated, and the company obtained it.

Because of the complex technologies in the plant—extruded saran tubing, flexographic tubing, and special-design bagmaking—it was decided that an analytical approach to job enrichment which incorporated both engineering and behavioral science was critical. David A. Whitsett, an associate and former student of Frederick Herzberg, who had been consulted early in the planning, was brought back into the picture. Whitsett in turn called upon Louis E. Davis, an international expert in job redesign who was located within a reasonable distance of the Camarillo plant.[18]

Whitsett reiterated that job enrichment is essentially a strategy for more fully utilizing the talents and competencies of employees by placing in their hands as much decision making and responsibility as they can handle. Davis agreed, and also added another dimension to the process of analyzing the plant's problem: He pointed out that in a technologically sophisticated environment like that at Camarillo, before turning over decision making and self-control to employees with the aforementioned hoped-for results, there was a need to be certain what the sources of variance in quality and productivity really were. Davis further noted that the most meaningful and productive kinds of responsibilities to be turned over to employees were precisely those that would help them recognize and control major sources of variance. Herzberg's concept of vertical loading was thus enriched by the analytical "variance analysis" approach, forming what later proved to be a powerful tool for job enrichment.

The Job Design Team Is Formed

The end-line process department, "Bagmaking," was selected as being the one that involved the greatest number of workers and

[18] Whitsett is a senior associate with Drake-Beam & Associates; Davis is chairman of the Center for Quality of Working Life, UCLA.

contributed most to the cost of the product. Not only was probability of success good, due to greater human resources, but program impact would be highly visible.

A job enrichment team was selected, composed of the first-line supervisors in the department in question. With the initial help of the outside consultants, the team members first studied job redesign philosophy and then met once a week for a full day, for some 20 weeks. Utilizing the Herzberg approach initially, they discussed ideas for making the work more meaningful, generating more than 100 possibilities in the first session alone. The team then set these aside for a time and employed the sociotechnical analysis of variance approach described above to pinpoint the many sources of technical problems affecting the basic tasks and hence the employees. Beginning at the end of the production process and working backwards from symptom to cause, the team initially defined some 150 key variables, screened them down to 48 "super" variables and analyzed these one by one. The criteria established for final inclusion in the new job structure were as follows:

Is it motivating? That is . . .

- Does it offer increased challenge to the incumbent?
- Does it provide a more complete task?
- Does it contribute to a logical work module, with a visible beginning and end?
- Does it offer timely feedback on how well the job is being done?
- Does it give the incumbent greater control over the work, including decision making?

New Job Structures Are Developed

Once the variance analysis hypotheses surviving the above screen were combined with those that had resulted from the discussion of general enrichment, a new job structure was developed. Work modules were ranked as to the degree of difficulty and responsibility, consistent with natural training approaches required for the employee starting a new job on the bottom rung of the ladder.

The issue of promotion and compensation arose early. The final policies developed incorporated a principle of promotion and pay based on demonstrated skills proficiency. With few constraints, an employee could progress as fast and as far up the training ladder as his individual ability and motivation would allow. Higher levels of proficiency were directly related to increased compensation. Training and compensation were thus individualized. Performance reviews, based on the considerable objective data available on individual productivity, were conducted on the principle of evaluation by mutually established objectives between employee and supervisor.

Shift Manning Changes

Having finally developed job structures, the job enrichment team worked out an action plan for the transition to a new mode of shift manning. Thus the Bagmaking Department changed from a three-on-two manning mode, with one operator and two inspector-packers manning two machines, to a one-on-one mode in which all but two employees were encouraged to learn the *entire* machine operation and handle it alone. This was done by means of a hierarchy of six skill levels, through which an operator was given opportunity to progress as fast as his or her ability to take advantage of training would allow. Compensation was thereby tied directly to contribution, since pay adjustments were made immediately upon demonstration of proficiency at the next higher rung on the job ladder.

The Program Is Expanded

Early in 1972, several key events resulted in the Camarillo program's being extended to all major departments in the plant. Thanks to the work accomplished under his predecessor, Plant Manager R. B. Fenyves was able to capitalize on the initial experience and begin immediately to focus his administration on a central theme: Camarillo's job enrichment program was to become not merely an experiment in reducing worker alienation, with hoped-for benefits in employee satisfaction and productivity; rather, it was to enlarge to a comprehensive, systematic approach to cost-effective management plantwide. Plant management had come to realize that significant progress in the redesign of jobs could only occur in a climate of organizational change wherein no departmental lines were sacred. For example, one job design team was struggling with problems of machine maintenance. Management realized that the team would be severely restricted in creating the most beneficial organization of tasks and assignments unless the members could work both for and with the production supervisor instead of reporting to an outside staff department. Following the transition, the maintenance force became an integral part of the production team, reporting directly to the production shift supervisor.

Fenyves had also learned as production manager that jurisdictional conflict between production departments reduces efficiency and constrains organizational development. Solution: Encourage job redesign teams elsewhere in the plant not to concern themselves with these artificial barriers to optimum human resource utilization. How? By simply eliminating the barriers themselves. As management promotions to other operations occurred, an opportunity to merge the remaining two production departments (Printing and Extrusion) presented itself.

Next, coordination of the newly developing approach to management was established throughout the plant. Each line and staff department was encouraged to begin discussion of its particular opportunities, needs, and problems in utilizing manpower, and to follow what had by now become a systematic, step-by-step program that went far beyond mere delegation of greater decision-making control to employees.

Capitalizing on the experience and mistakes of the experimental group, a job design team in the newly formed Press/Extrusion Department began work in the spring of 1972. A preliminary comparison of the results of the initial March 1971 organization and machine-manning mode with that of August 1972 shows that first and second level supervision was reduced by 50 percent, with the new department under the direction of only one production superintendent. As with Bagmaking, the maintenance workforce now reported directly to line management. The resultant reduction in workforce was from 15.5 nonexempt and 6 exempt employees per shift to 12.5 nonexempt and 2 exempt.

Such a dramatic change was not without its problems, particularly during a period when there was intensifying pressure because of a sharp increase in the volume of production.[19] To offset understandable feelings of threat associated with these changes, the new job design team decided to involve the employees to a much greater degree in the planning. A series of meetings was held to get the employees' reactions to the anticipated changes in organization and job content and to ask them for suggestions. By this time, many rumors were flying regarding the initial program in Bagmaking. The meetings minimized these, and succeeded in improving acceptance of change on the part of operating personnel.

The absence of any major morale or production problem in Bagmaking, coupled with the aggressive support of the program by both the plant manager and his successor as production manager, J. W. Scott, greatly assisted the team of supervisors to internalize the principles involved while reducing feelings of insecurity about their own future roles. The new system was perceived by most of them as *their* program—one designed essentially to free them from production "firefighting" and make them full-fledged shift managers by pushing down decision-making authority over production problems to the lowest level in the organization. While this did not erase their feelings of ambivalence, it tended to minimize their feelings of insecurity about their own future (a problem common to almost all reported experiments along these lines).

Results to Date

There have been overall organizational changes in the management structure as a result of the program. For one thing, the position of a quality control manager was eliminated. It became clear early in the program that one opportunity available was to eliminate inspectors—who, after all, could not inspect quality into the

[19] In March 1971, the average units-per-day volume was 250,000. By August 1972 it had increased to 420,000. By April 1973 it was close to 500,000.

product. By giving the production personnel timely feedback or information (through inspection of samples) regarding the quality of what they were turning out, responsibility for improvement was returned to those who made the product. Many quality problems were thereby solved. This enabled the plant to eliminate by attrition a number of quality control inspectors and to merge the quality control function into both line management and operating responsibilities.

A customer-account assignment program in Bagmaking was launched to give operators greater identification with the customer using their output. This included visits to customer operations by some operating employees. Integration of the quality control function with the operating duties did not result in a deterioration of quality. One key index: Flexographic print quality did not deteriorate, with the Camarillo facility winning five out of six print-quality awards given on an interplant competitive basis bimonthly beginning in the early fall of 1971.

The reduction in second-level production supervision and the shift in production maintenance from engineering to production were mentioned earlier. Other changes included the shift of production control to the direct cognizance of line management.

Notwithstanding two general wage increases during that period, a 28.6 percent improvement in units of output per direct labor dollar was achieved between March 1971 and February 1973. And, during a period when production output rose 68 percent, overall plant personnel was reduced 9.7 percent.

According to the team working currently in the newly formed Press/Extrusion Department, the performance in their area can be attributed to the following:

- More effective utilization of capital equipment (50 percent increase in run-time capacity).
- Increased output (a conservative potential of 50 percent).
- Reduced conflict between operating employees through more direct control over process variance.
- Increased skill utilization and flexibility.

Attitude Surveyed

Employees' attitudes, as measured in part by a recent anonymous survey, range from skeptical optimism on the part of some who are as yet uncertain how the whole program will affect them in areas where the program is only in its infancy, to strong endorsement in areas where it has matured. A significant example relates to the sensitive area of compensation. On this issue the survey reflected that by far the most satisfied group was the Bagmaking Department, where the concept of pay-for-skills-proficiency has prevailed the longest. The same group reported a higher perception of "opportunity for advancement" and a higher general feeling of identification with the company than any other production or maintenance group.

The attitude of management is perhaps best reflected in the comments of the new chief executive at the plant, R. B. Fenyves:

Effective human resource management is more than a pill labeled "job enrichment." Only when you begin to sense that it's the only sensible way to run a business and not merely another personnel program to make employees "happy" does this style of management cease to be merely a buzz word. We're not ready to export our program yet. . . . In fact, we may never suggest that other company units duplicate it at all because it must be customized to fit each situation, and they all differ. However, there are definite principles involved which demand hard work on the part of everyone. The program must cut across traditional thinking about total organization before the real potential can be tapped. Hence, it is a slow process but one with a measurable payout in benefits for everyone concerned.

Comment (by Robert Frame)

The Camarillo story has really only begun, but local CRYOVAC management believes that several preliminary conclusions are warranted for its own program:

1. Salaried status for blue-collar workers, though it minimizes dissatisfaction with differential treatment, is not in and of itself a motivational program.

2. If introduced into an otherwise unchanged organizational climate, such an investment is unlikely to produce hoped-for results in reduced employee alienation or measurable performance improvement.

3. Job enrichment, participative decision making, and similar programs aimed at dealing with a young workforce demanding more meaning from employment and desiring to achieve cost-effective human resource utilization are relatively unlikely *by themselves* to achieve the very ambitious program objectives outlined earlier.

4. The most powerful solution is to integrate such programs into an overall, systematic organization design effort, one which takes advantage of every personnel change and views it against the background of a master human resource blueprint.

5. The above implies at best enthusiastic top management support or at worst a "hands off" agreement until and unless any experimental group appears in serious trouble. Only in an organizational climate essentially free of serious doubts about top management interference or support can the grass-roots work progress effectively.

Corning Glass Works

The following is a condensation from *Improving Organizational Effectiveness Through Planned Change and Development* by Michael Beer and Edgar Huse, an unpublished study made in August 1970.

For the past several years a Corning plant has been the target and focus of an experiment in management. The purpose of the experiment has been to see if a planned and concentrated effort at developing an effective organization could alleviate two major crises facing contemporary organizations. First, work organizations (industry, government, universities, hospitals, schools, etc.) are facing a crisis in employee commitment and motivation. Lack of adaptability to change, both internal and external to the organization, constitutes a second major crisis for contemporary organizations.

We have been involved in a program of organization development aimed at putting into practice management patterns that could reverse these crises in organizations. This trend has been reversed in the plant we will tell you about. Through applying new management patterns in a planned and concentrated manner, commitment and motivation are high as exemplified through low absenteeism and turnover and a reduced need for supervision. Increases in productivity and high quality have also been documented. The ability of employees to respond to change has been demonstrated through rapid product introduction. The workforce is committed to attainment of plant goals and, through this, the attainment of their personal goals.

The Organization

The organizational development program has taken place in a plant manufacturing a variety of instruments for medical and laboratory use. The range of products varies from relatively simple to highly complex. There are approximately 70 hourly employees, mostly women with a high school education. There are approximately 35 weekly salaried technical and clerical personnel and 11 monthly salaried professional and managerial personnel.

Crucial decisions were in the making concerning the plant's methods of production, means of setting production standards and controls, personnel policies and practices, managerial practices and philosophy. These decisions were certain to be influenced largely by the traditions and practices of the parent corporation and stood the chance of being inconsistent in their basic thrust.

It became clear that a unique opportunity existed for bringing this process of decision making to a conscious level and consistency by getting the management team to develop a managerial philosophy and plan. Enough interest was generated by the personnel supervisor (there have been two others since) to start a series of seminars on current participative concepts in management. The purpose of the seminars was to contrast traditional approaches with approaches implicit in current organizational and behavioral research findings and theory.

The question, it seemed to us, was not really whether to implement participative management, but how much, how fast? At any given time employees are more or less ready or able to work effectively under participative management. The managerial approaches chosen not only should reflect the current state of readiness but should anticipate a direction of change (i.e., more participation) and lead the employees. Thus, the goal was a "positive snowball of change," heightened expectations and readiness for more change, further change, and so on.

The Means of Change

The emphasis was to concentrate on helping with present problems. The idea was to get someone or some organizational component to start implementing managerial concepts inherent in the ideal model of management. Access to these concepts came through our consulting on a specific problem they were facing, or may have come briefly but without full understanding through the initial few seminars that were held. The result was that there were a few individuals throughout the plant who began, with our aid, to apply some new concepts. As it turned out, most of these early experiments were successful, resulting in reinforcement for the individual and the organization, thereby enhancing interest and motivation to change.

What were some of the management patterns and organizational arrangements tried? We will summarize the new management patterns which were applied in two categories: those changes that relate to the behavior of individuals and groups; and those changes that relate to technology, tasks, and organizational structure.

Changes in the Behavior of Individuals and Groups

In this part of the program we wanted to work directly on organizational processes having to do with interpersonal and social variables: We wanted to improve the leadership and supervision potential in the plant; we wanted to improve communications; we wanted to establish and develop work groups that were effective in dealing with their jobs by themselves; and we wanted to improve intergroup relationships.

Communications

Although the plant already had the normal kinds of staff meetings and communications channels, we wanted to go further, particularly in improving the openness and quality of communication and making it two-way. What were some of the communications changes?

Departmental Meetings   The individual supervisors began, with relatively little training, a series of monthly meetings between each supervisor and his subordinates. This occurred at all levels of the organization, including first-line supervisors with their production employees. The format of these meetings, initially, was simply the supervisor telling his subordinates what was going on in the plant and in the individual department; what the monthly objectives of the plant were and how the plant was doing with regard to its objectives; how the department objectives fitted in with the plant objectives; and the like. At the same time, the supervisor tried to get feedback from his people, including comments, ideas, and suggestions regarding the things that had been discussed, and to obtain information about how they felt about the plant and what was going on.

How did the meetings go? They grew and developed over the next several years to truly involved, two-way communication. One of the interesting things that began to happen in the meetings is that, particularly at the production-worker level, the communications changed from "mini-gripes" to "mega-gripes"; that is, the discussions, questions, and comments changed from very specific topics, such as vacation and sick-leave policies, to areas of broader concern, such as: "What is our product being used for?" "Who is using it?" "What do they think of it?" "Are the quality standards that we are using high enough?" "What is the future of the business?"

"Coffee with the Boss"   A weekly communication meeting was set up between the plant manager and a sample group of hourly

and weekly employees (on a rotating basis) to close the communications loop at the top. Again, the discussion showed over time the same kind of shift that has already been described in the departmental meetings.

Other Approaches   As the meetings changed in content and openness, it became evident that employees at all levels wanted more information about their jobs and how they fitted into the organization, as well as how the business was doing. As a result, plant tours were initiated to show employees from one department what was happening in other departments.

In addition, charts were placed at the major traffic point in the plant. These charts, brought up to date monthly, show actual versus budgeted progress in areas such as sales, inventory, plant effectiveness, and the like. For proprietary reasons it was, however, necessary to leave actual dollar figures and similar information off the charts.

The process of increased and improved communication described above may seem deceptively easy to achieve and maintain. In retrospect the period during which communication was developing was a critical period; trust was building, and a culture conducive to further change was developing.

Leadership and Supervision

Leadership style not only is reflected in the nature of communication, job structure, and organization structure but is also affected by them. In short, leadership is not easily isolated from many of the other descriptive categories that we use.

Perhaps the most interesting aspect of the development of participative management was the early difficulties encountered by the managers in understanding the concept and applying it. After participative and supportive management had been discussed in the early seminars and with individual managers, we found that several individuals were interpreting this to mean a "hands off, be warm and friendly to everyone regardless of the situation" type of approach. That is, they were swinging from a hard to soft, from a directive to a laissez-faire style of management, in an attempt to find and establish a new pattern of management. When, not surprisingly, laissez-faire and friendliness did not work, increased frustration on the part of the supervisor would erupt into a new, tough, and quite unexpected (from the employee's point of view) approach to a problem. These swings were not surprising to the change agents and reflected a trial-and-error learning process on the part of the managers.

We pointed out that participative management is an integration of concern for people and concern for production through mutual involvement by boss and subordinate in goal-setting and major decisions affecting subordinates. That is, concern for people is not best expressed in a lack of attention to task and the development of a country-club atmosphere. Instead, concern for people is expressed through involvement in the processes of decision making and task and objective setting.

Such counseling led to the utilization of a management-by-objectives or work-planning approach at several levels of the organization. For example, production and other goals were mutually planned and set by the production superintendent and the production workers.

Other examples of a supportive, participative, and delegating but performance-oriented style of management also exist. Performance reviews are held with all employees, including hourly employees. These reviews are two-way discussions. The supervisor gives his impression of the subordinate's performance, and the subordinate gives his impression of his own performance, and in some cases that of his supervisor. A "Rate-Your-Boss" form was prepared, and several supervisors have asked subordinates to fill out the form and discuss it. Thus participation is carried over to a discussion of respective boss-subordinate performances.

Intergroup Processes and Relationships

Work on intergroup relations was important, we felt, because of the interdependence of departments in accomplishing plant objectives and the fact that differences between department goals and time horizons often create intergroup conflict.

A meeting was held with the department managers and the

change agents to discuss perceptions of their own departments and of the other departments. During that meeting frank discussions were carried on regarding what were seen as the good and bad points of each department.

Following that meeting it was decided that follow-on meetings of the same type should be held and that the format and style of these meetings should be expanded. As an example, cross-department meetings were established on a periodic basis. In these meetings the "monthly" personnel of a particular department would meet, in turn, with each other department to discuss expectations, perceptions, and strong and weak points. Although it is difficult to state precisely what the results of these meetings were, the general consensus was that they had been extremely helpful.

Group and Team Development   The plant manager and his staff formed themselves into a "board of directors" for the plant. As a group they would meet once a month to discuss a plant problem and try to develop a team solution to it. These and similar meetings were sometimes attended by one of us as participants, observers, and (occasionally) team facilitators and developers. In the latter role we sat in on meetings that managers had with their own staffs and, after the meetings, led a discussion of how they had gone and how they might be more effective. Openness between peers, as well as boss and subordinates, became more and more of a reality in the plant.

Changes in Technology, Jobs, and Organizational Structure

For change to last beyond the individual job incumbents, attention must be given to situational factors such as goals, measures, and controls; organizational structure; and the flow of information, materials, and ideas. For these reasons the development program has emphasized equally structural, job, and systems changes. In bringing about these changes we were striving to follow two principles:

1. *Job enrichment.* We wanted to change the structure of jobs to give individuals more opportunity to handle the whole job, with

responsibility for *planning, doing,* and *controlling* their own work. The objective was to create more interesting and challenging work. These changes, it was felt, would reinforce the evolution toward participative management and would further enhance employee involvement and motivation.

2. *Autonomous work teams.* We wanted to create cohesive work groups around interrelated or interdependent jobs. The purpose was to create further meaning in work through identification with a group. Group cohesiveness in turn could serve as an important positive influence on motivation and commitment.

Several of the structural and job enrichment changes are discussed below.

The Hot Plate Department

This is a department assembling a number of different models of hot plates for laboratory and hospital usage. It had already been pretty well streamlined into the normal assembly-line operation. There were six women, each of whom had a small part in the total assembly. The line had been balanced, and management was generally satisfied with productivity. After considering several alternatives and discussing them with other people, the first-line supervisor and the engineer came up with a design that was radically different from the assembly line. It was decided to give each of the women the responsibility for assembling the entire hot plate.

When the changeover was made, each woman was expected to do the whole job. No other changes were made in the department, and no change was made in personnel.

What were the results? First, the women responded positively to the change. As one women remarked, "Now, it's *my* hot plate." Second, there was a drop in controllable rejects (those within the control of the workers) from 23 percent to approximately 1 percent in the next six months. Absenteeism dropped from about 8 percent to about 1 percent in the same period of time.

What happened to productivity? The changeover occurred in mid-year. If one takes the average productivity for the first half of the year and compares it directly with the average productivity for the second half of the year, there is an 84 percent gain in productivity. If one takes the last three accounting periods (based on four-week accounting periods) in the first half of the year and compares these with the last three accounting periods of the year, there is a 47 percent increase in productivity.

The Glass Shop

The next step was in the Glass Shop, where women were working on lathes, forming glass for electrodes. The supervisor there decided that he was going to try the team approach to productivity.

His approach to his people was very simple. He told them, "Look, I think we ought to organize around teams, and you four women are responsible for the 'X' electrode. You are going to be responsible for the total task; and I want you to know that we're going to need 500 of these the next accounting period. You women decide who's going to do what and how you're going to do it, and you schedule it."

Not all the employees in the Glass Shop reacted favorably to the proposed change. Some saw it as a tribute to their ability and were very enthusiastic; others were not used to dealing with this type of climate or supervisory style and were suspicious. For example, with regard to doing their own scheduling, some individuals wondered if the supervisor was abdicating his responsibility. As it turned out, this particular change immediately resulted in an increase in productivity. There were rapid and lasting changes in the involvement and commitment of the employees and their interest in the work. For example, on occasion the women would stay in the cafeteria after work and after punching out, to discuss schedules and manufacturing problems over a cup of coffee. So that the schedules would look neat and presentable, one woman took them home at night to type, even though she knew she shouldn't work overtime without pay.

The Materials Control Department

The Materials Control Department has responsibility for the following functions: purchasing, inventory control, scheduling, and expediting. The department was functionally arranged; that is, there were people assigned to each of the four specialty areas. However, the plant was being plagued with parts shortages, which caused delays in the production of units needed for delivery. This was affecting the profit margin as well as service to customers. After enriching the job of his secretary and finding, to his surprise, that she was more involved in her work and liked it better, and he had less to do, the department supervisor decided that his organizational structure was wrong and that job enrichment could be applied to his whole department.

Rather than having each work group specialize in a particular functional area, he decided to organize his department around product-line teams. Each group would have total project responsibility for a particular product line, including all four functions: expediting, scheduling, purchasing, and inventory control. The supervisor felt that this would reduce his parts shortage problem, solve his communications problems, and make the work more interesting for his people.

Since this was a radical change, he moved slowly and discussed with the plant management, the change agents, and his people alternative ways of going about the structural change, the impact upon his people, and the need to go slowly and to keep the "back door open" in case he needed to retreat from the project-team approach.

When he made the change, people were ready. What were the results? In a three-month period of time, the parts shortage list was reduced from 14 IBM pages to less than one page. This was with the same volume of business. It must be pointed out that later, as the volume of business increased and as more complex instruments were introduced, the absolute number of parts shortages increased, although the relative number still showed a considerable net decrease. We also obtained very positive interview data on the involvement, commitment, and motivation of the employees in the department.

The Instrument Department

The Instrument Department makes complex devices ranging in worth up to $3,000. Here there have been both successes and failures in job enrichment and organizational development. Early in the development effort one of the supervisors was faced with the problem of which woman to assign to two different production areas. The supervisor decided to ask his people to fill out a sociometric questionnaire that asked, "Who would you like to work with most? Next most?" and so on. However, he did not prepare his people very well and had not yet established sufficient trust to carry it out. His employees rebelled and said, "I'm sorry, boss; that's your job to tell us who's going to work for whom; that's not our job." At a deeper level they were saying, "We're not ready for this kind of change yet; what are you talking about? This is not our proper role."

Some months later this supervisor left the plant for a better job and a new supervisor took over the Instrument Deparment. The new supervisor began by being extremely frank and open with his people, explaining why schedule changes were necessary and the like. At the same time he began to have discussions with his people as to how schedules could be met and began working toward involving his people in the planning process. He also began working toward what he calls the "total job concept." This is only a different term for what we have earlier called job enrichment. Over the last year he has been able to implement this concept so that he now has women doing individual, complete assembly of complex instrument systems with up to 500 parts and 12 printed circuit boards.

In addition to this, four new instruments were introduced on the manufacturing floor in three months. Rather than having a marked drop in productivity, as would be the case in most traditional electronics firms, productivity was reduced by only a slight amount. An engineer associated with the introduction of the new product asked one of the change agents how we knew that the total job approach (job enrichment) was equal to or better than the more traditional approaches. He indicated that he thought that it was good but he wasn't certain as to proof.

In reply, he was asked simply, "How would the Model X introduction have gone in any other plant where you have worked?" (Model X was one that, because of delays in design, was introduced to the floor only as a prototype, without manufacturing drawings.) After a moment's reflection, he replied, "It would have been utter chaos. Under the circumstances, we just couldn't have gotten a normal assembly-line process going. At least, with the women making the entire product, they learned about the problem quickly, you had fewer people to talk to and train, and they were so involved that if they had questions, they came looking for someone or, in most cases, solved the problem themselves by discussing it among themselves."

At a later date the plant accountant generated figures regarding the effect on productivity of the "total job concept" program. For comparison purposes he used a standard model which had been in production for more than two years prior to the change. The average productivity for the previous eight months was used as a base. Although the increase in productivity was not as dramatic as in the Hot Plate Department, gains were significant, resulting in productivity gains of approximately $1,500 per year per worker. To be more specific, productivity had increased by $1.75 per hour, or an increase of 17 percent. Quality had improved in similar fashion. The number of rejects had decreased from an average of 25 percent to an average of 13 percent, or an increase in quality of about 50 percent. Absenteeism was reduced from 8.5 percent per month to 3.4 percent, a reduction of over 50 percent.

The Matrix Organization

Another structural change now occurring is the introduction of the matrix organization and the integrator concept. In most industrial organizations, problem-solving or production meetings are usually attended by heads of different functional groups in the organization and by key production people. This plant was no different. For example, the daily production meeting was attended by the plant manager and by the heads of such departments as engineering, quality assurance, materials control, and the like. In addition, the individual first-line supervisors would come in, one at a time. The discussion would center on current production schedules, current production problems, parts shortages, and similar issues. Prior to the meeting each functional head and first-line supervisor would have a briefing with their own subordinates so they were up to date in their own area. After the meeting each manager would then go back with specific courses of action, which he would communicate to his subordinates individually or as a group. The meetings served to unify the plant, quickly disseminate information to the departments concerned, and ensure that the production schedules were met. However, the plant manager was not yet satisfied. For one thing, he felt that his time and the time of his managers could be put to better use in longer-range planning. For another, there were still communications failures, delays, and misunderstandings arising out of the managers' roles as "communications carriers" to and from their own departments.

The design of the matrix organization evolved. Each production supervisor was to be an integrator for a team consisting of representatives from each of the staff departments that service his production department. The individuals representing Engineering, Materials Control, and Quality Assurance were to be "doers" rather than supervisors or managers. A typical team might consist of a weekly technician from Quality Assurance, a weekly technician or engineer from Engineering, and one or more representatives from the appropriate product-line team in Materials Control.

The readiness of the plant's management for a major change of this type is evidenced by the relatively short period of time in which the new structure was discussed and a decision was made. Nevertheless, we cannot report a totally successful change to date.

Failure to prepare individuals effectively for the change and the new roles, skills, and relationships that are required in the matrix appears to be the main reason for lack of a totally successful change. The matrix structure seems to work best where the staff department representatives on the teams are most competent, motivated, and skilled in working in groups and have a good understanding of their roles. Where these are missing, the matrix has not worked well. The following also contributed to the difficulties in making the change: the lack of full commitment on the part of one functional department head to full delegation of responsibility to his subordinates on the teams; the lack of clear understanding of the integrator role by the integrators and the means of influence and control open to them; and the lack of attention and follow-up by the plant manager and the change agents (due to the time commitments on other matters).

Following a diagnosis of the problems and a subsequent discussion of the difficulties, it was agreed that most of the problems encountered could be overcome through more support from the consultants in role understanding and team development.

The introduction of the matrix organization, even though it has not yet been completely successful, is important in several respects. First, the fact that the organization was willing to undertake such a major change reflects management's adaptability and indicates that the top-level people have become fairly sophisticated consumers of new managerial methods. Secondly, the ability to examine failure and diagnose it reflects the openness of the plant and management's greater willingness to invest time in examining organizational processes, even when task pressures continue. Thirdly, the causes of failure cited above demonstrate that structural change must be preceded or accompanied by social and behavioral changes, such as changes in individuals' abilities, motivation, role understanding, or interpersonal skills. Finally, the potential for individual and organizational growth resulting from this structural change should be clear. The structural change will raise the levels of competence and motivation that individuals will be required to muster in order to function effectively.

Changes in Quality Control

One other fundamental change in job and organizational structure is under way and needs mention. For the past year the role of quality control has been changing from that of an inspecting department to that of a consulting department. More and more quality control is being performed by production workers. In the Hot Plate Department all routine inspection is being done by the production workers themselves. A full-time quality control job has been eliminated. In the Instrument Department many calibrations and checks previously performed by quality control inspectors are being performed by the production workers themselves. Thus, their work is enriched through further self-control, overhead is reduced, and the quality control job is upgraded in its level of challenge and responsibility. This change from external control to self-control is but another of the many interlocking structural and social changes which have created a new plant culture where individuals are growing in skills, knowledge, and need for achievement and involvement.

Summary and Conclusions

The management experiment we have described has been based on the assumption that employees in the plant desire responsibility, challenging work, and an opportunity for achievement. Over a period of five years a work environment was created based on these assumptions. Jobs, communications, organizational structure, and leadership, to name just a few dimensions of the organizational-development program, were shaped by the managers with the help of consultants to allow employees to satisfy these assumed needs while doing their daily work. This has resulted in increased involvement in work, commitment to the organization, motivation, and personal satisfaction. These positive changes have verified that the assumptions about employee needs with which we started were correct and/or the changes in work environment encouraged employees to develop the kind of needs we assumed them to have in the first place. In either case, employee needs and organization purpose are less in conflict at the end of the five-year period than they are in many other organizations, or than they might have been without the organizational development program.

The increased integration between employee needs and the organization not only has increased individual satisfaction and involvement in work but has also enhanced organizational purpose. The effectiveness of the plant organization is high. Voluntary turnover among hourly employees is considerably below that for the area; productivity and quality have improved as changes have been made in department after department; the plant handles more volume with less supervision and indirect labor; the plant has been able to introduce new products quickly and without drops in productivity; and its overall efficiency and financial performance have continued to meet the corporation's objectives.

Comment

In an article entitled "The Diffusion of New Work Structures: Explaining Why Success Didn't Take,"[20] Richard E. Walton describes eight unmistakable success stories, one of which has been Corning Glass. Yet in only one instance (Volvo) has diffusion been impressive. In Corning Glass, as Walton assesses it, "diffusion has been nonexistent or small." In an attempt to analyze the reasons for this all-too-frequent outcome, Walton comments as follows:

In the Norwegian projects, the researchers actually sought out the companies and persuaded them to collaborate in undertaking the projects. Similarly, in the Corning experiment, a corporate consultant began by stimulating interest among supervisors to try their own mini-experiments, which, if successful, could lead to plantwide work restructuring. Interestingly, although the management and worker members of the Norwegian and the Corning experiments subsequently came to "own" the projects, dependency upon outside experts long remained a factor in these cases, each of which resulted in little intracompany diffusion.[21]

Much more important than the above reason for nondiffusion of the clearly successful new work structure report in the Corning case is another observation that Walton makes, namely, ". . . no strong encouragement of diffusion came from the corporate level other than from organizational development groups."

The tendency for even clearly successful experimental projects in work restructuring to have a low rate of diffusion (either within the same firm or to other firms) represents an intriguing problem that seems generalizable, and by no means peculiar to Corning Glass. This will be discussed more fully in Chapters III and V of this book.

General Electric[22]

General Electric reports on a series of studies of employee motivation carried out by its Behavioral Research Service. An explora-

---

[20] *Organizational Dynamics,* Winter 1975, *3.*

[21] *Ibid.,* p. 7.

[22] Summarized from material provided by the General Electric Company. Used with permission.

tory study, reported on in 1966 in "Achieving Productive Motivation Through Job Design," stated:

Many jobs in the factory are designed in such a way that it is almost impossible for the individual to evaluate the real worth of his contribution. . . . Surveys have shown that hourly workers in many jobs feel that their work has little or no meaning and just seems to go on and on endlessly in a monotonous manner. This kind of work not only generates feelings of boredom, apathy, fatigue and dissatisfaction, but also leads to resentment and active resistance. Workmanship suffers, employee turnover becomes a serious problem, and work stoppages, slowdowns and strikes disrupt production.

In this study, the researchers attempted to measure the effects of various design characteristics on employee attitudes about their jobs and on quality of workmanship. Manufacturing shop operations and quality control managers in five departments were asked to identify work groups that were consistently high or consistently low in quality of output. Then, 25 groups at the high end of the quality continuum and 25 groups at the low end were selected for study.

The supervisor of each of the designated groups was interviewed for information on job-related factors such as cycle time, size of work group, training, and repetitiveness. In addition, a few employees from each work group, randomly selected by the researcher, were asked to complete a brief questionnaire dealing with pride in work, job meaningfulness, sense of accomplishment, monotony, identification with the product and the company, and attitudes toward management.

Because of the exploratory nature of the study, the researchers decided they would not attempt to articulate formal findings. Instead, they presented a series of provisional recommendations to the managers of shop operations:

1. Establish a formal training program for hourly employees beyond the required minimum.

2. Create subgoals to measure accomplishment in groups where repetition is high or where the employees do not ordinarily see the finished product.

3. Provide employees with feedback on the quality of their performance on a regular and frequent basis.

4. Have each supervisor put continuing effort into the maintenance of a very neat and orderly work area.

5. Arrange work areas to either make co-workers' conversation very easy while working, or make it virtually impossible for employees to converse while working.

6. Increase the number of operations performed by an employee whenever possible.

7. Structure jobs so that workers can, at least occasionally, move about the work area.

8. Explore ways to assign greater personal responsibilities to an individual.

Some of the recommendations of the foregoing study were further explored in a 1967 report entitled "Motivating the Hourly Employee." In assessing productive motivation, the company took into account the question of attitudes, as follows:

Attitudes or feelings about the work itself (job content):
> Enjoys work versus bored with work
> Pride in workmanship
> Sense of accomplishment

Attitudes or feelings about the work environment (job context):
> Perceived relationship between personal needs and department or company goals
> Identification with the department or company products
> Perception of general management
> Perception of immediate supervisor

These attitudes, in the opinion of the researchers, exert a direct influence on productivity (quantity to meet customer demand), quality of work (workmanship to keep customer satisfied), and labor relations (a working environment which minimizes income loss to employee and company).

The study undertook to observe and measure the following variables:

- Responsibility for own work (the extent to which an individual can use his own discretion)
- Shift work—repetitiveness of the work (a function of cycle time and the number of operations)
- Physical activity (is it sedentary work or does an employee move about area, use physical energy, etc.?)
- Rotation between work stations—goals (in terms of eventual use of product, customer, logical number of units to produce, etc.)
- Group structure (small work groups at interdependent stations versus individual work stations relatively independent of each other)
- Role-training (any informal or formal program which promotes insights into the importance of the job and encourages psychological investment in the work)

The following results were reported:

- Productive motivation was higher where employees had some discretionary responsibility in their jobs.
- Second-shift employees had more favorable attitudes than first-shift employees.
- Productive motivation was lower for employees in highly repetitive jobs.
- Regularly scheduled rotation was reacted to favorably while casual rotation had the opposite effect.
- The opportunity for relatively vigorous physical activity on the job was associated with greater productive motivation.
- Opportunities for social interaction seldom resulted in more favorable attitudes toward the job.
- Role-training and participation resulted in significant improvement in overall productive motivation.

In a third study, "The Effect of Employee Involvement on Work Performance," which was carried out by Personnel Research and reported on in 1969, General Electric explored the concept of stewardship. According to the report, "Stewardship denotes something more than merely adding responsibility. It implies having pride in doing the work properly, maintaining a sustained alertness for job improvements in all aspects of job-related functions, and a willingness to accept responsibility for related tasks which one has not previously or typically covered."

In one program, employees participated in a role-training program to help them understand how their work affected other groups in the plant. They were given a better understanding of the entire manufacturing process, the importance of each step in the process, and the problems encountered in manufacturing the product. They were also taken on tours of local businesses where their products were used.

Each operator was informed of the total output required for his unit, then asked to use this information to determine the order in which he would work on each of several items. To develop stewardship further, a graph depicting group performance to schedule was prominently posted each day in the work area. On the basis of this information, operators were encouraged to set their own quality goals in the form of number of defects per operator.

As a result of this program there were significant performance improvements. Defects per operator were reduced approximately 50 percent and productivity, based on dollar-output results, rose from a 25.7 average for the nine months before the program to a 46.7 average after its introduction.

In another aspect of the same program, the sequential assembly process was modified so that a single operator continued down the entire line with one production unit. This changeover in assembly substantially reduced the number of defects per completed units. There was also an improvement in productivity from 40 units, the monthly average produced in the nine months before the changeover, to 52 units in the first month after the change, 60 in the second, and 71 in the third.

Another example of the effects of added responsibility and a feeling of stewardship toward the job came in a department where most hourly employees were semiskilled equipment operators. In-line inspectors were taken off the floor and operators were asked to do their own inspection. In assuming this responsibility, the operators became more alert to problems of quality and scheduling. As a result, quality improved and the cost of direct labor was reduced. The self-inspection resulted in approximately a 25 percent reduction in the cost of product failures during the first year. The improved performance was sustained throughout the following two years.

In presenting its conclusions, the GE report stated:

Several conditions must be met if efforts to improve the motivation of workers are to be successful. In the first place, the program must be conducted by the immediate supervisors of the employees. An outside researcher, or even a local staff man, cannot conduct such a program successfully.

Secondly, the program cannot be based on a few mechanically applied gimmicks which would hopefully improve performance in some magical way. To be successful, such a program must be based on a genuine desire on the part of the supervisor to build the self-esteem of employees by demonstrating genuine trust and faith in their motives and in their abilities to contribute constructively to the objectives of the work group.

A third important condition of the success of a motivational program is that it must be carried out in an atmosphere of approval. It must not be seen by employees as any kind of admonishment for performance in the past. A punitive attitude on the part of the supervisor will only threaten, rather than build, the self-esteem of the employees. A natural reaction to a threat to one's self-esteem is to become defensive—to defend one's past performance and thus become unconstructive about possible improvement.

In 1972, *Business Week*[23] reported that General Electric was trying a task-force approach to make jobs more interesting and rewarding to workers, using teams of 5 to 15 persons to perform an identified task and giving them a maximum amount of responsibility. Welders in a fabricating plant were given the assignment of scheduling and planning their work, performing such tasks as estimating the time required to meet specifications on products necessitating special techniques. Their team was sufficiently experienced to decide which individual was best qualified to perform a particular task as well as to allot the required amount of time. This

[23] September 9, 1972, 143, 146.

freed methods engineers to work on new product models. As a result of their increased accountability, the men became personally more involved, and their efficiency and the quality of their work improved significantly.

GE has also involved approximately 2,000 foremen and supervisors in three- to four-hour training sessions in role-modeling to help them learn other methods of relating to workers. A supervisor plays the part of a worker who is requested to meet with his supervisor to discuss any one of a number of problems, such as inefficiency or absenteeism. This role-modeling is videotaped so that others in the training session may comment on the action favorably or otherwise. Most of those who have attended the sessions feel that a "tough" image is not the most effective one for use in their work. The idea behind this training program is not to change the behavior of supervisors by indoctrinating them with theory, but to develop in them an awareness of ways of dealing with people other than the punitive measures of the traditionally run shop.

Although this may seem simplistic, the results have been surprising. For example, a group of GE electronic components supervisors, ten weeks after going through the training, found that the workers under their supervision had raised their level of productivity by 20 percent. All the supervisors in that plant subsequently took the training program.

An Insurance Company Enrichment Trial[24]

Early in 1970, a large insurance company developed an interest in the concept that the work itself can motivate the workers. Two objectives of the job enrichment pilot study team were to test new approaches for the implementation of output of an Operations Improvement Program, and, at the same time, to improve the quality of work, to reduce absenteeism and turnover through the design of

[24] Summarized from R. Janson, *Job Enrichment Trial—Data Processing Department Analysis and Results in an Insurance Organization.* Paper presented at the International Conference on the Quality of Working Life, Arden House, Harriman, New York, September 1972. Used by permission. Janson did not identify the company.

more interesting and meaningful jobs, and to improve the job attitudes of the general workforce. A system was established to appraise each category for measurement purposes.

Selection of the test area was critical. The area had to have two similar operations in two separate locations for the purpose of comparison between the experimental and control (no job enrichment) groups, and it needed a progressive management that would be willing to accept changes. The trial started in July 1970 and was completed in July 1971.

Results

The results of the experiment were dramatically greater than the original expectations. Turnover was the only category that did not show improvement, but the turnover ratio at the outset at the first location was very low (15 percent). Table 2 gives the results of

TABLE 2

Summary of Results of Trial

	FIRST LOCATION (EXPERIMENTAL GROUP)		SECOND LOCATION (CONTROL GROUP)		DIFFERENCE
Current productivity ratio		104.0%		94.0%	10.0%
Absenteeism	Decreased	24.1%	Increased	29.0%	53.1%
Turnover	Increased	6.4%	Decreased	5.1%	*11.5%*
Attitude	Improved	16.5%	Improved	0.5%	16.0%
Throughput (cards keypunched per hour)	Improved	39.6%	Improved	8.1%	31.5%
Error or ratio change		35.3%		0.8%	34.5%

TABLE 3

	STAFF SAVED	ADDITIONAL POTENTIAL	ACTUAL SAVINGS	ADDITIONAL POTENTIAL
Measurable change:				
Attitude and quality	2	1	$11,354	$ 6,245
Selective elimination of controls	7	14	40,465	81,588
Absenteeism change	2	1	12,486	4,104
Total	11	16	$64,305	$91,937

the trial. The improvements resulted in an actual savings of $65,000 annually, with an additional potential savings of $90,000 annually made possible through expected increases in throughput (total cards processed per hour). The savings were determined on the basis of measurable changes in the quality and quantity of work as well as absenteeism and the elimination of certain controls (without eliminating responsibility). The quantifiable savings, including salary and machine rental, are illustrated in Table 3.

The following paragraphs treat the material in Tables 2 and 3 in greater detail and also provide background on the development of the results.

Quantity of Work

Two measures of productivity were kept in the keypunch groups: throughput rate and effectiveness ratio. The throughput rate is an expression of the average number of cards keypunched per hour of work. (Hours of work include keypunching and verifying.) Figure 3 shows the throughput rate results in the control and experimental groups.

The effectiveness ratio is an expression of the number of work hours required to complete a given number of cards as compared with the number of hours that should be required as established in

Figure 3

Throughout Percentage Increase or Decrease during Job
Enrichment Implementation Period, Compared with Base
Period (January 1970–July 1970) Average

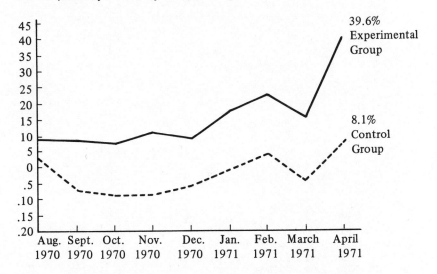

work measurement standards. At the start of job enrichment the
experimental group was at 78 percent of standard. At the conclusion of the job enrichment year this group was operating at 104
percent of standard, a 26 percent increase in effectiveness.

Job Attitude

When the job attitude survey was initially administered, both
groups showed nearly identical scores. Job attitudes could best be
described as average. Eleven months later, when the survey was
again given, the control group registered a score that was essentially the same as its previous one. The experimental group's score
had risen by 16.5 percent, which is a significant upturn for this type
of job. The change is highlighted in Figure 4.

Figure 4 Summary of Job Attitude Changes

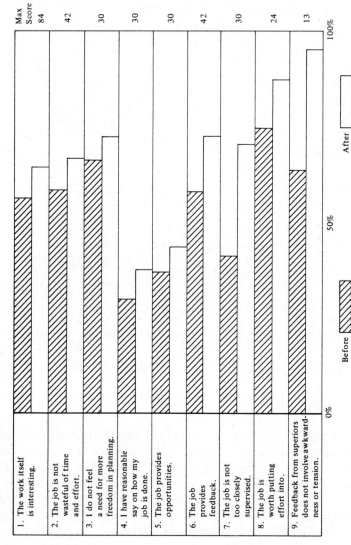

Quality of Work

Data were collected for approximately 40 keypunch operators in the experimental group who were keypunching before the job enrichment study and during it. All the operators were experienced. The data collected represented the number of cards that proved to be incorrectly punched. Data were not collected for the control group, since this would have affected other areas of the study.

For the two months prior to the study, the 40 operators had a collective error rate of 1.53 percent. For two months toward the end of the study, the collective rate had been reduced to 1 percent. Keypunching accuracy was rated as follows, with the numbers representing a range of percentage error in the work:

Outstanding	0 – 0.5% error
Acceptable	0.5 – 4.0% error
Poor	Over 4.0% error

By the end of the job enrichment year, there occurred a significant increase in the number of operators turning in outstanding work. The number of operators doing poor work had decreased. Figure 5 gives a graphic view of this improvement. Operators

Figure 5

Quality Improvements during Job Enrichment Trial

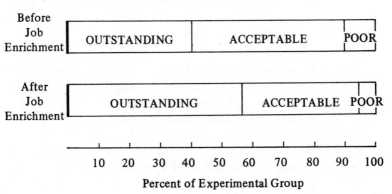

Percent of Experimental Group

achieving an "outstanding" rating increased from one-fifth to one-half. Operators receiving a "poor" rating decreased by one-half (11.1 percent to 5.5 percent).

These results were determined through the "effectiveness ratio" discussed previously. Credit was not given for reprocessed work, since this would have lowered the effectiveness ratio (volumes are repunched with no earned time credit). While error volumes decrease, the effectiveness ratio improves as time is spent on work with a time allowance.

Absenteeism

Absence statistics were obtained for both the experimental and control groups for two periods of time—the eleven months prior to the job enrichment study and the eleven months following the beginning of the study. All keypunch operators, leaders, and alternates employed at the end of a period were included. An absence was considered to be any sick time and any unpaid personal time. Changes in absenteeism were not reflected in the effectiveness ratio, since that ratio was a percentage figure, based on hours present.

In the experimental group, absenteeism improved by 24 percent. In the control group it actually *increased* by 29 percent, which in effect was a loss to the company. These changes are clearly illustrated in Figure 6.

Selective Elimination of Controls

This step involved removing controls—without removing responsibility or accountability—for those employees who demonstrated job proficiency. This change also does not appear in the effectiveness ratio, since it represents "eliminated work." It was assumed that 75 percent of the work could be processed this way, which was the equivalent of 21 employees. This has been achieved for seven positions with an additional potential of fourteen.

Figure 6

Changes in Absenteeism

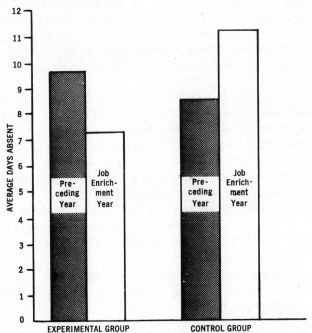

Other Benefits

Although the figures in Tables 2 and 3 speak for themselves, the most significant impact of the program was its effect on the organization. One dramatic change was in the behavior and attitude of the supervisor of the experimental group. Before the experiment, his was the first and only level where basic supervisory functions were performed. All 83 employees reported directly to him. Most of his time was spent reacting and responding to problem situations as they arose. Even casual observation of the unit indicated that each day was filled with continuing and recurring work crises. The supervisor was besieged daily by employees with salary grievances and personal problems.

As the experiment progressed, work was transferred from the supervisor to the unit leaders, and in some cases to the operators. The supervisor began rethinking all his responsibilities. As he worked with the unit leaders, he began to develop feedback systems, to establish work modules, and generally to spearhead the enrichment effort. Instead of supervising the behavior of his subordinates, he began to manage the work itself. Salary complaints dropped dramatically.

Before the trial, taped interviews were held with many of the operators. Most were found to be bored with their jobs, frustrated because of procedural and policy requirements, and generally apathetic toward their work. Interviews after the trial indicated marked improvement. Employees now talked about their work with family and friends, had better feelings because of increased responsibilities, and realized that their jobs were important.

The original list of changes, prepared from a brainstorming session of the supervisor and unit leaders, contained 73 items. This list was reduced to 25 for implementation, some of which were:

- Keypunch operators have become responsible for their own work. Included in their job is responsibility for scheduling—and for meeting those schedules.

- Operators now have been authorized and encouraged to correct obvious coding errors. Prior to this trial, they were told to punch information as they saw it. Since they know coding well, it was frustrating for them to punch the wrong codes.

- Each operator now corrects her own errors. Previously, the errors came back from the computer and were given to any operator to correct. The new system provides feedback and aids in training.

- Operators now deal directly with clients. Before the trial, work from unidentified sources was given to them in one-hour batches. Now an operator has her own customers, with full responsibility for those clients' jobs. If there is a problem, the operator, not the supervisor, discusses it with the client. (This approach brings in an aspect of entrepreneurship to the working levels.)

Motorola[25]

The Communications Division of the Motorola Corporation reports several successful innovations in the field of employee motivation. One represents a departure from the normal assembly procedure in the manufacture of a radio pocket pager. This innovation has resulted in employee job enlargement, increased efficiency, and better use of facilities layout.

Before the introduction of the new method, as many as 100 different individuals played a role in assembling, testing, and packing each pager. Today, one technician assembles, tests, and packs each pager by himself. This is made possible by a new design technique that resulted in a dramatic reduction in the number of components needed in the new paging device, from 210 to 80.

The direct involvement of a single employee in the completion of a finished product results, according to a Motorola spokesman, in "a turned-on group of individuals who enjoy their work and have a great deal of pride in their product. The key is involvement. If we're to achieve the quality and performance that our sophisticated customers demand, we must attract and keep bright, interested people and it is very difficult to be interested when you're inserting three or four parts into one printed circuit board after another."

The new manufacturing process revives a long-lost art: pride of workmanship. Now the assembly technicians have a true sense of relationship with Motorola customers. They are accountable for 75 percent of the final product and 100 percent of all line responsibilities. Compare this to the 1–5 percent accountability under the old assembly procedure. Thus, the assembly technicians identify with the customer (the technician's name is enclosed with each pager shipped) and increase their growth and learning skills through job responsibility. This responsibility, together with a sense of personal achievement and recognition, has produced such benefits as improved quality, increased productivity, and a reduction of employee turnover and absenteeism.

[25] From material supplied by Motorola.

Motorola admits there are problems associated with the new type of assembly. It is necessary to provide the assembly technician with supplementary training to familiarize him with all facets of the job. In the judgment of the Motorola management, however, the advantages far outweigh the disadvantages in terms of both human relations and cost considerations.

In another employee motivation project, Motorola sought to recapture the family spirit which it felt had been somewhat eroded by the fact that its employees now number in the thousands. Motorola was eager to test the management principle that most people are capable of contributing far more than what is required. To test this operationally, the company formed a team project that used the creativity of the individual and the team to find solutions to problems through involvement rather than imposed change.

The program was introduced when a new line of operators was trying, without previous experience, to build a complicated receiver. Many problems arose, and for a time it looked as if it would be necessary to shut down the lines completely. Supervisors and highly specialized engineering personnel had worked long and hard to find a solution, without tangible results. So the operators were brought into a session to discuss exactly what the problems were.

A major quality problem was the elimination of small metallic particles within the electrical circuits the team was building. These particles caused short circuits, making the entire circuit inoperable. Some workers had used air hoses to blow out the particles, others small brushes, but neither method was totally effective. After intensive discussion on possible solutions, the workers suggested using an air hose with a brush attached to the nozzle. It worked. The problem was solved.

From this small experience of successful participation, a sense of group cohesion developed. The ten women on the production line became eager to join in problem solving. Regular team meetings were scheduled. The ten women decided to take responsibility for checking their own performance, and developed a method for recognizing members who were outstanding in areas such as attendance and quality excellence.

Today there are more than 100 similar teams in Motorola's

Communications Division. As team members, employees have the opportunity to talk and be directly involved with managers, engineers, and other employees. Within the general framework of bettering themselves and improving daily operations, team members set their own goals, measure their own performance, solve their own problems, and, when the results are good, share in the feeling of accomplishment.

Each team elects a captain to help monitor and measure its effectiveness. The captains keep records of their reports and lead discussions on quality, cost, and attendance. In all major performance areas the team sets some goal or resolution so that, every month, they can work to improve themselves. Because the experience gained by a captain is invaluable for personal growth and understanding, new captains are selected every three to four months.

Each team is encouraged to determine in what ways it can best use meetings to help accomplish its goals. Team members view training films, hear talks about the functions of other departments, tour the plant, learn how a completed radio communications system operates, and engage in discussions with support groups.

At Motorola, management involvement started from the very top, and without the sustaining force of top management's commitment, any lasting application would be impossible. A motivational development department was organized under the direct control of the vice president of operations to serve the entire Communications Division, and seminars were developed to give management a better understanding of motivation in terms of philosophy, principles, and concepts. Though not all members of management were immediately converted, a climate supportive of real motivation has emerged.

Some tangible results of the team program as reported by Motorola on August 14, 1975:

1. Production has greatly improved.
2. Turnover has decreased in groups operating as a team for at least six months, compared to nonteam groups.
3. Rejects have been significantly reduced.

4. Average attendance has increased to 95 percent or more on most teams. Many teams consistently run above 97 percent.

A Motorola spokesman comments:

Today's employees are no longer content with a job that doesn't provide opportunities for expression of ideas, self-fulfillment, social activity, and participation in planning and controlling their jobs. The emphasis has been placed on the total work experience rather than a specific job. Work has been enriched to include the whole person and not just his mechanical skills. The feelings, ideas, and attitudes of the employee are receiving increased attention.

Texas Instruments[26]

A project was carried out at two divisions of Texas Instruments located in Attleboro, Massachusetts, involving approximately 1,500 employees. The essence of the program was a continuous cycle of meetings by a group of workers and their supervisors. At each meeting problems related to the work were identified, and one or more members of the group—either supervisors or workers—were assigned responsibility for solving these problems. In addition, reports were given by members on the progress made in solving problems identified at earlier meetings.

The objective of these programs was to increase the motivation of the workers. As those identified with the project stated: "The motivated worker can assume a part in the managerial functions associated with his job. He can share in planning, organizing, and controlling the work he does. His increased understanding and achievement, and especially his increased mental situation, combine to boost his morale and his company's profit."

The first step in launching the project was to enlist the sustained commitment of management. High-level management at Attleboro

[26] From W. Roche and N. MacKinnon, "Motivating People with Meaningful Work," *Harvard Business Review*, May–June 1970, 97–110. Reprinted by permission.

had the theoretical concepts underlying the proposed program explained to them in detail.

The next step was to familiarize supervisors with the new, less authoritarian style expected of them and provide them with the training necessary to carry out the style. Since supervisors would be called on to assume a new role as participants in the problem-identification and problem-solving conferences, it was recognized that they would be asked to behave in a manner quite different from what had been expected of them traditionally. The "emerging" style of supervision needed for this sort of motivation project was outlined as follows:

1. The manager works with his subordinates to identify and resolve work-related problems and guides and assists them in setting the standards and goals rather than dictating the goals, designating the basic methods of achieving them, and defining standards for quality and production.

2. The manager helps his subordinates set their own goals using their motivation as leverage, rather than using persuasion or other traditional methods of leadership to move his subordinates ahead.

3. The manager encourages his subordinates to evaluate their own performance, provide recognition for achievement, and promote open discussion of failures, rather than doing his own evaluation of performance in a judgmental fashion.

4. The manager provides the opportunity for his subordinates to develop and grow at their own pace, rather than taking the initiative in stimulating the development of skills among his subordinates and stressing promotional opportunities only for the successful ones.

5. The manager attempts to interpret rules logically and to explain the consequences of violating them, instead of disciplining subordinates for infraction of rules and for poor performance.

6. The manager encourages his subordinates to develop and install their own innovations, rather than imposing his new way of doing things upon them.

Texas Instruments provides no overall information on the effect of the programs on specific production goals, but they were reported to have improved both group morale and company profit.

Not all groups, however, did uniformly well during the two-year period. Within the first three months, in fact, they either made spectacular gains or manifested a pattern of failure. Some of the workers were uncomfortable in their new roles—and so were some supervisors. The supervisors had to take the initiative in helping workers identify problems, convincing them that they could really speak candidly and openly to employees on any level and providing them, between meetings, with the assistance they needed to solve the identified problems.

It was highly important that the supervisor performed in relation to the problem he and his group had undertaken to solve, so that the program became credible and the workers knew they could rely on the supervisor's participation and cooperation. A period of time devoted solely to problem solving was usually needed before the group had enough confidence to set goals for itself. Here, too, the supervisor had to provide confidence and initiative. It was very important that, at each meeting, everyone who had been assigned a responsibility for a problem was given the opportunity to report on it, so that nobody's efforts seemed to be discounted or belittled.

The following is quoted from the concluding section of the experiment.

The supervisor must:

1. Induce his work group to participate in identifying and solving problems, recording successes and improvements, and setting goals.
2. Make sure that the whole problem is solved in each case.
3. Make sure that the goals set are both attainable and challenging.
4. Work with the group to develop meaningful criteria for measuring its impact.
5. Report conscientiously on his own project and make sure that his workers report on theirs punctually.

Some ingredients for failure are also easy to list. They are:

1. Using short-term factors to measure management effectiveness.
2. Encountering supervisors' resistance to the change in management style.

3. Letting the meaningful work approach be viewed as "just another program."

4. Training the supervisor inadequately.

5. Concentrating on problems in areas over which the team has no control.

6. Setting unattainable goals.

7. Allowing early disappointments to discourage teams.

8. Allowing the supervisor to fail to follow through after problems have been identified.

In 1967, another Texas Instruments study was conducted at the company's headquarters in Dallas, where cleaning and janitorial services are contracted for with an outside building maintenance firm. TI's facility engineers evaluated the quarters as only 56 percent clean. The contractor's ability to do the job was aggravated by a quarterly turnover rate of 100 percent.

After careful planning and training, the following actions were taken in a test site with 120 maintenance personnel:

- Cleaning service teams of 19 people each were organized, with appointed supervisors. Each team was given a voice in the planning, problem solving, and goal setting for its own jobs.

- The whole group was held accountable for the overall job, but the means of getting the job done was left to the teams. It was their responsibility to act independently, devising their own strategies, plans, and schedules to meet the objectives.

- As individuals and as teams, the people were taught how to measure their own performance and were given the freedom to do so.

The results for the test site were:

- The cleanliness-level rating improved from 65 percent to 85 percent.

- Personnel required for cleaning dropped from 120 to 71.

- Quarterly turnover dropped from 100 percent to 9.8 percent.
- From the fourth quarter of 1967 until the fourth quarter of 1969, cost savings for the entire site averaged $103,000 a year.

Although only economic results were measured, the outcome in human terms can be inferred from the drop in the turnover rate.

In a further study, undertaken to cope with the many defective products coming off the assembly line, TI decided to delegate responsibility and authority for quality control down the ranks. Time clocks disappeared. The workers on the assembly line, who formerly had learned to perform small tasks, were reorganized into teams of seven, with each team responsible for producing a complete instrument. Distribution of tasks was left to mutual agreement.

Under the new system, man-hour productivity reportedly increased by 30 percent, customer reports of defective instruments decreased by 70 percent, and absenteeism fell to half the local average.

TRW Systems[27]

Companies employ a diversity of techniques for changing the attitudes of both management and employees. Since the early 1960s, TRW has been introducing job enrichment and organizational development programs for both salaried and hourly workers to provide an "atmosphere that's pretty open and encourages people to use their minds and imagination in a synergistic way without many of the constraints of traditional organizations."

TRW has had equally good experience with project teams. Thomas A. Wickes, TRW's director of organizational development, says: "Projects seem to get started faster, and we seem to come up with more elegant solutions than we did in the past, whether it's a manufacturing or management problem. We're convinced that in terms of productivity, the man who is most productive is the one

[27] Adapted from material supplied by TRW Systems. Reprinted by permission.

who is . . . in a job where he has control and influence, and one where he is measured on results."

In 1972, TRW created a semi-autonomous work team in one of its manufacturing plants. Workers were given responsibility for assembling a product as a team instead of working separately on assembly-line tasks. Once assigned a new project, they were allowed to set their own time schedules as long as they completed the job.

Response to the new plan was excellent. It was possible to eliminate the different shifts for a given task, since all members of the team worked at the same time, and working hours were staggered when necessary to fit personal needs of the workers. Team members began to take on tasks formerly regarded as "the company's responsibility"—for instance, the senior workers voluntarily spent extra time training younger team members. Enthusiasm for the work increased, and productivity reportedly rose by 15 percent.

The Systems Group at TRW is concerned with advanced products and services. The following description of its sophisticated organizational approach was provided by Berwyn Fragner, vice president of industrial relations at TRW:

The Systems Group conceives its organization as a total system of interfacing jobs, projects, spans of control, responsibilities, and relationships of people. There exist a large number of complex critical interdependencies. No one technical or administrative group is complete in itself. In getting a particular job done—for example, a project—the various resources throughout the company have to be called on to contribute. This requires an organization that affords a continuous open access between individuals and groups.

To help achieve these objectives TRW Systems has incorporated many behavioral science concepts in its operating style. The aim of this effort is the creation of an environment that encourages individual flexibility and increased interpersonal competence, which is seen as a requisite to the need for constant change and innovation. The behavioral science application is centered around problem solving and task accomplishment. Methods and techniques used at TRW Systems are not viewed as a single experimental program but as an ongoing process that is designed to reach the willingness, readiness, and needs of individuals and the organization alike.

Today there are numerous identifiable applications of the behavioral sciences in the organization. The following stand out most prominently:

1. *Matrix organization.* A project management system in which a work team is put together based on required expertise. A person may belong to several teams at once, or he may start on a project and then move to another because of his special expertise, because another project manager has asked for the individual, because the employee himself finds the work of the second team more attractive, or simply because he has completed his work on the first team. This system gives the employee some option to match project opportunities to his needs at the time, which includes an assessment in terms of his total self, his life-style, and his goals and objectives.

2. *Internal and external behavioral science consulting teams.* A permanent group of consulting behavioral scientists works with various levels of management, segments of the organization, and employee work groups both off-site and on-site.

3. *Team building.* A process wherein a manager and a consultant meet with the manager's work group for extended periods of time to identify and resolve problems directly related to their working as a team.

4. *Intergroup team building.* A step beyond team building, in which interfacing and interdependent work groups (including customer work groups) meet to identify and resolve mutual problems.

5. *Ongoing diagnosis.* An organizing process to evaluate the health and climate of the organization and to facilitate communication. In addition to traditional questionnaire techniques, a process called "sensing" is employed. Appropriate individuals are brought together face-to-face so that an individual or group may get a reading on a particular problem area or segment of the organization. For example, a senior executive periodically meets with and listens while persons directly involved in carrying out projects or programs discuss their problems and progress.

6. *Individual effectiveness training.* This refers to numerous techniques for developing greater competence in interpersonal skills, particularly as they relate to leadership and managerial effectiveness. Additionally, there are career development workshops designed to increase individual motivation toward achieving career goals.

There are, of course, numerous other activities which reflect the direct applications of behavioral science concepts within the organization. Those mentioned here, however, seem most directly related to the subject of organizational productivity and effectiveness.

No formal effort has been made to measure quantitatively the direct impact of any or all of these techniques in terms of productivity. However, over the years a climate has evolved in which managers at all levels of the organization continue to use the techniques described. Project managers continually call on the use of organizational development techniques and resources in their work with project teams. The teams seem to get started faster, produce more practical solutions and come to quicker and more effective conclusions. The influences of job enrichment efforts are also apparent, for example, in the manner salaries are administered, budgets are developed, and planning occurs. TRW Systems management is convinced that individual productivity and creativity are significantly greater in an atmosphere where people can share their ideas and have a sense of contribution and participation.

Kaiser Aluminum and Chemical Corporation[28]

The project involved 60 hourly maintenance workers in the reduction plant at the Ravenswood Works in West Virginia. The following changes were effected: The 16 maintenance men performed without a boss and with no time clock; worked the day shift only, though serving aluminum potlines that were in operation 24

28 From D. B. Thompson, *Industry Week,* February 14, 1972, 36–43. Used with permission.

hours a day; and, in cooperation with operating personnel, decided what maintenance jobs were to be done and in what order of priority.

The program was preceded by a management retraining program that involved weekly meetings for more than a year. The concrete results of the program were: Maintenance costs reduced 5.5 percent, four supervisory posts eliminated, uptime approaching 99 percent, no maintenance worker grievances filed since the program's inception.

The result of the program can be summarized in broader terms:

MANAGEMENT GAINS

Lower maintenance costs
Reduced downtime
Fewer grievances
Fewer supervisors
Improved maintenance performance
Higher employee morale

Better teamwork
Increased employee interest in reducing costs and improving efficiency
Foundation laid for related programs for improving productivity

WORKER GAINS

Freedom to exercise responsibility, initiative, and skills
Less direct supervision
No time clock
Fewer conflicts and aggravations
Opportunity to improve skills through specialization
Opportunity to specialize in work enjoyed most

Better understanding of relationship between efficiency/cost/profit and wages/job security
Growth of pride in workmanship
Growth of feeling of "ownership" of a particular work area

Chemical Bank of New York

One clerk who recalls her old job at Chemical Bank found it so boring that she was ready to quit after three months. She did nothing but pull invoices and checks out of envelopes, sort them into three piles, and pass them on to another person. Two years later, that clerk was still with the bank. Her job had been changed to include the processing of 22 corporate accounts, with varied duties ranging from crediting payments to returning unsigned checks. The work not only was more interesting but gave her a sense of accomplishment.

This job restructuring was just a part of the bank's job enrichment program, introduced in 1970, to add variety, interest, challenge, and a feeling of accomplishment to the task performed by the employees. The program resulted in a sharp decrease in the turnover rate, from 59 percent a year in the four years before it started (approximately twice the bank's overall rate of 30.9 percent) to 24 percent in just the first two years of its operation. This new figure more nearly approximated the bank's overall rate, which in the same two years had dropped to 22 percent because of the then-tight job market and various other factors.

Programs of this nature are enhancing productivity and greatly decreasing turnover at many corporations; many monotonous and unsatisfying tasks can be made much more rewarding. Furthermore, these changes are not limited to clerical and factory jobs. Supervisors, middle managers, and others may find that t'eir roles are the next to be enriched. Chemical Bank and many other organizations now know that boredom plays a large part in problems such as high turnover and absenteeism, which can be quite costly.

Procter & Gamble

Several Procter & Gamble plants have been experimenting with an overall job design and job enrichment system involving teams. In each shift, one complete team, made up of different work groups, is made responsible for a given type of production. For example, the "Liquids" team might be responsible for making, packing, and shipping liquids, not just making them.

Up and down the line, there is full and free communication of production information. The team meetings not only permit but value expressions of feelings and perceptions as well as task-oriented problem solving. Problems are discussed until there is general acceptance of the decision. Each work group has a measurable desired goal, which is stated in terms of cost, quantity, quality, and level of appearance.

At the "New Directions in the World of Work" conference conducted by the W. E. Upjohn Institute for Employment Research in 1972, results of the Procter & Gamble experiments were reported: "In its six new plants opened in the last year, the company has operated with 10 percent to 50 percent less overhead and operating costs, with technology constant." Writing on "democracy in the factory," David Jenkins says: "Without doubt the most radical organizational changes made on a practical day-to-day basis in the United States have taken place at Procter & Gamble . . . well known for its hard-boiled, aggressive management practices."[29]

The focus of Jenkins' report is the Procter & Gamble plant in Lima, Ohio. Interviewed by Jenkins, Charles Krone, the head of organizational development at Procter & Gamble's Cincinnati headquarters, said: "The plant was designed from the ground up to be democratic. The technology—the location of instruments, for example—was designed to stimulate relationships between people, to bring about autonomous group behavior, and to allow people to affect their own environment."

Jenkins continued:

The basic principle is that the human being has "growthful potential." And a key to the design and operation of the plant is that no barriers should be placed to hinder that growth.

Just as there are no physical barriers, so there are no barriers between jobs. Indeed, there are no jobs at all in the ordinary sense. . . . Not everybody can do every job, but every member of the community is constantly adding to his own skills in some specialized field. "You might be a laboratory technician," Krone says, "but you also handle operating jobs. Everybody carries the same minimum responsibility. No matter where you go, you always have to go back to the operation —you cannot become exclusively the specialist."

The workers have virtually complete control of the plant. There are no time clocks or other symbols of petty "class" distinction, and every-

[29] From D. Jenkins, *Job Power—Blue and White Collar Democracy* (New York: Doubleday, 1973). Used with permission of the author.

body is on straight salary. "The manager," says Krone, "has very little decision-making power. Usually, instead of being seen as a resource, he is seen as an invader, fulfilling a directive and controlling role—there is much less of that here." . . . I asked Krone if he and his fellow managers gave the employees complete financial figures. "Well, no," he answered, "they give them to *us*. One guy is interested in accounting and develops all that information. They draw up their own budgets and so on."

The plant's hard data are in fact easily understandable. Even though the pay scale is considerably higher than is customary, overall costs are approximately half those of a conventional plant. Much of this is because of the advanced technology. But this technology could not function properly if there were not, at the same time, an advanced social system. Quality is also affected, Krone told me: "It has the most outstanding quality record of any plant we have—it is virtually perfect quality."

The results have, in fact, been so good that the open systems principles have been applied in a number of other new Procter & Gamble plants constructed over the past few years, and the employees in such plants now total almost 10% of the company's 28,000 U.S. employees. . . . The open systems methods have proved quite profitable, so it is likely that this figure will rise in the future.

Federal Programs Concerned with Productivity[30]

The federal government has launched several programs relating to the issue of productivity. One is the Joint Financial Management Improvement Program, an ongoing, cooperative undertaking of the Office of Management and Budget, the General Accounting Office, the Bureau of Labor Statistics, the General Services Administration, and the Civil Service Commission.

[30] *Report on Federal Productivity*, Vols. I and II, Joint Financial Management Improvement Program, June 1974; *Report on Activities to the President and Congress*, National Commission on Productivity and Work Quality, July 1974; *Report to National Commission on Productivity re: Diagnostic/Job Enrichment Study in Social Security Administration*, David Sirota Associates, June 1974.

In June 1973, a joint project team of the Office of Management and Budget, the Civil Service Commission, and the General Accounting Office completed and submitted a final report on a project for measuring and enhancing federal productivity. Subsequently the director of the Office of Management and Budget authorized continuance of an annual productivity review. In June 1974, the Joint Financial Management Improvement Program issued the first of what will now be an annual series of reports on federal productivity. Volume I reports on productivity trends since the base year of 1967 and comments on the causes of productivity increases and decreases. Volume II consists of a series of productivity case studies.

Since the 1974 release of its two-volume *Report on Federal Productivity,* the work of the Joint Financial Management Improvement Program has been drawn together in a permanent cooperative program of the Central Management Agencies and the Bureau of Labor Statistics. Experimentation, evaluation, and information exchange on the quality of working life are the responsibility of a new Civil Service Clearinghouse on Productivity and Organizational Effectiveness. Elsa A. Porter, director of the Clearinghouse, recently presented the following insights related to the federal government's special efforts concerning productivity improvement:[31]

The Joint Financial Management Improvement Program is an unusual hybrid, and such collectivity has its strains. But in my view the joint program is succeeding not only to refine and perfect the system but, perhaps just as importantly, to draw together the highly fragmented, isolated parts of the government management team.

One of government's biggest problems, and a major contributor to low productivity, is the fragmentation of management itself. We have staffs for planning, budgeting, financial management, personnel management, management analysis, and audit that too often fail to talk to one another. In fact, they sometimes appear to be adversaries. What a perverse state of affairs! The interesting and exciting thing about the productivity measurement system is that it is forcing these separate groups to talk to one another and to see how each has an important role to play

---

[31] Excerpted from a paper prepared for a panel discussion on productivity at the annual meeting of the Allied Social Science Associations, Society of Government Economists, in San Francisco in December 1974.

—collaboratively—in the management of government organizations. The cause of this rapprochement, of course, is that the measures focus on mission accomplishment—and that is what each of us is there to assist.

Each of us, CSC (Civil Service Commission), BLS (Bureau of Labor Statistics), GSA (General Services Administration), and the JFMIP (Joint Financial Management Improvement Program) staff, which is housed at and led by GAO (General Accounting Office), has responsibility for a piece of the action. GSA issues the data call and has responsibility for improving capital investments and measurement systems. BLS does the statistical work with the data. The JFMIP group convenes the functional workshops and prepares the annual reports; they also are working to improve and extend the measures. We have responsibility for the people side of productivity improvement and are making some special efforts in that area.

Let me highlight them briefly:

- First, we set up a Clearinghouse to gather and exchange information on the practices in personnel management that might best contribute to productivity improvement.

- We have under way a communications program—an information campaign—trying systematically to reach key audiences with information about the measurement system and productivity improvement ideas.

- We have launched a long-range R&D program to gather evidence on the results of new managerial and behavioral science techniques and are encouraging *measured* experimentation in the agencies on such practices as flexible work hours, new incentive systems, participative management, and organization development. More than half our resources are being devoted to this R&D effort because we think that good measurement and evaluation of management innovations are sadly lacking in both the public and private sectors today. We have a lot of fads, a lot of missionaries, but little hard evidence of results.

- We are integrating the analysis of productivity data into our regular personnel management evaluation system, trying to find how, where, and when the information can be most useful for improving operations.

- We have revised our management training curriculum to focus on skills needed for measuring and improving organizational performance and are leading a government-wide effort to measure the productivity of the training function itself.

- At the state- and local-government level we are providing technical assistance and grants for improved personnel management under the Intergovernmental Personnel Act. . . .

The Office of Management and Budget (OMB), which has been conspicuously absent from our collective efforts during the past year, is now showing signs of renewed interest. And that is good news. Sooner or later the budget analysts need to join the team and factor the productivity data into their budget forecasts. Right now they constitute one of our biggest problems. From what I can see, they are still using the old meat-axe approach of levying across-the-board cuts automatically by fixed percentage on every budget request. And they compound the problem by calling these cuts "productivity factors." That kind of bludgeoning makes mincemeat of productivity data. It's a no-win situation for managers, it encourages them to fudge their data, which, in turn, undermines the whole system.

Another potential problem area is in labor relations. . . . Unions will certainly oppose unilateral efforts to increase productivity at the expense of government employees. They are looking for assurance that increasing their productivity won't mean working themselves out of a job, especially in today's depressed job market.

But they are not being unreasonable. After all, government employees are also taxpayers, and they know that there are mutual benefits to reducing the costs of public services and increasing their quality. What they want is bilateralism. They want a voice in the action. They want management to consult with them. And they want to bargain [with respect to] productivity gains. A few of them are already doing so. We recently surveyed more than 2,500 labor agreements now in force and found that 35 had productivity clauses. That's not much, but it is a beginning, and probably a portent of what is to come.

In short, productivity measurement in government is a reality today, and is on its way to perfection. The measurement effort, in turn, is providing a base for major new efforts in productivity improvement. The state-of-the-art is still in its infancy, but it is growing. And the beneficiaries are going to be the entire U.S. public, including you and me.

The National Commission on Productivity and Work Quality

The National Commission on Productivity was created by President Nixon in June 1970, and in 1974 it was renamed the National Commission on Productivity and Work Quality. The commission consists of 31 leading representatives of business, labor, the public, and government.

The commission has three board functions to perform:

To provide representatives of labor, business, state, and local governments, and the federal government the opportunity to search for ways to improve productivity and discuss constructively problems of productivity growth in which they share a common interest. This non-adversary approach, when backed by research and applied industry-by-industry and among sectors which must work together, tends to increase the possibility of cooperative action on many important issues.

To advise the government—at the federal, state, and local levels—on policies affecting productivity and to be an advocate for policies to improve productivity. The productivity implications of many government policies are not always apparent, and government programs sometimes inadvertently become an obstacle to progress.

To provide information and stimulation to the American people on the opportunities and benefits of productivity improvement.

During the year reported on, the commission focused on four major areas: food, transportation, health, and government. Its concern with the government sector extended to state and local levels as well as the federal level. To support its governmental studies, the commission conducted a Leadership Conference in June 1973 and has issued a number of publications, including *Managing Human Resources in Local Government: A Survey of Employment Incentive Programs* and *Handbook on Productivity Employment.* (The latter is addressed to mayors and provides guidelines for establishing local programs.)

Programs supported by the National Commission on Productivity and Work Quality are under way at the Social Security Administration, the Bureau of Printing and Engraving, the Naval Regional Finance Office (Alexandria, Va.), the Defense Construction Supply Center (Columbus, Ohio), and the Defense Contract Administration Services Region (New York). The entire five-agency program will cover nearly 8,000 federal workers, and its diagnostic survey outcomes will represent one of the largest consistent bodies of information about employees' perceptions of working conditions in a government setting.

Since the pattern of diagnosis and organizational remediation has wider application, the preliminary results have attracted the attention of state and local governments.

Social Security Administration (SSA)

An example of the way in which the commission serves as a catalyst in helping government agencies increase their productivity can be illustrated by the contract that was carried out by David Sirota for the benefit of the Social Security Administration. In his final report to the commission, Sirota stated:

The objective of the project was to determine whether job enrichment would be a useful solution to employee problems in the Division of Benefit Services of the Bureau of Disability Insurance (a bureau within SSA). . . . The philosophy underlying this project is that job enrichment is an important and valuable management tool provided it is applied to the specific problem it was designed to solve: the underutilization of worker talent because the demands of jobs are beneath the skills and abilities of the people who are doing them. Job enrichment is not a panacea for employee problems and can actually aggravate a situation, as when it is introduced among employees who are also expressing serious dissatisfaction with pay or job security. Nevertheless, when jobs are enriched under proper conditions these changes can produce striking and rather rapid improvement in both the performance and satisfaction of workers.

In carrying out his project, Sirota and his staff used interviews and questionnaires to arrive at a valid diagnosis of job satisfaction, analyzed the data, and supplied the information obtained to managers and employees. According to the analysis, 70 percent of the nonsupervisory employees indicated that their jobs did not fully use their skills and abilities. Employees were selected as job enrichment candidates and were matched with a corresponding control group. The job categories involved were: correspondent associate unit I, disability typing control unit I, incoming mail unit, special search unit I, and file subunit 12. A job enrichment training program was carried out involving both nonsupervisory and supervisory employees.

The following quotation, which describes the experience of one of the experimental units (special search unit I) gives an idea of the effectiveness of the program:

Before enrichment, employees in this unit received written instructions on an "852 form" filled out by the special search control unit, telling them what to do with special search materials. When they completed the assigned work it went to a technical assistant for dispatching. A control clerk maintained daily production reports for each clerk, and still other clerks told each employee how much nonproduction time to record, and when.

After enrichment the clerks in the experimental group were allowed to do some files work without the "852 form," deciding for themselves what needed to be done with the files materials. They also decided how and where it should be dispatched rather than giving it to a technical assistant. The clerks in the experimental group maintained their own daily work reports and nonproduction-time records.

In addition, an employee in this unit is assigned on a weekly rotating basis the job of unit captain. The captain's job each week includes screening and examining incoming work, dispatching certain material, assigning work to each member, combining the individual daily reports into an overall report, checking that the daily time and production record of each member is filled out correctly, taking calls from the other units regarding certain needed work and making sure that this work is completed and returned to those units, and making phone contacts with state agencies and payments centers as necessary.

These changes have given the employees responsibilities previously held by the unit supervisors or by higher-level employees in other units.

During the various phases of the study, there were a great many informal and anecdotal reports on positive changes in employees' attitudes toward their jobs. Many employees said their work was now more interesting and challenging, they were learning new skills, and they liked their new responsibilities.

In the concluding comments of his report on this project, Sirota said:

The experience in the Division of Benefits Services underscores the contractor's frequently reiterated contention that every organization contains employees with untapped talents who are perfectly capable with proper training of doing the kind of job enrichment and job reorganization that has been conducted at the Grade 2 to 4 levels in DBS. The Bureau of Disability Insurance now has a number of trained in-house resources on whom it can rely for an expansion of job enrichment to the control groups and to other parts of the Division and the Bureau.

Evaluation

Information concerning productivity and employee behavior was gathered at the conclusion of the active phase of the job enrichment experiment and a follow-up attitude survey was also conducted, using questionnaires and interviews. It was found that the experiment had mixed results. On the one hand, productivity had increased in the experimental groups, and absenteeism, employee turnover, complaints, and administrative disciplinary actions had decreased. These results were attributed to greater efficiency of the revised work procedures that had been introduced in the "enriched" groups, to improved performance feedback, and to competition. On the other hand, the experiment had not caused any significant change in employee attitudes toward their work, toward job environment, or toward management. This lack of change appeared attributable to these factors: there had been insufficient "enrichment" of the jobs (that is, the gap between worker talents and the demands made on people had not been sufficiently closed); and the workers in the "enriched" groups had not received tangible benefits as a result of their participation in the program. These findings indicate that the clerical employees involved in the experiment, although they want job enrichment, did not regard it as an end in itself, and that they would react more positively to it if it were more closely tied into the organization's reward system.

SSA comments pertinently about some of the problems related to productivity measurement in a federal agency in contrast to the measurements that can be applied by organizations in the private sector.

Productivity measurement is only one of several measures that should be used in evaluating an organization's total performance. Another measure frequently referred to in conjunction with productivity measurement is quality measurement. If productivity improvement is realized at the cost of deterioration in the quality of the service rendered, then the public is not being well served. Because the quality of the performance of SSA has a serious impact on the lives of individuals covered by Social Security, the agency is very mindful of the need to provide a high level of service to Social Security claimants and beneficiaries. . . . Among the types of measures of quality performance gathered in this system are:

1. The percentage of the initial claims and of subsequent beneficiary actions processed free of payment-related errors and the percentage free of procedural errors;

2. Data on the types of errors being made;

3. The average processing time in total and by major processing locations for claims and subsequent beneficiary actions; and

4. The number of beneficiary actions that are received and processed in time to prevent disruption of payment.

. . . The strong emphasis placed on achieving a high rate of productivity improvement must be counterbalanced with concern for quality of operations. The essential point, however, is that managers must have measurement systems for both productivity and quality; operation managers and review authorities must assess the impact that resource allocation divisions will have on these and other measures of organizational performance.

One bureau of the Social Security Administration—the Bureau of Retirement and Survivors' Insurance RSI—reports an especially interesting experiment designed to improve quality of service to the public as its first objective, and quality of worklife and productivity improvement as related secondary objectives. This case can be summarized as follows:

Background

Traditionally a program center is composed of several branches, each with several hundred employees and each responsible for a specialized function. After one of the necessary functions is performed—for example, authorization of the claim for payment, calculation of the benefit amount, and coding for computer input—the case is physically moved to the component responsible for the next step in the process. A problem associated with this traditional structure is that at each processing step a separate queuing point or backlog exists for the work of that component. This often results in intolerable delays between the receipt of a case and the completion of all necessary actions. Furthermore, an organization with approximately 2,000 employees, none of whom is responsible for performing more than a narrow range of functions, is not conducive to employee identification with either the program center or the work product.

The Pilot Test

Four basic organizational types are used to systematize business and government activities: functional, process, product, and clientele. At the Scott Plaza location of the Mid-Atlantic Program Center a modular component responsible for the full range of processing steps required for each particular case was instituted in April 1972, changing it from a functional type of organization to a clientele-centered or service-to-the-consumer type. The module consists of a team of 40–50 employees that includes specialists from all the major functional areas in the program center. Under the module setup, the first-line manager is responsible for a portion of the workload from its receipt in the program center to completion of the required action.

Results Achieved

(1) The time required to process a claim or carry out post-adjudicative action has been substantially decreased through reduction in queuing points and improved control of the workload. (2) Quality of service has been achieved with no increase in manpower. (3) Employee morale and feeling of team identity have been improved. (4) Clearer identification of effective managers has been made possible, since all managers are responsible for the same functions and have approximately the same resources available to perform their responsibilities. In summary, the modular organization offers better service to the public, permits a major degree of job enrichment for a variety of employees, and has improved managerial accountability for the performance of the organization.

Because of the success of the pilot experiment, new tests were established in the Southeastern and Northeastern Program Centers in November 1973 and March 1974 respectively. These quickly demonstrated the applicability of the modular organization to different locations and environments. Since June 1974, the six program centers and the Division of International Operations at headquarters have been converting to the modular form of organization in stages. The total project involves over 12,000 employees and is expected to be completed sometime in 1975.

SSA is doing a variety of things to improve organizational effectiveness and employee morale. The modular effort described above is but one example of SAA's attempt to improve its work environment.

Bureau of Engraving and Printing

The Bureau of Engraving and Printing (Department of the Treasury) is susceptible to productivity measurements not unlike those of many business operations, since it is actually concerned with the production of materials: currency notes, sheet postage stamps, and treasury bills. Between 1967 and 1973 this bureau registered a productivity increase of 26 percent.

Among the strategies employed to achieve this improvement has been a Human Resources Management Program that has involved labor-management relations with 18 employees' unions and the redesign of all personnel management systems. Following are excerpts from the bureau's case study, presenting the highlights of the program:

A. *Work performance.* Synthesized and coordinated performance evaluation and incentive-award plans have established good work performance as the common denominator for recognition and reward. Written tests, formal education requirements, and other extraneous criteria were either eliminated as non-relevant in the bulk of semi-skilled work situations or made secondary to the employee's work performance in eligibility for promotion, awards, etc.

B. *Training.* The strength of comprehensive training efforts is testified to by the fact that Bureau employees expressed in a recent attitudes survey an overwhelming belief that they are well trained for their jobs. Further, special supervisor training and stimulating employee productivity through such means as job enrichment, participative management, use of incentives, etc., are done on a continuing basis through established supervisors' seminar programs.

C. *Communications and feedback.* A variety of means—ranging from an 18 week series of Bureau-wide employees' seminars called "Employee Convention Days" to a recent, professional total employee opinion survey—have been employed to generate employee feedback, assess the effectiveness of policies and personnel programs, and help identify general managerial strengths and weaknesses. . . .

D. *Executive development.* A Bureau Executive Manpower Resource Board administers all executive development programs. The assessment center technique has been recently introduced for the identification of managerial potential among those who do not get visibility otherwise. . . .

E. *New productivity incentives.* Based on the confirmation in a recent attitude survey of high employee pride, quality awareness, and positive productivity inclinations, preliminary talks have been held with the National Commission on Productivity regarding the potential for a pilot installation of the Bureau's concept for an innovative incentive-bonus plan based on group productivity. Although such "Scanlon-type" plans have been used successfully in the private sector they have not been attempted in government. Therefore the Bureau is proceeding carefully in assessing the potential of such a challenging approach to improving the productivity of human resources.

Aside from formal or systematic efforts on the part of several federal agencies to achieve and measure productivity improvement, a number of individual managers are experimenting with their own informal versions of job redesign. For example, some are looking at jobs in their own areas of responsibility to see if the people can be organized into small work teams.

Ogden Air Logistics Center

From the Defense Department comes a provocative account of a job enrichment program carried out at the Ogden Air Logistics Center. The following is excerpted from a description by Major General Edmund A. Rafalko, Commander.

As Defense Department funds become tighter, management challenges of many descriptions arise within the functional agencies. At the Ogden Air Logistics Center, one of five centers which support the weapons systems used by the Air Force, a formalized effort to cope with such pressures was initiated in late 1972. The central themes were cost reduction and productivity. The study effort was titled High Payoff Investment (HPI) Study. . . .

Motivation enhancement was one of some 30 to 35 items identified as offering a high potential for maintaining support levels at reduced costs. . . . In September 1973 Dr. Frederick Herzberg was contacted to see if he and his staff would be available for assistance to the center. Dr. Herzberg was receptive, and a member of his staff, Major John Taylor, U.S. Army, was assigned as the military program coordinator.

A part of the Air Force Logistics Command, Ogden ALC is headquartered at Hill AFB, about 25 miles north of Salt Lake City. Last year was a prosperous one for Ogden ALC, with a $254,390,294 combined military-civilian payroll, a workforce of some 16,000 civilians and 3,000 military personnel, and a gross value of $2.4 billion, counting real estate, buildings, equipment, and inventories. The Ogden Air Logistics Center is "big business" in Utah. In fact, it is the largest business in the state.

Major mission assignments include systems support management of the F-4 and RF-4 jet aircraft, Minuteman and Titan II ICBMs, Maverick tactical missiles, simulators and training devices, aircraft landing gear, photographic equipment, airmunitions, and the provisional management responsibilities for the F-16, the new air combat fighter.

As in any large industrial complex, either in the government or the private sector, our problem, simply put, was to maintain or improve quality and at the same time increase productivity in the face of continuing cutbacks of funds and personnel. We had to determine how to increase motivation in the current economic climate with the ever-changing problems and needs of today's workforce.

. . . Dr. Herzberg's Orthodox Job Enrichment (OJE) approach is a process of restructuring jobs to provide patterns which increase opportunities to improve direct worker motivation. Dr. Herzberg's thesis has a basic premise supported by two separate tenets: First, that the opposite of job satisfaction is not job dissatisfaction but rather no job satisfaction. Next, and similarly, the opposite of job dissatisfaction is not job satisfaction but no job dissatisfaction. Further, he concludes that the conditions which lead to job dissatisfaction involve the environment in which the job is accomplished. He calls these dissatisfiers "hygiene" factors. The hygiene factors are company policies and administration of the policies, supervision, working conditions, interpersonal relations, money, status, and security. The conditions leading to job satisfaction involve the job itself. He calls these satisfiers "motivators." The motivators are achievement, recognition for achievement, work itself, responsibility, growth, and opportunity to advance.

Ogden ALC management decided to redesign jobs in order to create more elements of motivation and reduce the problems associated with hygiene. The guideline was to be sincere and credible with the workers, yet operate within the management and supervisory structure.

The strategy works two ways, in that it supports line management and presents a method to increase effectiveness while at the same time it offers increased quality of work life and a better job to the employee.

Dr. Herzberg suggests a number of additional ingredients that, from experience, lead to better jobs and better motivation. They are direct feedback, a client relationship, a learning function, the opportunity for each person to schedule his own work, the use of individual unique expertise, control over resources, direct communication, and personal accountability.

These ingredients of a good job directly relate to the motivators, and careful consideration of such factors assisted Ogden ALC's managers in the job redesign process.

In January 1974, a training contract between Herzberg and Associates and Ogden ALC was signed, and training of the first cadre of sixteen keymen began immediately. Keymen were selected on the basis of current managerial skills, broad knowledge of their organization, and a past experience of succeeding. They had to be able to learn the theory and application, assimilate and orchestrate it with previous management experience, and teach the principles to management and supervision. Keymen received comprehensive training in motivation-hygiene theory, the dynamics of how the motivation factors and the hygiene factors operate, and the specific skills associated with implementing OJE projects—about 120 classroom hours, which is the equivalent of eight credit hours in the graduate school at the University of Utah.

The classroom training, however, does not stand alone. The development process continued for an additional eight months and included some added guidance as the keymen worked on projects. Only then were they considered fully proficient.

In February 1974, the sixteen keymen selected eleven pilot projects. . . . Many areas were represented and involved over 350 direct labor workers to include mechanics, warehousemen, service people, and a variety of desk jobs.

The following data include results of the eleven pilot projects. Soft data (opinions, attitudes, and feelings) were encouraging in terms of reduced turnover, reduced sick leave, and improved attitude. Hard data (measurable, without question) showed more units produced and reduced manhours required.

. . . Figures aggregated to date reflect an investment of about $173,-000 compared to a return rounded out to nearly $290,000. Included in the investment figures are less than $13,000 out-of-pocket dollars for contract and training materials. The bulk of investment costs are for salaries paid to keymen and management personnel involved in the eleven projects.

Return data include such things as materials, fuel, increased units of production, and reduced personnel costs. It should be noted that the aforementioned figures are preliminary and represent a relatively short period of time. . . .

It would be a mistake to let you assume that all of this has been easy. There has been success, but also lack of it. No failures, but resistance to change or what I call the "sameness syndrome." Yet, on balance there are many more pluses than minuses. Management has not agonized over the lack of measurable progress in specific projects but has highlighted and reinforced the successes where found. It is now evident that management and keymen are more competent and confident in their ability to overcome areas of resistance and maintain the momentum. . . .

On the basis of these results, reinforced by the enthusiasm of top management and my own personal conviction that we can continue to improve, I have authorized the establishment of an organization designed to accelerate the expansion of success. Thirty full-time positions will be staffed by the most qualified personnel available. . . . The three lead keyman positions located in the Plans shop I'll watch very closely. They have the background, experience, and technical ability required to train and develop new keymen. The other 27 keymen are distributed in all major organizations, roughly proportioned to population and complexity. Twenty or more positions will be on a one-year rotational basis. This cycle provides an additive channel for expansion as the old keymen return to their former positions or to positions of increased responsibility. New keymen will be selected and trained three times a year to provide an orderly but controlled progression and expansion.

. . . Since last July, the program has matured beyond the test phase. Maturing projects added more "touch labor" jobs and the start-up of new projects now gives us a total of 29, involving more than 1,000 direct workers. Two hundred sixty-nine supervisors and managers are directly involved, and 36 keymen have been trained (21 are active, 4 have been promoted or transferred into supervisory positions, 8 have transferred into staff positions, and 3 have left the installation). Nine new keymen will be trained in March 1975 to continue the controlled progression and expansion.

Yes, we definitely need better measurement tools to more clearly see and differentiate among the many productivity programs we have going on. We need to be able to better judge how each of our efforts contributes to defense readiness. The management team at Ogden has roughed out a system to help provide that kind of visibility. We call it "Meaningful Measures of Merit," and it uses much of the existing management and productivity data. Many of those macro-level measures should, in the future, start to show the influence of the motivation-hygiene approach.

Even though I still call myself a "skeptical believer" when discussing OJE, I fully accept the notion that to increase productivity we must create a work environment in which each individual is first *allowed* and then *encouraged* to achieve his full work potential. It is this latent, unused individual talent, multiplied by the thousands of people we employ, that can give us major productivity increases. I believe we have applied a theory that will help create such an environment. We have adopted a management strategy which will reinforce job motivators. We have established an organization which will systematically review how we do what we must do. We must move closer to our primary objective of increased support to our combat forces at reduced costs. I believe OJE is an absolutely essential part of the "common-sense approach to people at work. . . ."

Comment

The federal effort to stimulate, achieve, and measure QWL and productivity improvement in its own agencies is heartening in several senses. For one thing, absence of the competition which besets non-government organizations tends to reduce the pressure for efficiency. More important, with the expense of government operation spiraling almost continuously upward, a means of management that offers hope of increasing employee ego-involvement, job satisfaction, and efficiency simultaneously seems on a creatively constructive track. It also constitutes appropriate role-modeling. And finally, productivity improvement efforts such as the three examples cited above demonstrate that much of value *can* be achieved in the direction of better agency management, and thus improved service delivery.

The creations of the National Commission on Productivity and Work Quality, and the new Civil Service Clearinghouse on

Productivity and Organizational Effectiveness should strengthen the federal government's ability to provide needed resource, catalyst and consultative functions to stimulate the spread of serious QWL and productivity improvement efforts—and to offer evaluation counsel as well. It might be still more effective and cost-beneficial in the national interest if the budget of these relatively small offices were enlarged to permit an offer of technical assistance to help organizations that indicated "readiness" to get started skillfully in developing their QWL program efforts.

The Tavistock Institute's Coal Mining Studies

From 1950 to 1958, the Tavistock Institute of London became involved in a number of studies in the British coal mines. Two of the studies are reviewed below (cited from Paul Hill[32]):

The Longwall method of coal-getting. This was a semi-mechanised system involving automatic coal cutters and a conveyor-belt for filling and loading the coal, which had replaced the old traditional hand-got method. The Longwall method had encountered many difficulties, but some changes in manning arrangements had emerged in some pits which were giving more promising results. One purpose of the study was therefore to examine what these changes were and to determine to what extent they might be more generally applicable in other pits. The study included what was the first "socio-technical" analysis of a productive system. In other words, it made a detailed study of the technical system, not merely as background to examining the set-up of the social system, but in order to see how appropriately the two had been related to each other.

In their report on this study, Eric Trist and K. W. Bamforth (1951) show first how the organisation of work in the old hand-got method was ideally matched to the nature and the demands of the task. The miners had developed over generations a system where small groups of two or three men per shift worked their own narrow face. Every man

---

[32] P. Hill, *Towards a New Philosophy of Management* (New York: Barnes & Noble, 1972). Reprinted by permission of Barnes & Noble Books, a division of Harper & Row, Publishers, Inc.

was capable of doing all the tasks involved in the three main phases of the work, breaking up the coal face ("preparing"), moving the coal to the tubs and filling ("getting"), and then fixing pit props and moving forward to the new coal face ("advancing"). Thus, at whatever phase of the job one shift finished, the next shift picked up the work and carried on. They were self-selecting groups and shared a common wage packet. They needed no external supervision to direct their activities, which was as well, considering the dark, remote and physically cramped conditions in which they worked. Furthermore, as a small, mutually-supporting and autonomous group, they were well sùited to withstand the danger and the stress of their underground task.

By contrast, the way in which the work organisation had been set up to deal with the semi-mechanised Longwall method was not at all well suited to the demands and nature of the new technical system. Mechanisation made it possible to work a single long face of up to 200 yards in place of the many short faces of the hand-got method. This meant that as many as forty or fifty men over three shifts were engaged on the face, and the quantity of coal to be handled by the system was greatly increased.

Faced with the problem of creating an organisation to cope with this new and more complex situation, management and engineers turned to the conventional pattern of production engineering. Thus each of the three shifts was allocated one of the main phases—"preparing," "getting" and "advancing." Within each shift, the work was further broken down into specialised tasks and men were assigned to a specific task group. There was no self-selection. Each group was paid separately. Responsibility for co-ordination between the task groups and between shifts was not vested in the men, but placed with external supervisors.

The effects of this system of working were damaging both to productivity and to the morale of the men. As they were restricted to, and paid for, a single specialised task, each group tended to concern itself only with its own task, at the expense of the overall objective. Delays and difficulties on one shift would hold up and disrupt the following one. Conflict between task groups, and with supervisors whom the men now held responsible for delays, caused high absence and accident rates, and low morale.

The changes in the social system which had begun to emerge in some pits were in the direction of creating groups with more flexible skills who would not be limited to a specific task. The next study goes further and shows how the same Longwall technical system could be operated much more effectively by a social system derived not from production engineering, but from the characteristics of the old hand-got method of mining.

The Durham studies. In studies in the Durham coal mines, Eric Trist and his colleagues located within the same seam, and using the same Longwall technical system, two quite different work organisations. They were able to compare the functioning and effectiveness of the two systems over a period of two years. The results are reported in their book *Organisational Choice* (1963).

The first system was the conventional Longwall organisation with specialised tasks, described in the previous section. The second, which they called the composite system, had been developed largely by the miners themselves and incorporated many of the features of the old, hand-got working methods. Thus, in the composite system, the men were multi-skilled and able to move from role to role. The group accepted responsibility for the deployment of its members. There was also rotation over shifts, so that no man was pinned to a particular shift or task. Payment was on an overall-output basis for the whole group of forty men and divided up by them, usually in equal amounts. Men were thus committed to the overall task, not only to a specific part of it.

The differences in the effectiveness of these two systems, both operating with the same technology in the same seam, were striking, not only in terms of productivity but also of response to stress, as indicated by levels of sickness and absence. For example:

	CONVENTIONAL SYSTEM	COMPOSITE SYSTEM
Productive achievement (as per cent of coal face potential)	78%	95%
Ancillary work at face (hours per man-shift)	1.32	0.03
Per cent of shifts with cycle lag	69%	5%
Absenteeism (per cent of possible shifts):		
No reason given	4.3%	0.4%
Sickness or other	8.9%	4.6%
Accident	6.8%	3.2%
Total	20%	8.2%

Conclusions

The coal mine studies were of great importance and enabled Tavistock to draw the following main theoretical conclusions.

The concept of the socio-technical system. The need to study a production system as a whole and to understand the interrelatedness of all its aspects. Trist and Bamforth wrote: "So close is the relationship between the various aspects, that the social and the psychological can be understood only in terms of the detailed engineering facts and of the way the technological system as a whole behaves in the environment of the underground situation."

The organisation as an open system. In connection with the above, Tavistock argued that it was no longer adequate to consider an organisation as a closed system, sufficiently shut off within its own boundary to enable its problems to be analysed without reference to its external environment. It must be seen as an open system in constant interaction with its environment, and this must be taken into account in the analysis of its problems.

The principle of organisational choice. The importance of matching the social and the technical systems together in the most appropriate way had been conclusively demonstrated. (Tavistock termed this "joint optimisation of the socio-technical system.") This clearly had implications for the design of new systems or the revamping of old ones.

The importance of autonomous groups. It had been demonstrated that when men formed an autonomous group with a degree of responsibility for a major section of the task, where the group sets its own target and managed its own internal relationships, the most favourable results were achieved.

Alienation from work. Poor morale and lack of motivation were directly engendered by the type of work role created by the prevailing standards of production engineering, which were exemplified in the conventional Longwall system of working. This led Tavistock to develop some general theories on the psychological conditions under which people could be motivated at work.[33]

---

[33] These theories were to be built into another Taxistock case, Shell UK Limited, described later in this chapter.

Imperial Chemical Industries, Ltd.[34]

A group of studies was carried out in Britain to cross-validate some of Frederick Herzberg's influential theories of motivation. In each experimental situation, management had identified problems of morale and performance: For example, a group of laboratory technicians were believed to be suffering from low morale because of their lack of status compared to the scientists with whom they worked. They felt that their technical abilities were wasted and that channels for promotion within the plant were limited.

A group of sales representatives were selected as targets for another experiment because, in the management's opinion, they were not competing successfully for their share of the market. A third group—design engineers—had problems with an increasing workload and recruiting; developmental work in the organization suffered as a result.

Two final studies concerned factory supervisors—one group of production foremen and another of engineering foremen. In these cases, management was concerned about the recent erosion of the traditional role of the foreman. The men had fewer opportunities to make decisions on planning, technical control, and discipline, and were isolated from critical work. The day-to-day relationship between the foreman and his men, it was believed, had been weakened. The methods and results used with each of the groups are summarized below.

Laboratory Technicians or "Experimental Officers" (EOs)

There was an experimental group of 15, and two control groups totaling 29 EOs. The changes made were:

Technical. The EOs were encouraged to write the final report on any research project for which they had been responsible.

[34] Based on W. Paul, K. Robertson & F. Herzberg, "Job Enrichment Pays Off," *Harvard Business Review,* March–April 1969, 61. Used by permission.

Such minutes carried the author's name. The EOs were also involved in planning projects and experiments, given more chance to assist in work planning and target setting, and, upon request, given time to follow up their own ideas.

Financial. EOs were authorized to requisition materials and equipment, to request analysis, and to order services such as maintenance, all on their own signature.

Managerial. Senior EOs were given responsibility for a training program for their junior staff, were involved in interviewing candidates for the job of laboratory assistant, and took part in staff assessment of their own assistants.

Results are reported only in general terms. It was felt that reports written by EOs compared favorably with those of scientists. One original idea that was followed up on resulted in an important discovery with possible applications in certain kinds of national emergencies. It was the feeling within the company that the members of the experimental group showed definite evidence of growth and improvement during the experimental period.

Sales Representatives

There were 15 in the experimental group. The 23 other members of the sales force served as the control group. The following changes were made:

Technical. The sales representatives were relieved of writing reports on every customer call, but were required to pass along information when appropriate or to request action when it was required. They made their own records for staff review and themselves decided how frequently calls were to be made. Contact between sales staff and the technical service department was direct, paperwork being cleared subsequently; service calls from sales representatives were given top priority.

Financial. Sales representatives were authorized to make immediate settlement of customer complaints up to $250, and to buy back surplus stock. They were given a discretionary range of about 10 percent on the prices of most products.

The resulting sales for the experimental group increased by almost 19 percent over the same period of time in the preceding year; for the control group, sales declined by 5 percent.

Design Engineers

The sizes of the experimental and control groups are not reported. The changes were:

Technical. Engineers were given greater independence; situations in which consultation with a supervisor was obligatory were reduced to a minimum. Engineers were encouraged to become departmental experts in particular fields and to follow up on completed projects as they thought appropriate. They made the choice with regard to outside consultants.

Financial. Engineers were given considerable latitude in spending money, provided they adhered to the project budget.

Managerial. Engineers were involved in the selection and placement of designers (draftsmen), ratified the allocation of any new employee to their jurisdiction, and made initial salary recommendations for their junior staff members.

No statistical backup on results is provided, but the descriptive account indicates improved performance. The increased autonomy was well handled, and supervisors were freed to give more time to technical development.

Factory Supervisors

The supervisors were production foremen in one company, engineering foremen in the other. In these cases, too, the sizes of the experimental and control groups are not reported. The changes were:

Technical. Foremen were involved more in planning and were assigned projects on specific problems, such as quality control. Production foremen were authorized to modify schedules for loading and sequencing. Engineering foremen were consulted more about organizational development.

Financial. Both categories of foremen were given greater control of certain categories of expenditures.

Managerial. Foremen were given expanded authority with regard to hiring, disciplinary action (except for dismissal), and training. Engineering foremen, in addition, worked jointly with union officials on a job appraisement program.

In only one instance was a dollar value placed on the results of this program. The foremen developed solutions to long-standing technical and organizational problems that resulted in estimated annual savings of more than $125,000. Beyond that, managerial personnel reported that the foremen in the experimental groups demonstrated that they were able to absorb their additional responsibilities creditably.

Analysis of Findings

An analysis of the ICI studies arrived at these conclusions:

Generality of Findings

1. The findings of job enrichment studies can be applied to a variety of types and levels of jobs in a wide range of industries. The researchers believe that the findings are relevant wherever people are being managed.

2. The scope for change is wide and the need is deep. Almost any type of job offers the potential for job enrichment.

3. Significant results can be obtained in a variety of situations, regardless of whether the job involves large numbers of people all doing the same work or a few people in highly diversified tasks. Managers reported that job enrichment programs made

possible methods of measuring individual performance that had not existed before and that often led to better diagnosis of technical as well as personnel problems.

Feasibility of Change

1. It is doubtful that any situation exists in which the operational risk is so high that it would be foolhardy to attempt to pass responsibility and scope for achievement down the line. Although there were considerable risks involved in the experimental projects—particularly with respect to the latitudes given employees in financial matters—no disasters were reported. As the researchers put it:

> When a man is given the chance to achieve more, he may not take that chance, but he has no reason to achieve less. The message of both theory and practice is that people respond cautiously to new responsibility. They feel their way and seek advice. When responsibility is put squarely to a person doing a job, he is the one who wants and needs feedback in order to do the job. . . . Mistakes are less likely, not more likely, than before. Those which occur are more likely to be turned to account, learned from, and prevented in the future, for they are seen to matter.

2. It is not necessary to make changes selectively, despite the fact that people's ability and sense of responsibility vary markedly. The researchers concluded:

> We are in no position to decide before the event who deserves to have his job enriched and who does not. . . . Some people who had been thought to be sound and responsible under the old conditions turned out merely to have been yes-men once those conditions were changed; their performance was the same as it had always been, but now compliance was no longer valued so highly. At the other extreme was a classic example of an awkward employee, about to be sacked, who turned out to be unusually inventive and responsible when he was given the opportunity to be so. . . . When changes are made unselectively, the genuinely good performers get better. Some poor performers remain poor, but nothing is lost.

3. Not all employees are uniformly receptive to a job enrichment program, but this lack of enthusiasm on the part of some is not likely to impair the program itself or to diminish the level of performance of either those who are receptive or those who are apathetic.

4. The imposing of new responsibilities on employees does not inevitably lead to demands for higher pay or better conditions. There is not necessarily a price tag attached to changes in working practice. In the researchers' words, "Higher pay may temporarily buy more work, but it does not buy commitment."[35]

5. Participation is not necessarily the route to motivational change. The researchers are quite convinced that the employees themselves should not participate in deciding what changes are to be made in their job.[36] The researchers do not totally dismiss the value of participation as a component of job enrichment, but feel that meaningful participation consists of consultation sought by the employee with his superior.

In consultation upward there is no ambiguity; tasks and roles are clear. Both parties are motivated, the subordinate by the need to make the best decision to satisfy himself, to justify the trust placed in him, to enhance his professional reputation; the manager by the need to develop his staff.

The researchers believe conversely that when management seeks consultation from employees it is often a patronizing gesture, or an attempt to lend credibility to a job enrichment program that is not essentially a valid one.

[35] On the other hand, if a job enrichment program does in fact result in sustained, significant increases in productivity and profitability, why not share this increased harvest with all concerned, including customers? —*E. M. G.*

[36] As noted earlier, most other researchers disagree with this observation and cite evidence that employee participation in job changes helps to support and implement those changes. —*E. M. G.*

Participation is indeed the best route to motivational change, but only when it is participation in the act of management, no matter at what level it takes place. The test of the genuineness of that participation is simple—it must be left to the subordinate to be the prime mover in consultation on those topics where he carries personal responsibility. For the manager as well as for the subordinate, the right to be consulted must be earned by competence in giving help.

Expected Consequences of the ICI Experiment

1. Despite the many potential difficulties associated with job enrichment programs, it can be expected that the gains will be significant rather than only marginal. For example, it was estimated that in the experimental programs reported above, the annual savings would be more than $200,000.

2. Contrary to some people's expectations, the gains from the programs related primarily to performance rather than to job satisfaction. In the opinion of the researchers, this is accounted for by the fact that performance gains can be measured immediately, whereas changes in attitudes tend to be delayed. The researchers are confident that ultimately the job satisfaction gains also would be appreciable.

3. The fact that the jobs of subordinates were enriched does not necessarily mean that the jobs of supervisors became impoverished. Rather, the supervisors found they had time to do more important work. The researchers explained: "Fears that the supervisor may somehow miss out are based on the premise that there is a finite pool of responsibilities in the organization which is shared among its members. In practice, new, higher-order responsibilities are born."

4. The researchers see a new role for management as one of the consequences of motivational change. "The main consequence is that management becomes a service. Its purpose is to enable, encourage, assist, and reinforce achievement by employees. Task organization and task support are the central features of the manager's new role."

In September 1972, *Business Week* magazine, in a special issue on productivity, took a look at the expansion of productivity programs throughout ICI. The following is a condensed version of that account.

"It was a real sweatshop before, with the management up there, us down here, and those bastards, the supervisors, in the middle," says a local union leader who has worked 20 years for Britain's Imperial Chemical Industries (ICI). "We have proved that we don't need supervisors, and we have proved that work can be more than just a pay packet at the end of the week."[37]

According to a later report on the ICI program, "So far, the company is getting a productivity improvement of about 11 percent."

In connection with the Weekly Staff Agreement, which ICI instituted in an effort to remove restrictive work practices, an ICI spokesman observed: "When you open men's minds . . . you can't close them, either. You have to find new ways of maintaining the dialogue, or you're in trouble."

As *Business Week* further observed: "Union officials have already given ICI plenty to think about. They have told management that the next logical steps are to develop a new system for promoting men from the shop floor, provide more operational and financial information about the company, and introduce workers on the board of directors."

Shell UK Ltd.[38]

In 1955 Shell UK Ltd., which operates oil refineries and chemical plants at four locations in Great Britain, launched a long-term program to improve company performance by creating

---

[37] *Business Week,* September 9, 1972, 119.

[38] The substance of this report is taken from P. Hill, *Towards a New Philosophy of Management.* Abstracted with permission of Barnes & Noble Books, a division of Harper & Row, Publishers, Inc.

conditions in which people at all levels might become better motivated and more committed to their tasks.

For more than a decade, Shell had been less than successful in persuading employees to work effectively. Among other problems, there were continuing difficulties in union negotiations. Overall, management judged productivity to be low and labor costs excessively high.

The first step toward change was an employee relations planning team (ERP), formed in 1964. One year later, aided by social scientists from the Tavistock Institute's Human Resources Center, the team presented Shell with two proposals. Twin lines of action were suggested to deal with two main problem areas:

1. *Attitude change.* If management allowed workers more participation in the running of the company, there would be a change in worker attitudes. It was proposed, therefore, that the ERP team should draft a statement of objectives and management philosophy. If accepted by management, the statement would serve as a focal point for discussion and debate, not only by groups of managers and supervisors but by all employees throughout the entire organization.

2. *Productivity bargaining.* To deal with the unsatisfactory terms and conditions of employment for unionized employees, a number of study teams should be set up to investigate in depth the implications of all the changes which the company would hope to see introduced as a result of eventual bargains with the unions.

After considerable and thoroughgoing discussion, plus some clarification, the ERP proposals were accepted by Shell's entire management team. Trade union officials and shop stewards at the plants were then involved in similar debates. In time, the senior shop stewards expressed their understanding of the company's new philosophy (made explicit in a "Statement of Objectives") and supported it as a statement of intent.

Implementation of the new development program involved four components:

1. *A pilot project* to provide people with jobs which, while effectively meeting the technical requirements, would provide sufficient psychological satisfaction for them to become committed to doing their tasks well.

2. *The use of department managers as change agents* to put the ideas of the philosophy statement into practice, to examine how well existing jobs met psychological needs, and to make changes so these needs could be more effectively met.

3. *The designing of a new refinery* to offer an opportunity to put into practice the ideas of the philosophy statement on job design and a chance to establish a set of working conditions and practices that could serve as a model for the older refineries to follow.

4. *The establishment of joint working parties* to pave the way for productivity bargaining with the unions, and the negotiation of new agreements that would incorporate radical change in the terms and conditions of employment of unionized employees. It was hoped that the results of the productivity bargaining would clear the ground of restrictive practices, making it easier to introduce new methods of work and to redesign jobs.

At the end of 1966 a questionnaire was distributed to all department managers—the first assessment of a just-beginning, long-term project. The data showed that substantial changes had been made in the desired direction and that the tempo of change far exceeded that of previous years. There was a wide variation in the progress of individual items, but, taken together, they represented a clear and positive movement toward the objectives in the philosophy statement.

While the overall results were very positive, a few negative points also emerged. These indicated a need to reinforce understanding of the key concepts of the philosophy and to provide help to department managers wishing to bring about change.

By 1967, the program had created a climate throughout Shell that supported efforts to put its concepts into practice. The statement of philosophy was seen as a framework of values within which a variety of experiments could be tried out. Early in the development program, however, the need to incorporate the philosophy within the company—to create policies and procedures that would reflect its values—was recognized. This was accomplished by:

1. *Staff appraisal* to assess annually a person's performance in achieving previously agreed-upon work targets. Each year new targets would be agreed to, against which performance would be reviewed and assessed.

2. *Management by objective* to ensure that the system was consistent with the philosophy and not used to enforce more autocratic control over people's performance.

3. *Trade-union agreements* to induce a maximum sense of joint responsibility between company and unions for assuring adherence, reducing the area of conflict, and facilitating change through some form of joint problem-solving mechanism.

4. *Communications* effectively handled through departmental meetings with representatives from all employee levels.

5. *Induction and training* to introduce new employees to the history of the development program and take them through the main points of the philosophy statement.

6. *Participation* of people on the shop floor in the planning and design of projects.

7. *Job enrichment* to explore alternative methods of redesigning jobs.

8. *Supervisors' role enrichment* to provide wider areas of discretion and an increased level of responsibility.

Comment

The impressive effort reported here began when Paul Hill was personnel manager at one of the Shell refineries. It was Hill who, with the help of consultants from the Tavistock Institute, developed the "Statement of Objectives," and sold the plan to top management of the Shell parent company.

Hill's objectives and the underlying philosophy were worked through in the conferences described in his book, then became company policy for all Shell UK refineries. The plan also won the support of the union representing the shift workers (those with the skills to make the refinery run), though not that of the majority of the craft union day workers such as electricians, painters, and plumbers.

Hill's change strategy seemed to work. The Shell organization changed; the counterproductive disturbances also reportedly changed, although this has not been measured in any precise way. But change lasts only as long as the company remains committed. In 1968 Shell International reorganized, and old managerial lines were reestablished. According to personal correspondence from Ted Mills, director of the Quality of Work Program:

The turned-on managing director who had steadfastly stuck by the Hill plan was replaced by a new hard-liner who *had never heard of* the effort, let alone been involved in or conversant with it.

In the reorganized Shell UK, the effort was given no managerial push anymore. The union representing the shift workers . . . exercised no leadership in insisting on maintaining or strengthening the many positive job enrichment and social gains made before the reorganization. The craft unions, which had resisted the change from the outset, were of no help.

Hill resigned from Shell two years later, when it became evident that the new management, unlike the former management, was simply uninterested in the entire philosophy of the highly successful operation. He and I discussed at length how, had there been a committed and demanding union leadership, it could have bridged the management change and continued to keep and increase the quality of work effort in the refineries, by making such gains an expressed and dynamic factor of union bargaining.

In a May 1973 conversation with Mills, Hill said be believed that perhaps 50 percent of the affected employees were still psychologically committed five years after the effort had been let die.

Unfortunately, the manager who guided the experiment at the largest refinery involved says he has no way of proving how much impact the total effort had had on productivity. As Hill put it:

The qualitative impact is still there in things like morale, attitude, and Shell being a good place to work, with little turnover, whereas before it was bloody awful. But I have no way to measure the impact on productivity. Our technology has changed so since 1966 that it may be technology, it may be attitude and work change, or it may be both which lets us make do with fewer redundants [British term for surplus labor]. We have no records whatsoever, though, which we can use to show other managers how effective the effort was—or wasn't.

Norsk Hydro[39]

The Norsk Hydro fertilizer company of Norway was facing steadily tougher competition. Profits were decreasing, and co-operation between labor and management was considered by management to be unsatisfactory. In response to this situation the company selected a fertilizer processing plant with about 50 employees for experimentation. The following organizational changes were made:

- The shifts were organized in flexible subgroups that were responsible for production in assigned work areas. (Individual workers were not given specific jobs.)

- The organization was built up without "first hands" (i.e., supervisors).

- Each worker was given the opportunity to learn all the tasks within his subgroup through job rotation and mutual aid.

- It was left to the worker to decide how quickly and how much he wanted to increase his competence, thus leaving little chance for too much or too little variation in a job.

[39] N. Herrick & M. Maccoby, "Humanizing Work: A Priority Goal of the 1970's." In L. E. Davis & A. B. Cherns (Eds.), *Quality of Working Life* (New York: The Free Press, 1975). Copyright © 1975 by Louis E. Davis and Albert B. Cherns. Reprinted with permission of Macmillan Publishing Co., Inc.

- The idea behind the organization was that every man should be able to get help from others when his own abilities were not sufficient, and vice versa.

- A bonus system was installed which paid the workers according to factors they themselves could influence, such as quantity produced, cost, loss of materials, and working hours. The bonus was paid to all workers in the 50-man plant, in order to stimulate cooperation.

- Basic wages were paid according to the number of jobs in the plant that a worker was able to do rather than the actual work he did.

The human outcomes of this participative work restructuring were measured by asking the workers involved whether their jobs were satisfying or not satisfying in general and with regard to variety, learning, responsibility, and security. This was done for their previous jobs and for their new jobs after the experiment had been under way for one year. The percentage of workers expressing satisfaction increased from 58 to 100 on general view, from 45 to 85 on variety, from 33 to 96 on learning, from 42 to 96 on responsibility, and from 39 to 73 on security.

The economic results were that production costs per ton steadily decreased by about 30 percent during the first six months of the project, and absenteeism in the experimental factory was 4 percent as compared with 7 percent for the controlled factory and 7.5 percent for the firm as a whole.

Norsk Hydro has since been extending this participative management experiment throughout the company. Top management sums up its reaction with "It is not only the production that matters; human values become more central."

However, a more recent account of this project, prepared in a Work Note from Thoralfvirjk Qvale, February 1973, states that "the workers' involvement and general satisfaction with the project seem to have been failing." This phenomenon is interpreted by observers of the project as a result of learning possibilities being exhausted within the given frame.

One observer states:

The first year, and particularly the first few months after starting up the plant, the workers experienced an immense growth in terms of learning. The learning in work was supported by the training courses and vice versa, and led to a great enthusiasm among all employed in the fertilizer area. Expectations for further growth were therefore also strong. What should have been done . . . was a change in the role of the supervisors. As it is now, the supervisors have tended to take over many of the decisions earlier made by workers, as the workers' involvement and interest have been going down. At least temporarily, therefore, the change process seems to have lost momentum. . . .

Seen from the Industrial Democracy point of view, the project demonstrates that under certain conditions workers are interested in taking over responsibilities for decisions affecting their own daily work and in participation in the development of the total organization. But so far, it does not seem fair to take conclusions from this experiment very much further. It is still too early to see whether this is the big leap forward toward industrial democracy, though it may show some important conditions for it.

Olivetti

Since 1961 Olivetti management has been aware that job monotony affects work morale and production volume. Absenteeism and requests for job shifts seemed to correlate with monotony and boredom in the assembly-line environment. Management decided that an enriched job experience would have to occur in the context of a reorganized manufacturing system.

By 1967 Olivetti had arranged for variation in job function by allowing three-member teams to perform all the required steps in a mechanical series: setup, operation, and inspection. Workers also learned different machine tool operations. When this aspect of the industry became computerized, workers were retrained to understand computer designs and tapes. Sharing in professional goals enhanced work quality and reduced substantially the number of defective end products.

For the new Auditronic accounting system, initiated in 1969, Olivetti used worker teams to help construct equipment such as keyboard and printer modules. The team worked around a table, with each member given a job taking up to half an hour rather than just a few minutes as had previously been the case, and also given the responsibility for testing his own product. Because of its success, this flexible organization is now used throughout the Auditronic Division.

Olivetti has started using worker teams to plan larger, more complex projects on modules for memories and printers for electronic desk calculators. The new system has provided great flexibility in this high-technology field, which frequently involves product changes. Workers trained to perform several industrial tasks no longer become dead weight on the payroll if their machine is modified or their work role shifted. (In Italy, it is almost impossible to fire anyone.) This is in comparison to the old assembly-line method, under which it took several months to introduce an innovation. As a result, partly finished equipment piled up, and it was difficult to retain workers because they were accustomed to performing only one operation.

Results

Benefits to Olivetti include a more rapid introduction of new industrial processes as well as a higher quality of work. There is also reduced absenteeism and a lessening of fatigue in the workforce. People's increased involvement gives them a heightened sense of their own value and of the significance of the product they help to create. As of 1972, this program had raised productivity 15 percent, due largely to fewer rejects.

Volvo[40]

In the late 1960s structural changes in Swedish society became evident, such as the higher educational status of youths entering industry and the greater numbers of women and older people in the labor force. In 1969, certain events—such as alarming per-

[40] From material provided by Volvo, Sweden. Reprinted by permission.

sonnel turnover and absenteeism, a few wildcat strikes, and an unstable workforce situation—triggered Volvo management to set up a task force[41] charged with investigating possible corporate actions. The recommendations of this task force have led to integrated sociotechnical-administrative changes in the assembly operations of a number of different Volvo plants since 1969, with the responsibility and initiative delegated to individual plant managers.

For example, changes in the technical system have dealt with the physical environment (e.g., improvements in building design, layouts, noise level, ventilation, lighting, job safety, rest areas) and the assembly line (e.g., tilt features to eliminate workplaces under the car, individually controlled platforms to provide for flexibility). Changes in the social system have resulted in:

1. *Joint consultation:* works councils with representatives from management and the unions, joint consultation groups at the "grass-roots level," union representatives in steering committees for projects.

2. *Formal organizational changes:* decentralization of the organization, with more responsibility and power to line management and with specialists (such as the industrial engineer) in a service role to a foreman or some other appropriate line manager/ supervisor.

3. *Work organization changes:* in the Torslanda plant, jobs are rotated within groups of 9 people, with inspection part of the rotating scheme; the interval of rotation is between two hours and two weeks. At the Kalmar plant, the group size is 15–25 persons, with each group assembling a complete function in the car. At the Skövde plant, there are 4–6 persons in each group, with an individual operator able to assemble almost a complete engine.

4. *Work content changes:* flexibility in the amount of time an individual would spend at a given work station, depending on type of product, number of variants, and training methods.

[41] The system of works councils is based on a national agreement from 1947.

Changes in the administrative control system have led to group responsibility, follow-up of short-term objectives, fast feedback of results, new types of computer systems to provide the necessary information for such controls, and so forth.

Some key guiding concepts in the development of Volvo's job redesign and quality of worklife improvements have been:

1. There is no single "Volvo model" for the design of assembly operations. Developments should be tailored to the "readiness" and conditions at each Volvo plant, with due consideration for product types and volumes, plant size, available workforce, social environment, cultural traditions, and management style.

2. While small group task teams have often proved to be a suitable way of organizing work, and while experiences with such teams have been good, each individual situation needs to be analyzed in terms of its own specific requirements. Successful solutions in one situation cannot just be transferred uncritically to another situation. Thus, the adoption of group production methods, while utilized, is not a well-defined technique at Volvo and is not regarded as an objective in itself.

3. Change requires freedom of action and time. When change is seen as a searching and learning process extended over time, the chances for lasting effects are increased. When we tend to formalize and routinize change—creating projects and requesting targets and quantifiable results too early—the chances for desirable, lasting effects are decreased.

4. Volvo sees the initiative for change as a line responsibility, with specialists as speaking partners and supporters. Volvo management regards this concept as a major reason for the company's achievements so far in the redesign of work. Top management feels that changes introduced and run by specialists in staff positions—whether they be technical people, personnel people, or behavioral scientists—may have immediate effects but not lasting ones.

5. Isolated, "nonsystemic" trials that introduce simple, specific changes—such as job rotation—are not likely to yield much of

lasting value. It is when an organization accepts that changes require a total approach, a "systems package" of activities introduced over time, that it increases its chances of success. The package might include: delegation of responsibilities; co-influence on the job situation, such as participation in decision making related to the design, structure, and organization of the work; job enlargement; job rotation; and changes in physical environment. An integrated sociotechnical-administrative approach, as Volvo terms it, increases the chances of success.

6. Changes that evolve "naturally" in the normal course of constantly seeking better ways of operating—without special projects, without scientific sophistication, and without necessarily reporting them to anybody—should be encouraged.

Clearly, Volvo has given a good deal of thought to the *change process,* and its concepts are in accord with findings from a distillation of the literature on the subject.

Comment

An evaluation of all this activity is still in progress. However, in groups where a certain degree of self-regulation has been achieved and where as much consideration as possible has been paid to the degree of competence possessed by the individual members of the group, there has been a clear decrease in absenteeism and personnel turnover, and increased interest in the job.

At the time project work started for another new factory at Kalmar early in 1972, Pehr G. Gyllenhammar, managing director of Volvo, said, "When a product is made by people who find meaning in their work, it must surely be a product of high quality." He also set up the following targets for the project work: "We must create a factory which, without sacrificing efficiency and economic results, provides the possibility for the employees to work in groups, to communicate freely, to carry out job rotation, to vary their rate of work, to feel identification with the products, to be aware of quality responsibility and also be in a position to influence their working environment."

The special interest in and dramatic commitment by the managing director of Volvo to the concept and practice of work restructuring are major reasons for its diffusion and variability within that organization. The fact that the early experiments at Volvo were initiated with labor union support, and involved technologies typical of the larger system of which they were a part, further helped diffusion to the other parts of Volvo.

It should be kept in mind that some of the tasks involved in automobile manufacturing *are* rather monotonous. The Volvo arrangement tends to reduce that monotony, and certainly the superior working conditions contribute to improved quality of worklife. The creation of production "buffers" between the various segments of operations allows work teams to vary their pace during the day. Rest and recreational facilities, such as saunas and coffee lounges, are provided for employee use, and there are advanced training programs for those wishing to learn other skills. Team members cannot, however, just "up and leave" early because they have completed a quota, and Volvo thus far has no cost-savings-sharing plan.

There are individual differences in the desires of people regarding work arrangements, work speed, task variety, degree of responsibility required, and so on. Perhaps different teams composed of "kindred spirits" with regard to some of these style preferences could provide an interesting way of considering another dimension in the organization of work—namely, deliberate attention to sociometric factors (that is, ascertain who would prefer to work with whom and try to arrange for persons who are particularly attracted to each other to work together).

Saab-Scania

In 1970 Saab-Scania initiated a program to improve the quality of worklife at its new $10 million Saab-99 engine plant in Soedertaelje, near Stockholm. The new assembly operation allowed small teams of three or four workers to produce a complete four-cylinder engine rather than just one segment. Swedish unions, which in the late 1960s had actively begun to press the issue of putting an end to fragmented, repetitive, dull assembly-line jobs, supported the new plan.

Saab had not produced Swedish-built engines since the late 1960s, and it was expected that the new plant would enable them to discontinue the purchase of engines from England.

Certain items, such as motorblocks, crankshafts, connecting rods, and cylinder heads, were obtained from outside foundries, to be machined and completed at Soedertaelje. Items not requiring additional labor were sent directly to assembly. A great deal of preliminary work and some mounting and assembling were handled as before, but final work was accomplished by means of a new plan involving seven teams of three or four workers each. A team member might choose to work individually on an engine assembly, or members might elect to pair up or otherwise organize themselves.

There were difficulties in developing a pay rate on a team basis, as against the usual combination of hourly and piece-work rates. Saab and its unions discussed this problem as well as a premium rate for the maintenance of high-quality production.

The unions regarded the new production theory as an initial step in the proper direction. For some time the consideration of working environment has had a high priority in Sweden with the public as well as with the unions. Although he recognizes the Soedertaelje program as a beneficial one, Arne Gustavsson, chairman of the local trade union, stated:

Now we have to see what we can do in other parts of the plant. There is still much hard physical work to be done, and there will still be a high-tempo work that will have psychological effects. . . . There will be monotonous tasks to be performed, and thus it is necessary that the union take an active role in organizing the work to make sure that monotonous jobs are eliminated as much as possible.

According to a 1973 management report, first-year results of the Saab experiment were mixed. Absenteeism and turnover remained the same as before—and the capital cost was higher. On the plus side: Labor was attracted to the new work arrangement, and the production group system gave the company more labor flexibility.

In a June 1972 speech, UAW vice president Irving Bluestone commented favorably on the Swedish experiments:

Humanizing the job must be related philosophically to democratizing the workplace. Not only must it embrace the normally recognized amenities of life at work, but it must move to a higher plateau and create job satisfaction, a closing of the widening gap between the ever-increasing mechanization of production and the participation by the worker in the decision-making process.

An experiment of enormous potential aimed at this goal of democratization is currently under way in Sweden, where the Swedish labor movement and the Swedish employers' association have joined in a cooperative effort to test ways and means of democratizing life in the workplace. They are jointly financing an organization called Development Council for Collaboration Questions, which acts as a catalytic agent for experimentation in worker participation in decision making. In 1971, this Council issued a paper describing certain areas for exploratory experimentation as follows: "Each of these experiments takes its premises from one of the following areas: job design—the organization of work in production; the supervisory function; the planning, processing, and work-study functions; personnel policy; the firm's long-range planning; the development of representative cooperation; the economic budgeting—accounting function."

It is immediately evident that whatever the results, there is no gimmickry, no manipulation of people and ideas, but rather a recognition of the seriousness of the problem and a comprehensive probing for solutions. It is significant too that the areas of study go far afield, involving not only the job itself, but the management of the total enterprise.

Comment

Detroit auto makers have taken a dim view of the Swedish experiments. They argue that U.S. production rates are too high for group assembly. One American plant can produce 200,000 cars per year—more than are turned out by the entire Swedish auto industry.

The General Motors Truck and Coach Division has experimented with team assembly of motor homes, involving 300 workers at the Pontiac plant and 100 employees at their Gemini operation. Six-member teams were organized to handle body trim and fitting work; three-member teams assembled the chassis.

According to *Business Week*[42] the experiment was not successful, and GM abandoned the team approach and is now concentrating on attempts to reorient supervisors, teaching them to "open the doors and give people an opportunity to improve the quality of what they do." One result to date is that GM has begun to consult more with workers about the structure, layout, and organization of their jobs. The long-term effects remain to be seen.

In a study funded by the Ford Foundation and carried out under the direction of Professor Arthur S. Weinberg (coordinator of Worker Exchange Programs at Cornell University), six American auto-assembly workers—four men and two women—spent four weeks in Sweden. They spent three of these weeks on the shop floor at the Saab-Scania plant in Soedertaelje, learning and applying the worker-participation method to group assembly of engines. According to Weinberg:

Each of the six was involved in a three-day (November 12–14, 1974) orientation program in New York City. This initial program attempted to acquaint the participants with the concepts of job design, job enrichment and enlargement, industrial democracy, and Swedish life and culture, and to prepare them for what they might expect at Saab-Scania. This was followed by a two-day orientation program by Scania in Södertälje. They began work on the 20th of November, 1974, first in engine pre-assembly and then followed by assembly of the Model 99 engine.[43]

The criteria for selection of these particular six workers were diversity of age, sex, and race, and the presumed "ability to articulate their work experiences and how the work related to their

[42] May 12, 1973, 144.

[43] A. S. Weinberg. *A Worker Exchange Program at Saab-Scania.* Report for Cornell University School of Industrial and Labor Relations, Metropolitan District, New York, New York, 1975. Used with permission.

lives." The information available about these six persons is noted in Table 4.

TABLE 4

Information About Auto-Assembly Workers in Ford Foundation

NAME	AGE	RACE	RECENT EXPERIENCE IN MOTOR ASSEMBLY	EDUCATIONAL LEVEL	ACTIVE TRADE UNIONIST
William Cox	33	Caucasian	Utility man on motor assembly (Chrysler)	High school graduate	×
William Gardner	42	Black	Assembly lines (Pontiac)	Attending university at night, third-year status, working toward business administration degree	×
Herman Lommerse	53	Caucasian	Utility man on motor assembly (Cadillac)	Completed 10th grade	
Joseph Rodriguez	35	Mexican-American	Utility man on motor assembly (Ford)	High school equivalent (G.E.D.)	
Ruth Russell	31	Caucasian	Assembly line (Cadillac)	High school graduate	

TABLE 4 (*continued*)

NAME	AGE	RACE	RECENT EXPERIENCE IN MOTOR ASSEMBLY	EDUCATIONAL LEVEL	ACTIVE TRADE UNIONIST
Lynette Stewart	20	Black	Assembly line (Cadillac)	Attending junior college part-time, first-year status, working toward nursing degree	

Based on R. B. Goldmann, *Work Values: Six Americans in a Swedish Plant.* Ford Foundation, March 1975. Supplemental information supplied by Professor Weinberg.

The job called for working both day shifts (5:00 A.M. to 2:00 P.M.) and night shifts (2:00 to 11:00 P.M.), alternating on a weekly basis. The Americans noted that only a small part of the plant (about 50 out of 300 workers) was engaged in group assembly of engines. The others were engaged in processes that seemed to operate along traditional assembly-line principles.

At the end of the visit, five of the six expressed a preference for the conventional American production line. It had been expected by Weinberg, and perhaps by others, that the workers would find group assembly of engines under the Saab-Scania arrangement more challenging and gratifying than the monotonous work routines prevailing in the U.S. auto industry; however, only one person (Ruth Russell) had an unqualified positive reaction to the question (asked on December 7, 1974), "If you had to make a choice now, from the point of view of group assembly only, between Detroit and Soedertaelje, which would it be?" Ruth Russell reported a greater sense of accomplishment, no boredom, and some relief from feeling pushed. Bill Cox said he would choose

Soedertaelje if he could work at a normal pace. Herman Lommerse and Bill Gardner said they would choose Detroit. Lynette Stewart said that she would choose Detroit, but stated that given time to get accustomed to the pace, group assembly might be more attractive. Joseph Rodriguez had trouble with the question.

Several of these workers reportedly were willing to accept boredom as a trade-off price for the freedom to lose themselves in their own thoughts while working rather than confront a work situation that demanded greater concentration and a faster pace. One worker felt that despite the greater job satisfaction, boredom could still be a factor in the long run. The American workers also felt there was more paternalism at Saab-Scania, compared with greater freedom "to be one's own person" in Detroit. With regard to external conditions, all six said they were impressed by the cleanliness, lighting, safety precautions, lower level of noise and air pollution, and general attractiveness of the Scania plant compared with U.S. auto plants.

All participants emphasized that their impressions had resulted from a brief stay and might have been modified after a more extensive experience with the Swedish work system.

The press conference called by Saab-Scania was held at 9:00 A.M. on December 11, 1974. It was attended by Messrs. Cox, Gardner, and Rodriguez and by Professor Weinberg. The other three workers were interviewed on the job. The three press conference participants may have felt some annoyance, since they had just come off a night shift, which they detested, and had had about three hours sleep in the past 24 hours. Following that conference and the subsequent write-up in *The New York Times,* the three worker-participants expressed irritation that only their negative comments had been reported.

Part of Weinberg's general overview statement was as follows:

Most workers, whether native or Finnish, felt no identification with the Production and Development groups, and none expressed any feeling of participation in union activities or in the Works Councils. American workers were quick to cite what they perceived as a rather formal relationship between foreman and worker. At the time, the visiting workers were bothered by the fact that they had to call foremen by their full surname. Their observation was that the Swedish foreman had disciplinary authority which exceeded similar powers granted to a Detroit counterpart.

Among the observations by the American visitors was the ethnic togetherness of each of the major groups of workers in the plant, i.e., Swedish and Finnish workers. Even though Scania management had developed extensive housing facilities, language training, and educational programs to promote integration, social contacts are largely ethnically determined.

. . . There was a negative reaction by the visiting Americans to mandatory shift changing. Scania workers and the Americans worked both day and night shifts, alternating on a weekly basis. Management explained this procedure as a tradition in Swedish industry. It became obvious over time that the work-shift procedure had never been expressly accepted by Scania workers. They frequently expressed dissatisfaction over this issue.

The mandatory shift change each week does in fact constitute an unpleasant condition, especially if it is not a tradition to which one has become accustomed.

A highly interesting comment in Weinberg's report should be noted: "From an American trade unionist's viewpoint, the mutually respectful relationship between management and labor at the Works Council rather than an adversary relationship was disturbing." This seems to imply that an adversary relationship between management and labor is more desirable than a mutually respectful relationship. Is that necessarily so? Perhaps that depends on one's value system and what sort of management-labor relationship is likely to be beneficial to all concerned over the long run.[44]

Conclusion

Little or nothing can be generalized from this particular sample of six American auto workers spending three weeks in a Swedish auto factory, because of the various atypical circumstances and

[44] Weinberg explains that from an American trade unionist's viewpoint, the union leaders at Saab seemed too ready and willing to go along with management on issues or questions of working conditions that the American United Auto Workers would press hard to resolve in their favor.

conditions. The project was designed mainly to raise questions on certain issues. With regard to that objective, it appears to have been successful.

Robert Goldmann, in his report, summarizes some discussions he had with the six Americans and with a Swedish worker and a Finnish worker (both female) at the Scania plant:

> What emerged from all this was that the group assembly at Saab-Scania seems to have limited appeal; that it does not appear to meet the needs of young people or of men of any age; and that it attracts the most work-oriented, responsible and highly motivated individuals. In short, it is a work design that demands a high measure of commitment and expenditure of effort. And while these observations are limited to one plant, they may have something to say to production engineers and managers who have become so wrapped up in their commitment to and rhetoric about work reform that they have lost sight of some fundamental worker needs and perceptions. They may need to review their programs and revisit with the workers.[45]

A member of the Swedish Employers' Confederation made the following comments about the perceptions of the "Detroit Six":

> Hundreds of workers have all the time lived and worked within the change process and perceived changes. They have expressed their thoughts in the local discussions from day to day, and they have continuously affected the project's development. Six American workers arrived at Sodertalje and three weeks later they are telling the world that the assembly lines in Detroit are much more human than the famous group work in Sweden. They have also found that Finns and Swedes hate each other, that Swedish trade unions are weak, silent and incapable, and that Swedish companies have a bad management. From this time every report from Saab-Scania becomes dominated by the report from the tour of these American workers. You may understand that there are mixed feelings about this and that we sometimes think that this report has gotten more attention than it deserves.[46]

Weinberg reports that so far as he could learn, no systematic, anonymous survey of all employees' perceptions and opinions

---

[45] R. B. Goldmann, *Work Values: Six Americans in a Swedish Plant* (New York: Ford Foundation, March 1975), 45.

[46] Personal communication to the author.

of the Saab work setup, or of job satisfaction at Saab—including aspects liked, aspects disliked, recommendations for improvements, and so on—has ever been undertaken. It might be interesting if this were done. Evidence from other companies and other studies generally supports the finding that not all workers like an enriched job that calls for greater concentration and responsibility. But most do, in situations where they feel they can influence decisions about the design, structure, and organization of the work rather than having those decisions made for them—even if benevolently. And acceptance appears greater if there is a financial incentive or reward system encompassing cost-savings sharing as well (as in the Donnelly Mirrors case). Undeniably, there are real difficulties in designing work in ways that are responsive to varying individual needs and values. And as Robert Goldmann notes in his report, "The roots of alienation are not clearly defined, and . . . the workplace accounts for only a share of what's good and bad in life."[47]

Sweden's Development Council[48]

The importance of involving unions and union officials in changes in work organizations has already been mentioned in connection with the American labor movement. This is especially the case in Sweden, because of the high rate of unionization. As David Jenkins explains:

Though there are no closed shops, the rate of unionization in the manufacturing industry is about 95%, and it is about 70% in the white-collar area. Industrial unions are affiliated to the Swedish Confederation of Trade Unions (LO). Its counterpart on the white-collar side is the Swedish Central Organization of Salaried Employees (TCO). There are also smaller unions for persons with advanced educations, for supervisors, for government employees, and other groups. Though there is some overlapping, as a rule all union members in a particular industry

[47] Goldmann, op cit., 59.
[48] This section draws on material supplied by the Development Council for Collaboration Questions, Stockholm, Sweden.

belong to the same union, and there are therefore few jurisdictional disputes.

All these factors are of relevance. Because of the unions' strength, they can watch to see that new management or production methods are not used against the best interests of employees. The absence of jurisdictional disputes, of course, is of considerable value in organizing group working methods, where workers learn several jobs. The unions have been generally positive to the introduction of new working methods, and union officials have even occasionally criticized companies for not moving more aggressively in this area. There is a long tradition of labor-management harmony and understanding in Sweden, and this is true in the field of work reform as in other areas.[49]

In 1966, LO, TCO, and SAF (Swedish Employers' Confederation) established a new joint body: the Development Council for Collaboration Questions. A major aim of the collaboration program is to improve productivity as well as job satisfaction, reflecting Sweden's growing interest in corporate democracy. A number of experimental projects directed toward this aim are now going forward under a special unit of the Council devoted to research. This research arm keeps track of experimental projects but does not actively intervene. Once an experiment starts, any decision to change it must be made jointly by the management and employees of each company, in consultation with the researchers.

As of 1972, experiments were being followed by 30 researchers and consultants. They included:

1. *Work organization and job design.* A number of workers employed in the assembly department of an engineering company have formed a team, which is divided into small groups. The employees circulate between different tasks within and between the groups. A similar experiment is in progress at a chemical products company. In both these cases, principal interest focuses on: giving the individual more influence over his own job; vesting the individual with more responsibility; including in

[49] Editor's note in R. Lindholm, *Job Reform in Sweden: Conclusions from 500 Shop Floor Projects,* D. Jenkins (Ed. and Trans.) (Stockholm: Swedish Employers' Confederation, 1975). Reprinted by permission.

tasks a higher degree of problem-solving and self-enriching elements; and improving the meaningfulness and esteem of the job.

2. *The supervisory function.* The focal problem at a steel mill and an engineering plant is how to develop the supervisory function by means of systematic collaboration between the "parties at interest" in this function. The parties are chiefly concerned with design and specification of the supervisory role, recruitment and selection of people for the supervisory function, and training and development of supervisors.

3. *Production planning.* At a mining and manufacturing company, production engineers and operating personnel are engaged in further developing the collaboration forms for purposes of planning and production. Among other things, new measurement and control methods, organizational patterns, and wage-payment plans are being tried out. This project is meant to obtain knowledge about the design of production planning, the causes of organizational changes, and opportunities for the individual to influence his own work and the work of those around him.

4. *Organizational development—white-collar firms.* An experiment at an insurance company is seeking to achieve organizational forms for office work that will facilitate co-determination —that is, permit employees to participate with management in the determination of business policy. Toward this end, the employees and the management staff have jointly appointed a project group to propose a new organization for one division of the company. One of the questions posed in the project is: What factors of corporate structure, administration, and long-term planning would help change the organization in the direction of greater co-determination?

5. *Personnel policy.* Experiments in this domain are under way at an engineering plant and a rubber products factory. Principal interest focuses on the individual's influence over determination of personnel policy. Also of interest is his influence over the application of this policy (i.e., personnel administration). The

project is based on the assumption that it will be feasible for employees to take a generally active part in and exercise influence over these areas.

6. *The representative system.* Three in-house systems are being studied at an engineering company: the administrative, the representative, and the sociotechnical. Emphasis is put on the representative system, which refers to works councils, subcommittees, and the like. The project keeps track of the channels chosen by the parties at interest in the company to develop the representative system toward greater co-determination.

In addition to providing coordination through its research unit, the Development Council provides a range of supportive services, such as training, exchange of information, and counseling.

Excerpts from the September–October 1974 Forum on Humanizing Work: Swedish-American Experiences[50]

The selected quotations below are taken from papers presented at the forum by Erik Karlsson, information secretary, Swedish Confederation of Trade Unions (LO), and Fingal Ström, Ministry of Finance.

Before citing from these papers, it should be noted that in 1973–1974 the Swedish parliament passed "An Act Relating to Allocation to Work Environment Fund." The act requires "limited companies, incorporated associations, and savings banks, which are in principle engaged in carrying on business, agriculture, or forestry," to make allocation to the work environment from annual profits in amounts corresponding to 20 percent. Most of the provisions of the act concern legal and technical details of its financial administration, but the following paragraph makes clear the act's basic purpose:

His Majesty's Government, or the Swedish Labour Market Board acting in accordance with an ordinance of His Majesty's Government,

---

[50] Used with permission of the authors.

may on application from the company permit that moneys, which have been paid into the work environment account during the time and under such conditions in other respects as are determined thereby, may be used for expenditure on investments for work environment or . . . to improve the conditions of employees in the company in other respects. If permission is to be granted, the application must have the approval of a majority of employee representatives on the safety committee or the works council of the applicant company. In the event that there exists neither a safety committee nor a works council, the application shall be approved by the safety representative of the company in question or, where there are several such representatives, by the chief safety representative.

Democratization and Reorganization—E. Karlsson

The debate on conditions in the job world and on the situation of employees in the workplace is being waged in ever-widening circles and with mounting intensity. In this debate the main focus is on work structuring and job design. Several investigations have clearly shown that the present state of production technology, with its tightly controlled, machine-paced processes, highly fragmented tasks and virtually no opportunities for the employees to take their own initiatives, generates big problems for the people concerned and thus for the employing enterprises as well.

As a matter of course, the trade union movement in Sweden also thinks a better work structure is needed. We therefore welcome the intensified debate, and as regards the experiments that are being made in Sweden and in other countries, we are both direct participants and interested observers. But we also feel that an altered work structure is not enough. The change must not be limited to creating another design of the work process and then trying to prevail on the employees to accept it. As we see it, the most important thing is for the employees themselves or their elected representatives to be brought in as equals towards shaping the means of production. The prevailing structure of power must be changed.

. . . The findings of investigations to date show that today's dominant production technology is shot through with major flaws . . . and that the flaws are caused by letting the technical function of work run the show, while the social function of work has received far too little attention.

It is quite clear that these two functions of work have long been out of kilter. But the solution cannot lie in now creating a similar imbalance, though with the pivotal weight shifted in the opposite direction. It is scarcely realistic to imagine abandoning modern technology to return to old-fashioned production methods. What we must find is an approach that will let us keep the benefits of production technology intact while attenuating its drawbacks.

What do we want to change?

Many factors can be shown to have negative consequences, some more and others less. One and the same factor may also be negative in varying degree, depending on the form of business organization. It is scarcely feasible or necessary to count up all the factors, but let us have a go with an enumeration that looks like this:

- The corporate hierarchy.
- Highly fragmented, individually bound work tasks.
- Tightly controlled production flow.

The experiments so far completed have found that certain conditions must be met in order to achieve job satisfaction. These conditions are:

- The job shall be full of variety.
- The job should contain elements which enable the worker to learn more. That is to say, he should be made more knowledgeable about materials, products and technical equipment that are in his direct charge. He should also be enabled to know more about tasks performed at adjoining work stations.
- The job shall afford the worker room to take initiatives on his own. It shall enable him to participate in planning, problem solving, decision making and assumption of responsibility.
- The worker should be enabled to understand how his job and the adjacent jobs fit into the big picture.
- The worker shall be able to see a future in what he does.
- The worker shall be enabled to influence those changes which his job is constantly undergoing.

In discussing how to go about restructuring work, Karlsson states that one should begin with a group that has several work tasks or operations. With such a group as "partly self-governing," the tasks assigned should provide scope for planning and initiative. The important thing is for the group to busy itself with a number of tasks which will still form an aggregate work effort even though they vary in character.

Karlsson states that the remuneration system, which needs to be modified from the prevailing piece rate (in Sweden), should be designed in mutual understanding with the union. He summarizes the matter in the following words:

We know that a great deal has gone wrong in the job world. Technology has given us a material standard of living that lies on a high level. But in too many cases the price paid for that "blessing" has been much too high. Work is supposed to be a vital ingredient of the human condition, but it has been transformed into a mere instrumentality, the pay envelope that provides the necessary income. Soulless, monotonous jobs in a destructive environment degrade the human being.

The hierarchy

Most types of private enterprise are structured with a hierarchic pyramid divided into command levels. Communications between the levels are limited, especially in the upward direction but also, though to a lesser degree, in the downward direction. Those who occupy the higher rungs of the ladder are perceived by their subordinates to be players in the power game rather than fellow workers in the enterprise, which is what things ought to be like.

To be able to tap the experiences of all employees and get them to feel like participants in all the affairs of the enterprise, it is necessary to disintegrate the hierarchy to some extent.

Although abolishing the hierarchy altogether is surely impracticable, it should be feasible to reduce the number of levels and improve relations between the levels in both directions.

The work tasks

The most conspicuous elements of modern production technology is the breaking down of processes into small, compartmentalized work tasks. When the technology was first applied, it was seen to offer prospects for speeding up the individual work pace by making tasks simple and highly repetitive. We see the result today: monotony, cramped working postures, physical and mental strain. Another result has been to isolate the individual. On top of that, the potentials inherent in human capital have been turned to very poor account, which makes for widespread job dissatisfaction.

The production flow

Hear the phrase "controlled production flow," and the first image that springs to mind is the assembly line. This technique seeks to standardize the work pace and wherever possible to prevent variations from one person to another. The assembly line, in combination with short work , passes, has routinized the job even more.

How do we want it?

It is not very hard to point out these and even more shortcomings. The really hard part will come when one is called upon to present other solutions. In saying these words, I don't want it to be inferred that any solution sought is supposed to make a universal fit for all time to come. Far from it: the idea is to enlist co-determination from all groups of employees to promote a development that aims at adapting work to Man. We know pretty much about the causes of this development. We are beginning to learn what is needed to turn it right again. The changes are impacting on more and more enterprises. But one thing is extremely important in this development.

We must not repeat the mistake of fashioning a production method which is then merely applied to members of the human race. Instead, we must let everybody working for the enterprises get in on the act, towards making each and every one a co-worker in the true sense of the word. Without that kind of worker participation the job will remain alien to everyone who is called upon to perform it.

The democracy that all of us otherwise consider indispensable cannot be ordered to halt outside the plan or office. Open the doors and let it come in.

Co-determination for Government Employees in Sweden—F. Ström

Representing a government committee, Ström takes up the same theme of shared responsibility in decision making on the part of workers and management:

The new fundamental philosophy (developed by a government committee) vests the employee with a *right* to take personal part in determining personnel policy as a whole, not only rates of pay, vacations, hours of work and the like. Even if the sphere of collective bargaining is broadened, there must be guarantees to ensure the enforcement of contracts under employee influence. Experiments have therefore been mounted whereby special units have been set up inside the government agencies for taking decisions of this kind. The employees are members of these units. No personnel problems can be settled by the employer alone, as in the present system. In other words, the employees are entitled to participate directly in the decision-making process on virtually all personnel matters where the employer used to have the total responsibility. Co-determination is meant to guarantee the employees the same influence as the employer over personnel policy. The right of co-determination is exercised by special decision-making units in which the employees get to appoint half the number of members, while the employer appoints the rest. The trade unions appoint those who represent the employees; the employer appoints his representatives.

It follows that the new decision-making units replace the top man or boss who used to take these decisions all by himself. In the new system that is being tried out, this boss will become *one member* of a collective that is going to take those decisions he used to take alone. The once unrestricted decision-making power of the employer, and of the boss to whom that power was delegated, is abolished in the experiments and is democratically shared out to a group in which the employee representatives wield the same power as the executive staff of the government agency. . . .

With the aid of experts—sociologists and administrators—one general model has been developed. (As regards the *industrial* program, efforts to put the model into practice have bumped up against certain obstacles. Corporate managements have sometimes reacted negatively to overly far-reaching changes which might impair competitiveness and efficiency. Lively debates have been waged on these matters.) The experiments in the government sector have now reached the point where certain lessons can be drawn, but these must be regarded as highly tentative. Yet this much is clear: the results are positive.

In conclusion, Ström asserts:

Every employee must become a co-worker, and this not only in a psychological sense but also in a real one. He must be assured of the power to control his personal situation. The only means towards that end is co-determination: this is my conclusion based on the experiments we are now making in Sweden's civil service. Not until every employee—whether directly or indirectly—shares in the actual exercise of power over every aspect of industrial relations can he be called a co-worker in the true sense of this word. And when that happens, industrial democracy will become a reality. My belief is that this will also become a guiding model for the coming century.

Quality Control Circles in Japan[51]

One movement that has contributed to an impressive increase in productivity in Japanese industry is the phenomenon known as QC (quality control) circles.

These groups of workers, initially concerned solely with quality control, now have expanded their activities. The QC movement started in 1962. Within five years 10,000 circles were reported in operation and, among the companies where the circles operated, $30 million worth of improvements had been achieved.

The significant characteristics of a QC circle are:

1. It is made up entirely of nonmanagement people. No one above the rank of foreman is included, and most of the people are workers at the operator level.

2. Membership is voluntary.

3. The activities of the circle are carried on outside of regular working hours.

4. Compensation for the time spent on QC activities ranges from full time to no compensation at all.

Management devotes considerable effort to training workers for their added responsibilities: books, audiovisual devices, discussions of cases worked out in other companies, and discussions of internal

[51] Based on J. M. Juran, "The QC Circle Phenomenon." In *Quality Progress,* January 1967, 329–336. Reprinted by permission of the American Society for Quality Control, Inc.

quality control problems, both those that have been solved and those that are yet unsolved. Since 1962 there has been a Foremen's Quality Control Conference held annually in Japan; one of the rewards of companies achieving success through their QC circles is the privilege of presenting their case material at these conferences. J. M. Juran notes:

Beyond improvement or control, a gratifying proportion of the projects are of a breakthrough nature—by systematic study they take the department to better levels of performance, levels not previously attained.

The intangible by-products of the foregoing results are evident but not measurable:

- The foreman's ability to control and lead his department is increased. . . .
- The operators have greater interest in their jobs and a higher morale. . . .
- The relationship between the staff people and the line workers has improved noticeably. . . .
- There is being developed on the factory floor a generation of workers with successful experience in the use of what have today been regarded as management tools. . . .

In projecting the broadening of the QC circles, Juran, in the 1967 article summarized here, predicted that this movement would extend into improvements in cost, safety, and productivity as well as quality, and would strengthen relationships between the company and the employees. At the same time he was skeptical that this kind of participation could work in Western industry. Juran cited the difference between Japanese orientation to work and what he considered the prevalent attitudes in the United States and in other industrial countries of the Western world. The priorities of the Japanese worker were, in his judgment:

1. Improving the company's performance
2. Self-improvement
3. Recognition

4. Creativity amid boredom

5. Money incentives

These priorities, as we have seen,[52] are not so markedly different from those of American workers as might have seemed in 1967.

Table 5 gives Juran's summary of the differences between QC circles and more conventional motivational plans.

[52] See Table 1, pp. 15–17.

TABLE 5

QC Circles versus Conventional Plans

	AS PRACTICED IN . . .	
	CONVENTIONAL MOTIVATIONAL	
ELEMENTS OF PLAN	PLANS	QC CIRCLES
Choice of projects	Left up to employee to identify his own project	Some projects identified by management; others identified by the QC circle
Training in how to analyze a project	None provided	Formal training program provided—out-of-hours; voluntary
Analysis of the project	By employee himself or with such aid as he can muster; otherwise by formal suggestion which is analyzed by someone else	By the QC circle, out-of-hours, using training tools previously provided
Payment for time spent	None	Varies from no pay to full pay for hours spent

TABLE 5 (continued)

	AS PRACTICED IN . . .	
	CONVENTIONAL	
	MOTIVATIONAL	
ELEMENTS OF PLAN	PLANS	QC CIRCLES
Payment for successful idea	Definite payment, varying with value of idea	No payment; indirect effect on company profit and resulting bonus which uses one formula for all employees
Nonfinancial incentives	Opportunity for creativity and recognition; pride of workmanship	Opportunity for training; opportunity for creativity and recognition; membership in a group; response to company leadership

The QC movement is still functioning effectively in Japanese industry. *Business Week*'s special productivity issue[53] reported that Nissan Motor Company workers are organized in such teams. During the past five years, according to that account, the company has cut its unit manpower requirements in half, and, in one plant alone, cost savings as a result of these worker circles were estimated at $350,000 annually.

Toward the end of 1973, six people from Lockheed Aircraft Corporation visited Japan as a team to study and get firsthand information about the operation and efficacy of QC circles, and consulted with Juran in the United States before their departure. Following are some highlights from their report in January 1974 to Lockheed management:

[53] September 9, 1972.

- Over and over we heard that the QC Circle must be used to develop workers. "If a people-building philosophy exists the program will succeed. If a people-using philosophy prevails the program will fail."

- The Japanese manager said . . . that while many production jobs are repetitive, routine, and devoid of motivational content, the worker finds job satisfaction and an outlet for his creative and innovative drives through participation in his QC Circle. . . . We saw production employees working at an enviable pace . . . and doing so with an unmistakable feeling of enthusiasm and mental engrossment in their work.

- In trying to implement a QC Circle program, two key pieces of advice were "Go slowly; start with one Circle," and "The real purpose must be to develop the worker. It must be aimed at his betterment in order for him to be motivated from within."

- At Toyota . . . over 90% of customer complaints were assigned to QC Circles. The remaining 10% were retained for resolution by the professional staff. The results were gratifying.

- A QC Circle usually selects its own project. A common technique to do this is brainstorming. Occasionally management suggests a project to the Circle.

- An important factor in the success of the quality assurance effort is the *extensive training of production personnel* in elementary statistics, quality, and problem-solving techniques.

- Training should be directed toward the foreman, who ideally should be the first Circle leader. The *foreman then assumes the role as instructor for members of his QC Circle.*

- Toyota estimated that their Circles have saved almost $3 million each year.

- Four pitfalls can spell the death-knell of a Circle. They are: (1) Lack of understanding and support from top management. (2) Lack of training in QC Circle techniques. (3) Lack of leadership and competence on the part of a QC Circle leader. (4) Lack of vitality: Circles have their highs and lows; during a low period management should innocuously intervene to revitalize the Circle with a request for aid on problems.

- QC Circles are likely to be more effective in companies with "Theory Y" (participative or consultative) management than in companies with "Theory X" (authoritarian or "just do as the boss directs") management. The higher levels in the organization need to be favorably disposed toward participative management and job enrichment.

Worker Management in Yugoslavia[54]

The Yugoslavian experience is not a case history per se. It is presented here because of its relevance to the issue of productivity, and because it is viewed by many as a trend-setting development in participative management.

It should be kept in mind that one should not draw facile parallels between the experience in Yugoslavia and potential applications elsewhere. For one thing, the ideological climate in Yugoslavia is markedly different from that of the United States and most countries in Western Europe. The industrial scene there is characterized by a weak union structure and by a pervasive role assumed by the Communist Party. Furthermore, the dramatic improvements in productivity have to be assessed in terms of the ravaged condition from which Yugoslavia started after World War II.

The self-management system has been evolving since 1945, when the Federal People's Republic of Yugoslavia was established. At that time, most of the country's industrial plants were destroyed and many of its managerial and professional people had been killed in the war. In the process of industrial evolution since, there has been a constant diminishing of state intervention in the work structure. The present system of self-management dates from 1956 and undergoes constant revision to keep pace with political and economic realities.

The Yugoslavian system combines two classic approaches to

[54] W. Glueck and D. Kavran, "Worker Management in Yugoslavia," *Business Horizons,* February 1972, 31–39; W. Glueck and D. Kavran, "The Yugoslav Management System," *Management International Review, 1971–72,* '3–17; C. Cvlic, "Yugoslavia," *The Economist,* August 21, 1971, v-xlii; B. Horvat, "Yugoslav Economic Policy in the Post-War Period. Problems, Ideals, Institutional Development," *American Economic Review,* 1969, 71–169.

increasing productivity: economic incentives and participation in decision making.

Ownership of most business enterprise in Yugoslavia is vested in society. The workers are considered trustees for the people. All those working in an enterprise belong to a collective that elects workers' councils (with membership limited to two-year terms) through which self-management is administered. The council in turn elects a board of management (also limited to a two-year term) and appoints a manager who faces reelection every four years. The council makes long-term policy decisions, the board makes short-term decisions, and day-to-day decisions are delegated to the manager.

Although there is some variation between individual plants, and some gap between theory and practice, the system on the whole assigns comprehensive control to the workers through their councils. This includes decision making on production, prices, distribution of income, and personnel policies.

There seems to be little doubt that the system has yielded impressive gains in productivity. Between 1956 and 1963, economic growth in Yugoslavia was 14 percent each year. Since 1963, growth has been between 12 and 16 percent annually—a more rapid rate of increase than in any country except Japan. This has been accomplished in a country in which, before World War II, 85 percent of the workers were in agriculture. The standard of living reportedly has improved with the quality of products.

Some observers have warned that self-management should not be viewed as an eternal panacea, and that even now the trend in Yugoslavia may be ebbing. As the industrial pattern becomes more complex and the nation grows more concerned with international competition, the center of power is shifting from the workers to a new bureaucracy of managers and technicians.

Other problems are also cited: Many workers are losing their enthusiasm for endless discussion, even though it gives them control over their working life; internal disputes develop over whether excess revenue should be allocated to capital investment or bonuses, with workers often voting for bonuses to the long-term detriment of the company; the system is not subject to audits or other types of financial surveillance; bribery and corruption have surfaced; interference by government bureaucracy is still present.

Evidence that self-management is not the ultimate, across-the-board solution is found in the fact that the government has decided that this approach does not work in the service industry, and is turning this industry over to the private sector. In spite of the problems now surfacing, however, self-management in Yugoslavian business enterprises still presents a persuasive model.

Europe Likes Flexi-Time Work

In September 1972, at the conference in Paris of the Organization for Economic Cooperation and Development (OECD), about 150 labor market experts from 22 countries gathered to hear about various experimental programs for varying the traditional eight-hour day and five-day week without loss of productivity. In Europe, the most prevalent variation is flexi-time, which allows workers a few hours' latitude in starting and stopping work each day without reducing the actual total amount of working time. Currently, 30 percent of Switzerland's industrial labor force and 5 percent of Germany's total workforce operate on flexi-time systems, and extensive experimentation with the system is under way in Holland, Scandinavia, France, and Japan. So far, according to the OECD reports, the novelty offered by flexi-time has paid off in tight labor markets where employers are under pressure to create pleasant working conditions for their employees or want to lure employees away from other companies. The employees like their new freedom, and the employers like the increased productivity that has resulted from it. U.S. delegates Janice Hedges and Jack Meyer, both Labor Department officials, were sufficiently impressed to urge U.S. companies, which have been experimenting mostly with compressing the 40-hour week into a few days, to give flexi-time a try.

Switzerland has been a leader in implementing the new concept. In the summer of 1972, Omega Watch extended its pilot program to cover 90 percent of its 2,500-man workforce. Workers must be on the job during two set time blocks in the morning and afternoon, each of a few hours' duration, but the remaining work hours can be put in at any time the plant is in operation. The assembly-line co-ordination problem was solved by building up a "buffer stock" at each point along the line. Although Omega officials report that production dropped slightly, improvement in quality has been so substantial as to produce a net gain. Another Swiss company, Sulzer Freres, Switzerland's largest producer of machines and pumps, has also expanded its pilot program to include more than 8,000 employees, or 90 percent of its payroll. Sulzer's toughest problem —how to apply a flexi-time schedule to the foundry where teams of men were required to operate large furnaces—was solved by the creation of "floating" teams. Each team member agrees on the next day's starting time before quitting each day.

Other European countries are experimenting with flexi-time as well. In France, L'Oréal, the major cosmetics manufacturer, is gradually introducing flexi-time to its 9,000-member workforce. According to President François Dalle, "This flexibility does away with the anxiety that, for example, a mother would suffer if her child were suddenly taken ill in the morning when it was time for her to go to work." In Germany, major employers such as Lufthansa, Siemens, Messerschmitt-Bolkow, and Volkswagen have implemented flexi-time variations for large numbers of their personnel, and a pilot program of the Ministry of Transportation and Communications now in progress may be extended to all government employees in the future.

The U.S. delegates were impressed by the pilot studies of flexi-time scheduling, which differed from the experiments prevalent in major U.S. firms. The latter have focused mainly on compressing the workweek. The U.S. delegates noted that several New York banks and insurance companies have created a three-day workweek of 12½ hours per day for their computer data processors. This has been found to reduce errors, which occur most often at the moment of shift changes, but more research must be done, say the delegates—especially on the health factors—before the efficacy of a compressed workweek can be measured. According to their report, two assembly-line operations had already tried it and dropped it.

Members of OECD came out with disapproval for this compressed workweek. Pessimism was expressed regarding the effect the longer workday has on family life, as well as on how workers will spend their spare time; Allan Porter of the Canadian Labor Department envisioned the production of "a race of people that spends seven hours a day, three days a week, watching television." It was also pointed out that the compressed workweek ignores consideration of health and safety standards that the unions fought for in establishing an eight-hour day.

As of 1974, the United States has begun to adopt flexi-time scheduling. An increasing number of companies are trying it, and most reports have been favorable, though it doesn't seem to work for all conditions or all people.

Concluding Comments

Not described in this chapter, because we have to stop at some point, are a number of other organizations that have reportedly undertaken QWL and productivity improvement programs of some kind; for example: Alcan; American Bank Note; American Velvet; Arapahoe Chemical; Bankers Trust; Bank of New York; R. G. Barry Corporation; Black & Decker; Chase Manhattan Bank; Chesapeake & Potomac Telephone; Chrysler Corporation; Cummins Engine; Dana Corporation; Detroit Edison; A. B. Dick; Eaton Corporation; Exxon; Fieldcrest Mills; First National City Bank, New York; General Motors, Detroit plant #23; Georgia-Pacific Corporation; Harman International Industries (formerly the Jervis Corporation); Harwood Manufacturing Company; Hercules, Inc.; Hewlett-Packard; H. P. Hood & Sons; Humble Oil; Inbelco (Belgium); Indiana Bell Telephone; IBM; Internal Revenue Service; International Nickel; Jervis International; Levi Strauss & Company; Lincoln Electric Company; City of Jamestown, New York; Lockheed Missiles & Space Company; Maytag Company; Mead Corporation; Merrill Lynch, Pierce, Fenner & Smith; Monsanto Company, Chemical Textile Division; Nobo Hommelvik; Northern Electric Company; PPG Industries (Lexington, N.C.); J. C. Penney Company; Philips (Netherlands); Pillsbury Mills; Polaroid; Precision Castparts; Prudential; Qantas Airways,

Ltd. (Australia); Ralston-Purina; Reader's Digest; Rockivell, Ltd.; Rushton Mining Company; Saga Administrative Corporation; Sandia Laboratories; Sherwin-Williams; Sonesta (Hotel Corporation of America); Sisak Ironworks (Yugoslavia); Sony; South Central Bell Telephone Company; Southern New England Telephone Company; Standard Oil Company of New Jersey; Syntex Corporation; Sunkist Growers; Tennessee Valley Authority; Tokyo Gas Company; Toyota; Union Carbide; United Airlines; Valley National Bank (Phoenix, Ariz.); Weldon Manufacturing Company; Western Union; Weyerhaeuser; and Xerox.

The case literature reporting the experiences of different types of organizations in quality of worklife programs is bound to increase.[55] The more case literature there is, the more experience can be shared among those who would start new programs or improve those which are well (or not so well) established. Each worklife situation is unique to some degree. When a large number of such situations are studied together, however, certain common features become apparent to a practiced observer. It is these continuities that suggest to behavioral scientists and other interested persons new approaches or new models for program change. Periodic program reporting, therefore, is important to enhance the resources of researchers, practitioners, and administrators concerned with problems of human motivation and organizational development.

Robert Merton has observed:

In the world laboratory of the sociologist, as in the more secluded laboratories of the physicist and chemist, it is the successful experiment which is decisive and not the thousand-and-one failures which preceded it. More is learned from the single success than from the multiple failures. A single success proves it can be done. Thereafter, it is necessary only to learn what made it work.

[55] For further reference, interested readers may refer to the summary of 34 quality of worklife case histories listed in the appendix of U.S. Department of Health, Education, and Welfare, *Work in America* (Cambridge, Mass.: MIT Press, 1972); and to 183 case abstracts listed in a paper by J. C. Taylor, *Experiments in Work System Design*. Tech. Report No. 75–1. Los Angeles, Calif.: UCLA, Institute of Industrial Relations, June 1975.

While agreeing with Merton that success stories provide more impetus for introduction of QWL programs than failures, review of the latter can be helpful for determining what existing conditions and/or introduced innovations are not conducive to successful programs. A discussion of some of the problems confronted is found in the following chapter.

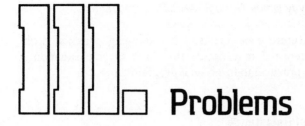

Problems

Although there is heartening evidence that lower production costs and superior products can go hand in hand with efforts to improve the quality of worklife, it should be noted that there are also cases on record in which such attempts have not worked out well. There are cases in which programs that aroused enthusiasm because of early success seemed to "lose impetus" and were not sustained, so that things returned to their former style and state of operation.

It would be an error to think of any specific management style as a panacea for solving either morale or productivity problems in an organization. The reasons for any given instance of poor motivation, alienation, or low productivity need to be studied in depth before a well-founded plan for improvement can be developed. And even when such a plan is developed, it requires sustained commitment and support from a power source to keep it functioning.

This chapter identifies some of the major pitfalls found when quality of work programs have been introduced without adequate regard for resistive forces, so that the same mistakes can be avoided or reduced in future experiments. After studying potential problems, those interested may decide that in a specific situation it would be more practical to forgo such programs.

Organizational Resistance

David Sirota, a professor at the Wharton School of the University of Pennsylvania, and Alan Wolfson, a consultant in the application of behavioral science research, have pointed out[1] that anyone who is planning a quality of work improvement program should be aware in advance of the following management obstacles to such programs:

1. *Educational.* Training in job enrichment is not customarily a part of management's preparation. Managers often lack the necessary skills to plan and carry out job enrichment.

2. *Ideological.* The more conservative members in a company's management tend to think of job enrichment as an additional employee benefit. Accordingly they begrudge it.

3. *Organizational.* Job enrichment programs often challenge vested interests. Functions are taken from one unit of the company and given to another. Further, if a manager does not expect to be in a job for long, he has little interest in installing a job enrichment program which may not pay off until after he has left the organization.

4. *Managerial.* The manager tends to have the classic resistances to change. For example:

   (a) he feels that it is safer to do what he has always done than to change his procedures;

   (b) change may be an admission that he has been wrong in the past;

   (c) change may reveal his inadequacies.

[1] "Job Enrichment: What Are the Obstacles?" *Personnel,* May–June 1972. © 1972 by AMACOM, a division of American Management Associations. Reprinted by permission of the publisher.

5. *Technological and financial.* Technology often imposes very real constraints upon job design. There are times when job enrichment cannot be carried out in any significant sense without investment in new equipment for facilities. Management is usually reluctant to undertake those investments.

6. *The employee.* Although most employees have demonstrated that they are willing and able to handle increased responsibilities, management tends to be doubtful of their potential and motivation.

7. *The enricher.* The job enrichment practitioner is cautioned not to downgrade management's past efforts as he attempts to bring about a change.

8. *Diagnosis.* There is a critical need for competent diagnosis before job enrichment work is undertaken.

9. *"Prove it here."* Management tends to think that its own organization is special and that job enrichment programs which have worked elsewhere cannot possibly be applied there.

10. *"Nothing new here."* Management contends that they have been carrying out a job enrichment program for years. What the job enrichment practitioner offers them represents nothing new.

11. *Time.* Few job enrichment programs are allocated enough time needed for planning, idea development and actual implementation.

The author's own experiences support the Sirota-Wolfson findings—with the addition of two vital points:

1. *Equity of reward opportunities.* When job enrichment is undertaken in only one part of a company, and the workers involved like it a great deal or have a special opportunity to earn more money, other employees often become jealous. Planning, then, should consider ways of expanding the program to the entire workforce if the pilot experiment proves clearly successful.

2. *Feedback, follow-through, and recognition for achievements.* There needs to be a performance feedback system, with positive recognition from management for desirable results achieved and consistent follow-through on all ideas submitted by members of the workforce.

The author also feels that the Sirota-Wolfson paper overemphasizes job enrichment as such. There are other possible job-related change options that are not necessarily job enrichment *per se*. A list of such options, taken from the National Quality of Work Center's QOWP Statement of Intent, is found in Appendix B.

W. E. Reif, D. N. Ferrazzi, and R. J. Evans, Jr., in a recent study, mailed a questionnaire to a random sample of 300 of *Fortune*'s top 1,000 industrial firms. Usable responses were received from 125 companies (42 percent of the sample group). Some of the questions were aimed at finding out what problems, if any, were being encountered by workers in adjusting to enriched jobs. The responses indicated that some employees were having difficulty. Reif, Ferrazzi, and Evans reported:[2]

Their problems include reluctance to accept added authority and responsibility; difficulty in adapting to changes in job content; and difficulty in adjusting to self-supervision and self-control. These and similar responses would tentatively lead to several conclusions:

Companies do not adequately prepare employees psychologically for the greater autonomy, responsibility, and expanded scope of enriched jobs.

Employee training and development is not given sufficient attention during the implementation of job enrichment; thus, workers do not feel they are qualified to meet the performance standards of the enriched jobs.

Organizational support for enriched job holders is not forthcoming. This is characteristic of firms that are only concerned with changing job content and do not give adequate attention to the relationship between the job and the total work environment.

Industry has done such a good job of conditioning men to perform like machines that employees now are having a difficult time performing like whole beings at work.

An analysis of the respondents' remarks suggests that employees of companies with formal programs have less difficulty in adjusting to enriched jobs than their counterparts in firms that are practicing the concept on an informal basis.

[2] "Job Enrichment: Who Uses It and Why," *Business Horizons,* February 1974. Used with permission.

One explanation for this is that firms that have formally committed themselves to enrichment as a philosophy of job design are willing to spend the time and resources necessary to properly analyze the situation prior to introducing enriched jobs and to provide the orientation and training that is crucial to success. In this way many potential problem areas, both of an individual and organizational nature, are anticipated and dealt with before or during implementation.

On the other hand, the same study revealed that "most firms practicing job enrichment, formally or informally, are experiencing benefits both in terms of increased *job performance* and *job satisfaction.*"

David Whitsett notes:[3]

The growing popularity of job enrichment as a problem-solving technique has led some organizations to believe that it can be applied anywhere, anytime. Not so; when the organization is beset by certain severe difficulties—such as widespread dissatisfaction over pay levels—job enrichment naturally has little chance to flower. But more to the point, the procedure can be incorporated only where poorly designed positions exist. The author lists and describes 11 structural clues for spotting opportunities to improve the shape of the job and the productivity and satisfaction of the person filling it.

J. Richard Hackman summarizes his view as follows:[4]

Job enrichment rapidly is becoming one of the most widely used behavioral science strategies for organizational change. And there is scattered but compelling evidence that, under certain conditions, the technique can lead simultaneously to both improved productivity and to an increase in the quality of employee work experiences. Yet observations of ongoing job enrichment projects in a number of organizations suggest that the approach is failing in practice at least as often as it is succeeding—and that its future as a strategy for personal and organizational change may be bleak. This report (a) explores a number of

[3] D. Whitsett, "Where Are Your Unenriched Jobs?" *Harvard Business Review,* January–February 1975, 74–80. Reprinted by permission.

[4] J. R. Hackman, "On the Coming Demise of Job Enrichment." In E. Cass, *Man and Work in Society* (New York: Van Nostrand Reinhold, 1975). Reprinted by permission of the author.

frequently-observed errors in implementing job enrichment that can lead to "failures" of the technique, and (b) identifies a number of ingredients found to be common to most of the "successful" job enrichment projects that were observed.

. . . In this paper, I report some observations and impressions about work redesign as a strategy for individual and organizational change —with particular emphasis on factors which determine whether it will succeed or fail in a given instance. These observations are based on experiences my associates and I have had in fifteen to twenty organizations over the last two years. We have been developing and refining an instrument for the diagnosis of jobs and the evaluation of job redesign projects. . . . In the process, we have visited numerous organizations where job redesign activities were being planned, implemented, or gotten over. We have talked with workers, managers, and internal and outside consultants. In several cases, we have used our instrument to make quantitative evaluations of organizational change projects involving the redesign of work.

Hackman gives what he feels are five compelling reasons for why work redesign should survive, namely:

1. Changing jobs changes the basic relationship between a person and his/her work.

2. Work redesign changes behavior, and does so directly.

3. When behavior is changed through the redesign of work, it tends to stay changed.

4. Work redesign offers—indeed, often forces into one's hands— numerous opportunities for initiating other organizational changes.

5. Work redesign, in the long term, can result in organizations that can rehumanize rather than dehumanize the people who work in them.

Hackman then observes:

As described above, the potential of work redesign as a strategy for change may sound absolutely glowing. It should. The evidence—although it presently is scattered and sadly nonsystematic—is convincing that job redesign really can "work" in the sense of leading to the kinds of positive outcomes suggested above. Yet the emphasis, for now, must carefully be placed on the word "potential"—because that potential infrequently is realized in work redesign projects being undertaken in contemporary organizations. Let me turn now to what I believe are some of the major reasons for this state of affairs.

. . . There is an almost endless list of things that can go wrong when a work redesign project is carried out in an organization. Listed below are seven pitfalls I believe to be especially serious, and which often were encountered by the organizations we observed:

1. Sometimes the work itself does not actually change.

2. Even when jobs are changed, their positive effects sometimes are diminished or even reversed by insufficient attention to the impact of the changes on the surrounding work system.

3. Rarely is a systematic diagnosis of the target jobs undertaken prior to planning and executing the actual changes.

4. Rarely is the work system surrounding the focal job assessed for its "readiness" for change prior to work redesign.

5. Rarely are work redesign projects systematically evaluated.

6. Neither consulting staffs nor line managers nor union officers are obtaining appropriate education in the theory, strategy, and tactics of work redesign.

7. Work redesign projects often are themselves managed in accordance with the dictates of traditional bureaucratic practice.

Hackman concludes with the following list of ingredients that he found common to many of the more *successful* projects.

1. Key individuals responsible for the work redesign project move *toward* the especially difficult problems, and do so early.

2. Management undertakes a theory-based diagnosis of the target job(s) prior to implementation.

3. Management ensures that specific changes are planned explicitly on the basis of the diagnosis, and are done so publicly.

4. The people responsible for the work project prepare contingency plans ahead of time for dealing with the inevitable "spin-off" problems and opportunities that emerge from work redesign activities.

5. Those responsible for the work redesign project are ready and able to evaluate, iterate, and evaluate again throughout the life of the project.

Resistance of Organized Labor

As outlined in earlier chapters, obstacles to job enrichment often come from the suspicion—and sometimes the overt resistance—of labor. During an Upjohn conference called "New Directions in the World of Work,"[5] Mitchel Sviridoff, vice president of the Ford Foundation and formerly a top union official, observed that comments by the union representatives attending showed their uneasiness at the drift of the discussion. In all the cases the "new directions" in the world of work were described by management people, often supported by the academicians present. Most of the proposed solutions also came from the management side. The union representatives felt there were anti-union attitudes behind the job improvement initiatives reported on at the meeting. Sviridoff's remarks clearly pinpoint the nature of the conference deadlock:

The anxiety here reveals that union representatives are clearly suspicious of an analysis that challenges the fundamental precepts of the trade union movement. . . . When you suggest that the basic problem has to do with the nature of the job and the way the plant is structured, rather than wages, fringes, and other things basic to the bargaining process, then union representatives understandably get nervous.

Frank Pollara,[6] the AFL-CIO's assistant director of research, also sums up labor's fears: "Everybody would like to see his job enriched. But when you're talking about productivity, you're really talking about cutting the number of jobs, so workers will look on this with suspicion."

By way of contrast, UAW President Leonard Woodcock has

[5] C. R. Price, *New Directions in the World of Work*. A Conference Report. Kalamazoo, Mich.: W. E. Upjohn Institute for Employment Research, 1971.

[6] *Business Week*, September 9, 1972.

shown an open-minded attitude about government and management efforts to improve the quality of worklife. In a February 1973 speech, Woodcock said:

We've had a lot of discussion with regard to this within our union. It's not the sort of thing, really, that should be a problem of confrontation and collective bargaining. If any of the companies suddenly said to the UAW, "O.K., we agree: We want to humanize the workplace; you do it," we wouldn't even know how to begin. . . . What we would say, I think, is, "We want experimentation involving both management and the union, and [we want] the workers to try to find answers."

Sometimes it is as simple as asking a group of workers, "We're going to bring this product into production—how would you do it?" Then the workers tell the engineers and the supervisors, "This is how we think it should be done."

The end result may not be much different than if it had been laid out for the workers by management, but because the workers had a voice, they will take a different attitude toward it.

On the other hand, *Business Week* in its December 9, 1972, issue reported that after 16 months of experience, the joint labor-management program to boost the steel industry's productivity had been disappointing. "The program has produced more confusion and uncertainty than gains in productivity."

Although I. W. Abel, president of the United Steel Workers, had urged union support for the plan, there had been considerable rank-and-file resistance. The reasons behind the resistance were the classic ones: fear of working oneself out of a job; fear of being victimized by speed-up tactics.

One United Steel Workers official commented, "If the members aren't getting cooperation on other things, they might use this productivity clause as a wedge." In short, he was implying that cooperation to increase output could be made conditional on concessions from management, such as the clearing up of accumulated grievances.

One of labor's most vigorous opponents of the drive for job enrichment is William Winpisinger, general vice president of the International Association of Machinists, who is quoted in *The*

Wall Street Journal, February 26, 1973, as saying that job enrichment is just "a stopwatch in sheep's clothing." Mr. Winpisinger continues, "If you want to enrich the job, enrich the paycheck. The better the wage, the greater the job satisfaction. There's no better cure for the 'blue collar blues.'"

Since there is little evidence concerning the views of local union officers and the rank and file with regard to quality of worklife improvement efforts, Kochan, Lipsky, and Dyer[7] conducted a study in 1975 focused on three main questions: (1) How do local union leaders and members rate issues of quality of work as compared with traditional issues of collective bargaining, and is there general concordance of views between management and union on quality of work issues? (2) How effective are collective bargaining channels for achieving different types of aims? (3) Should quality of work issues be handled by traditional bargaining methods, or is there a need for innovative approaches to union-management relations?

The 221 participants in the study were a mixture of local and district-level union leaders and active rank-and-file unionists (stewards, committeemen, etc.), all enrolled in the Cornell Labor Studies Program. Most participants were white males, and their median age was 40. The typical participant had a high school diploma, held a blue-collar job, and earned $200–250 per week.

Participants were asked to complete a questionnaire in which they ranked items falling roughly into the categories of traditional union issues and quality of work issues. Results of the study are summarized below:

1. Without exception, respondents ranked the traditional bargaining issues (e.g., work standards and benefits) higher than the quality of work issues. Certain quality of work issues were ranked as somewhat or very important: Employees did wish to have more influence on how operations are carried out and to improve conditions felt to inhibit the work process. It is

[7] T. Kochan, D. Lipsky, & L. Dyer, "Collective Bargaining and the Quality of Work: The Views of Local Union Activists." *Industrial Relations Research Association, Proceedings of the 27th Annual Winter Proceedings* (Madison, Wisc.: IRRA, December 1974), 159–162.

interesting to note, however, that the somewhat related issue of improving company productivity was given significantly lower rankings by union activists, suggesting that the area of productivity was felt to be management's concern and unlikely to be in union's best interests.

Whereas there seemed to be general agreement on the importance of traditional bargaining issues, there was considerable difference of opinion in the ranking of quality of work issues. The confusion surrounding these more humanistic concerns became apparent when people were asked the extent to which their union and management were attempting to achieve the same or conflicting goals on each issue. These results were surprising. It had been expected that the union people would see wide gaps in union and management stands on hard-core bargaining issues and narrower ones on quality of work issues; however, the opposite proved true. Possibly this trend resulted from people's familiarity with the outcomes of disagreements on traditional issues and their lack of familiarity with quality of work issues that had not been generally handled over the bargaining table.

2. In general, collective bargaining was seen as most helpful on issues that were ranked most important (i.e., traditional union issues). For two highly ranked quality of work issues that centered on adequate resources and control of work, collective bargaining was not considered especially helpful. The one issue that might serve as a bridge between the traditional and quality of work issues is that of workload, already the subject of collective bargaining and also very central to the quality of work controversy.

3. Issues related to the quality of work movement, such as resources and control of work, offer some potential for union-management joint programs. However, a large percentage of union activists do not consider that these issues are as important as traditional issues. Thus, evidence is not encouraging for advocates of quality of work improvement through innovative union-management cooperation outside the traditional bargaining framework.

According to Kochan et al., the results of this study point to three guidelines for joint-program attempts. First, the scope of any joint program should be kept narrow, centering on quality of work issues and avoiding the entrance of traditional collective bargaining issues. Second, these joint ventures must be identified as supplements to and not replacements of traditional collective bargaining procedures. And finally, given the skepticism of union activists concerning employers' goals on quality of work issues, unions will probably be hesitant to enter into any cooperative efforts unless they are given a strong voice in defining the program's goals.

Unions' fears of increased worker exploitation in the guise of measures to improve quality of worklife are not as great as the fear of their position being weakened on two fronts: first, that by offering benefits to workers which have not been demanded by the union on their behalf, management weakens their claim to be the sole protectors of workers' rights and interests; and second, that as management and workers learn to work together in close cooperation, workers may question their need for the union and, as a result, be weaned away from it.

Furthermore, labor fears that the result of inviting workers' ideas for improved productivity will be layoffs that would not otherwise have occurred. It would hardly be reasonable to expect many people to facilitate their own unemployment. Both labor and management should examine the experience of companies that have increased productivity without layoffs. The Black & Decker Manufacturing Company is a good example. This tool company keeps constant and careful control of the interacting factors of costs, pricing, and sales volume. The firm has supported rising production by consistently reducing prices to stimulate sales: Its ¼-inch drill, for example, was introduced in 1946 for $16.95 and sold for $7.99 in 1972.[8] In the past five years Black & Decker sales have nearly doubled. In spite of marked productivity improvements, it has been necessary to hire more employees to keep pace with the expanding market.

A noteworthy effort at QWL improvement that evolved from the lower levels of the company with full union (UAW) support has

[8] *Business Week,* September 9, 1972, 110.

been at the Bolivar, Tennessee, plant of Harman International. Here, worker participation programs have opened up avenues of respectful and cooperative communication which bridge the gap that traditionally has existed between management and labor, especially in the American automotive industry. Departmental "working committees" composed of management and employee representatives create and implement their own work improvement programs. Innovations such as utilization of worker production teams with flexible hours so long as production standards are met, instead of traditional single-operation assembly-line procedures with set hours, not only have improved employee attitudes but have, in the process, increased company productivity as well.[9]

Failure to Accommodate to Changing Trends in the Labor Market

Columbia University Professor Eli Ginzberg[10] argues that current approaches to improving the quality of working life do not fully take into account changing trends in the labor market. Ginzberg lists seven: (1) the shift from a goods-producing to a service-producing economy; (2) the need for an expanded number of educated and trained personnel; (3) the increased participation of women in the labor force (chiefly on a part-time basis); (4) the later entrance and earlier withdrawal of people from the labor force; (5) the increased movement toward a "second career"; (6) the shorter workweek; (7) the increased growth and centralization of organizational units, including the trend toward mergers.

Says Ginzberg:

If work structuring represents managerial and societal efforts to make more imaginative use of technology and organizational powers [in

[9] For further review of the Harman International QWL project at Bolivar, Tennessee, see "How Workers Can Get Eight-Hours Pay for Five," *Business Week,* May 19, 1975, 52 V ff.

[10] E. Ginzberg, *The Manpower Connection: Education and Work* (Cambridge, Mass.: Harvard University Press, 1975). Used with permission of the author.

order] to provide greater autonomy for the worker and to elicit greater commitment to the organization, these efforts must be placed along-side labor market trends which are also acting to transform the work environment. Our review suggests that these manpower trends do not speak with one voice either to the subject of autonomy or commitment. In fact it suggests that the framework established for assessing the subject of improving the quality of working life must be broadened. From the viewpoint of manpower and the labor market it should be in the following dimensions. First, it is essential to recognize that the adjustment of people to the world of work changes as they change. Hence the need for a longitudinal perspective that allows for such changes. Next, it is an error to neglect differences in the way in which men and women workers approach the problem of jobs and careers. The implications of the vastly extended period of education and training prior to entrance into the world of work upon the skills workers have to offer, upon their expectations about work, and upon their value orientations must also be part of any comprehensive approach studying the quality of working life. And finally, a broadened framework must allow for the interplay and interpenetration of the work and non-work aspects of a man's life.

Although it may be well to keep these labor market trends in mind, so long as QWL programs only invite but do not require active participation of workers, the author sees no conflict between the trends that Ginzberg identifies and work restructuring efforts.

Alleged Incongruity between Individual Needs and Organization Goals

Thomas Fitzgerald, Chevrolet's director of employee research and training activities, finds current approaches to employee motivation inadequate.[11] He wonders whether it is possible, given the present structure of business organizations, to achieve anything but superficial solutions to the problem. "How much personal freedom is possible in a hierarchical, bureaucratic authority sys-

[11] T. H. Fitzgerald, "Why Motivation Theory Doesn't Work," *Harvard Business Review,* July–August 1971, 37–44.

tem?" he asks. "At what point does individual style become incompatible with order?"

Fitzgerald agrees with other experts on the necessity of eliminating monotonous, repetitive jobs, and considers it inevitable that such operations will ultimately be automated. But beyond that, he believes today's job enrichment does not take into account individual differences.

"The job Jones finds moronic and insufferable is okay with Smith, yet too much for Brown," Fitzgerald explains. "Restructuring and/or enlarging jobs are brave attempts to fit the job to the man, but *which* man? Do we have different sets and sequences of the same operation for people of varying competence, interest and drive? Does turnover then imply continued rearrangement?" He further believes that there are recognizable limits to how much job enlargement will satisfy the worker and speculates that perhaps the added challenge provided will be only a temporary phenomenon.

Fitzgerald says enhancing supervisory skills and improving the climate of communication "does not get at enough of the basic incongruence between individuals' needs and organizational goals." He argues that it is inherent in our organizational structure for supervisors to be authoritarian, that the models of success presented by our society encourage them to be "bossy, condescending and insensitive," and that they derive rewards of both money and status by maintaining their traditional roles.

Some of Fitzgerald's points are valid. At the same time, he is setting up some straw men. It is true that some people do not want more responsibility in their jobs, but the evidence suggests most people do. A thoughtful, successful job restructuring effort takes individual differences into account. It considers intellectual, physical, emotional, social, and technological factors. The evidence presented in *Work in America,* in three papers presented at the 1974 Convention of the American Psychological Association by Michael Brower, T. G. Cummings, and Raymond Katzell, along with evidence presented in this book and the published work of Louis Davis, Eric Trist, and Richard Walton, among others, all tend to support the contention that sociotechnical, economic, and individual difference factors can be, should be, and *are* taken into account. Generally the only demand made of an individual worker in an enriched job setting is that he satisfactorily perform the tasks for which he is paid. When there is a commitment from top management to sponsor and support a system where ideas and suggestions are invited from all concerned and where workers have a substantial voice in decision making, there is less divergence between individual needs and organizational goals. Perhaps the key problem Fitzgerald poses is how to get a larger proportion of managers and supervisors to relinquish a portion of their traditional authoritarian role and to develop an attitude of *wanting* to encourage and reward those below them who are willing to move toward optimum work within their capabilities or practicable potential for learning. What divergence does remain should be dealt with openly, as part of the real world in which we live.

Fitzgerald is even less optimistic about the feasibility of participatory management. It is, he contends, "an open question whether any significant percentage of the workforce even wants to participate, other than perhaps for the novelty of doing so." Fitzgerald foresees the possibility of continuing pressure for more involvement, ultimately bringing the judgment of employees to bear on issues considerably beyond their ability, and predicts an ensuing disruption of order in our increasingly complex organizations where order is imperative.

Michael Brower offers a broader view of the issue of worker participation, noting its relation to work redesign, productivity, and quality of working life.[12] Six of his nine conclusions are as follows:

1. Employees at all levels of an organization have more to contribute to its success than just their physical energy. They have brainpower as well as muscle power, they have ideas and they have specific knowledge of value to the organization, often knowledge unavailable at upper levels of management.

2. It is therefore both logically to be expected, and empirically verified, that efforts to involve employees in participation in decision

[12] M. Brower, "Relations Between Work Redesign, Worker Participation, Productivity, and the Quality of Working Life," paper presented at the meeting of the American Psychological Association, New Orleans, August 1974.

making can result in increased productivity for the organization and in lowered costs due to such factors as turnover and absenteeism.

3. Redesigning work, through job enlargement or job enrichment without involving workers in participation may also increase productivity and lower costs. But it is my own judgment, difficult to document at this point, that such changes are more likely to offer only limited and temporary gains. Such more cautious and more limited change programs, introduced from the top down and dealing with individual jobs as separate entities, are more likely to fail, and if succeeding, more likely to level off with acceptable but not dramatic benefits.

4. Efforts to improve the quality of working life, especially those relying heavily on employee participation, are likely but of course not certain, to lead to increases in productivity and to cost savings. But they may not lead to increases in "job satisfaction" narrowly defined, since aspirations of workers may be raised more rapidly than fulfillment, with a resulting decline in some measures of satisfaction.

5. Contrary to what was once widely believed, increasing job satisfaction is not necessarily a road to increasing productivity. More satisfied workers are not necessarily harder working or more productive workers. The opposite causality may be more true: higher productivity may lead to increased satisfaction. And in many cases, if the two increase together, it is probably due to the common impact of third factors.

6. Despite the fact that scores of U.S. companies and perhaps several hundred worldwide have experimented with one or another form of job enlargement, job enrichment, worker participation, autonomous work groups, open systems planning, etc., we know really very little about which methods have what results in which circumstances. We badly need carefully monitored longitudinal studies in which adequate baseline data is gathered on both economic and human aspects of the enterprises, in which careful records are kept of changes and change processes, and in which follow-through studies of economic measures and employee attitudes are taken every year or so for several years (pp. 24–25).

Although disruption of order has occurred in some situations, evidence from companies in which participatory management has been tried suggests that a substantial majority—over 70 percent of the workforce—does want to participate and to continue to do so over the long run. The argument that disruptions have occurred is valid only as a warning. Any tool can be misused or used unskillfully. People cut themselves with knives every day, but that is hardly a good argument for not using one for an appropriate purpose.

Another critical (and somewhat dyspeptic) appraisal of many reported successes from job enrichment programs, which often are part of but not synonymous with overall quality of worklife improvement efforts, is offered by Mitchell Fein.[13] To cite Fein's concluding statement:

Solving problems in the plants must start with the question: Why should workers want enriched jobs? It is readily apparent that management and the stockholders benefit from increased worker involvement, which leads to reduced costs. For their part, if all the workers get is reduced hours or even layoffs, they must resist it. It is futile to expect that workers willingly will create more for management without simultaneously benefiting themselves. *The most effective productivity results will be obtained when management creates conditions which workers perceive as beneficial to them.* The changes must be genuine and substantial and in forms which eventually are turned into cash and continuity of income. Psychic rewards may look good on paper, but they are invisible in the pocketbook. If workers really wanted psychic job enrichment, management would have heard their demands loud and clear long ago.

Change must start with management taking the first steps, unilaterally and without *quid pro quo*. There must not be productivity bargaining at first. Management must provide the basic conditions which will motivate workers to raise productivity: job security, good working conditions, good pay, and financial incentives. There must be a diminution of the win-lose relationship and the gradual establishment of conditions in which workers know that both they and management gain and lose together. Labor, management, and government leaders are very concerned that rising wages and costs are making goods

[13] M. Fein, "Job Enrichment: A Reevaluation," *Sloan Management Review,* Winter 1974, *15,* 2, 86–87. Reprinted by permission.

produced in this country less competitive in the world markets. Increasingly all three parties are engaging in meaningful dialogue to address these problems.

There are unquestionably enormous potentials for increased productivity which workers can unleash—if they want to. The error of job enrichment is that it tries to talk workers into involvement and concern for the nature of their work when their memories and experiences have taught them that increased productivity only results in layoffs. Only management can now create conditions which will nullify the past.

Companies which are experimenting with new work methods probably will increase their efforts. As viable methods and approaches are developed, more companies will be tempted to innovate approaches suited to their own plants. The greatest progress will come in companies where workers see that management protects their welfare and where productivity gains are shared with the employees.

Fein makes some good points, but with reference to certain statements his facts are incorrect. For example, elsewhere in his article he asserts that all job enrichment experiments have been initiated by management, never by workers, and that "practically all experiments have been in non-union plants." Not quite so. We have only to look at the exciting examples of Harman International, Rushton Mining, and the city of Jamestown, New York, where union and management are engaged in collaborative efforts to improve quality of worklife. Nor do productivity increases necessarily lead to worker layoffs. There are a number of recorded cases where productivity increases have led to lower prices, expanded markets, and *increased* employment (as in the Black & Decker case cited earlier). But Fein interprets the evidence correctly when he says, "The greatest progress will come in companies where workers see that management protects their welfare and where productivity gains are shared with the employees." The Donnelly Mirrors case cited in the preceding chapter is one excellent example of this.

Levitan and Johnson[14] offer a sobering analysis of some limi-

[14] S. Levitan & W. Johnson, "Job Design, Reform, Enrichment: Exploring the Limitations," *Monthly Labor Review,* 1973, *96,* 35–41.

tations in the possibilities for humanizing work due to the social demand for continuation of certain intrinsically unpleasant tasks and also due to the difficult or unpleasant requirements of certain technologies. However, they nevertheless conclude: "Despite all this, improvements *can* be made by rotating workers among jobs, by enlarging jobs, by expanding responsibility. Generally managements (and unions) have done too little to change working conditions which could be improved."[15]

Katzell and others[16] suggest that relatively limited programs, such as job enrichment, participation in decision making, or incentive pay plans, seem unlikely by themselves to create large or enduring improvements in both productivity and job satisfaction; they are better regarded as possible ingredients in redesigned sociotechnical systems of work. The evidence suggests that to achieve both sustained quality of worklife *and* productivity gains, behavioral science or human factors, plus learning and motivational considerations, need to be blended with production engineering principles and economic requirements of work organizations. Enduring gains are most likely to come from a *systems* approach, in which all important considerations or variables receive simultaneous attention. Einar Thorsrud has remarked:

Job design may degenerate into a mere gimmick if it is not part of both a comprehensive new policy concerning the use and development of human resources and a comprehensive new philosophy of management. But as a corollary—and illustrating the inherent interdependence of these three factors—the most advanced policies and philosophies cannot impinge on real life unless we learn more about job design and apply it better. The relationship between man and his work is basic to his relationships to himself and to his fellow men. If we cannot improve these basic relationships, I doubt very much whether we can even turn our attention to more global problems.[17]

[15] Levitan & Johnson, op. cit., 39.

[16] R. A. Katzell & D. Yankelovich, *et al., Work, Productivity, and Job Satisfaction* (New York: Harcourt Brace Jovanovich, 1975).

[17] Cited by Levitan & Johnson in L. Davis & J. Taylor, *Design of Jobs* (Baltimore, Md.: Penguin Books, 1972), 41. Used by permission of E. Thorsrud.

Along similar lines, in a Conference Board report on management applications of the behavioral sciences[18] Harold Rush summarized the evaluation responses of the 302 firms that cooperated in the study as follows:

The companies expressing the most satisfaction with their behavioral science programs are those that do not view them as programs at all. Instead, they see them as a completely different way of improving and managing the enterprise. These firms are trying to impact the total organization by applying behavioral science principles at all levels. Their behavioral science applications extend beyond trying to develop managers. Instead, they encompass every facet of the company's operations in terms of meeting such objectives as long-range planning, career development, productivity, and profitability.

Pitfalls in the Introduction of Organizational Development Programs Noted by GM Personnel Administration and Development Staff

In the GM Assembly Division, efforts to improve the quality of life at work have involved what the company calls organizational development (OD). This is a long-range program to improve the effectiveness of the total organization at all levels—work group, department, plant, or staff. A number of OD efforts have been made to promote a "people-oriented" management philosophy. This philosophy, if spelled out in appropriate directives for action, may well inspire new management attitudes and behavior that will persuade workers to care about their work because they have the opportunity for a significant voice in the organization.

GM has used OD only recently, but results have been favorable. Nevertheless, GM did find that, as with almost every other introduction of change, their system has potential pitfalls. Some of their experiences are summarized in a GM brochure entitled "Our People Do Care—If We Care About Them." In this brochure, it is

---

[18] H. M. Rush, *Behavioral Science: Concepts and Management Applications* (New York: The Conference Board, 1969).

emphatically stated that OD will work in a plant only if it starts at the top and goes down, and it is recommended that a long preparatory period be spent with supervisors before the plan involves hourly workers. One of the pitfalls cited is the danger that a superintendent or general foreman may perceive a new program as having the potential of solving all his problems. In other words, it is important not to build up unrealistic expectations concerning the introduction of OD. The need for patience is also stressed. One must expect that hourly workers will express some resistance to the change and will not automatically develop a high level of motivation simply because a new program has been introduced. It is also important that no single department or section in a plant move ahead too rapidly. The total organization has to be geared to the program if it is to be successful.

Case Report Illustrating Problems of Job and Organization Design in a Corporation

A detailed look at some very important problems that may be encountered in trying to introduce work teams and job enlargement comes from William Lytle, a human behaviorist in a major U.S. corporation. He gives unusual insights into what might be considered a failure experience at an unnamed company.

In 1969, the corporation under study created the beginnings of a manufacturing organization which, it was planned, would eventually produce a new line of corporate products. Lytle had served as an internal consultant to company management from the beginning of this new project, attempting to help top management explore and utilize a diversity of job and organization design concepts. Despite Lytle's efforts, however, the ideas and processes that he introduced seemed to have little impact on the two factories that were to manufacture the new product; when they proceeded into full operation, they were using traditional human systems.

The two plants in question had projected workforces of 600 and 1,200 employees, respectively. The parent company, located in a major Eastern metropolitan area, was a large U.S. corporation. It had been primarily research-based but was now becoming more manufacturing-oriented, and was noted for its unique products. The company was not unionized, but had liberal employee policies and practices, and ten years before Lytle was called in, it had made a major attempt at job redesign.

Lytle analyzed the reasons for the limited accomplishments, including a frank critique of his own performance as a consultant, and from his conclusions was able to make several observations for future projects. Some of these observations are summarized below:

1. When an organization is operating under stress, the possibility of incurring what it may perceive as additional stress is likely to act as a deterrent to adoption of innovations. Although the results of such adoption may be potentially worthwhile, they cannot be achieved without a substantial initial investment in planning, and that time/energy investment, aside from other resistances to change, is likely to be perceived as additional stress, and thus something to be avoided.

2. Unless management deliberately specifies the type of organization it wishes to have, it will end up with a traditional bureaucracy. The organization will build from the top downward, and consequently will lose its chance to focus on its functions (e.g., manufacturing processes and tasks). If an attempt is to be made to innovate at the lower levels of the organization —through changes in workflow, jobs, and so forth—the management structure must be designed to support this. The values, norms, and leadership patterns found throughout the organization need to be consistent.

3. Although appropriate technology designed by sensitive engineers is necessary to promote worker motivation, group formation, individual identification, trust, and cooperation, it is not sufficient in itself to ensure this—skillful management and mature employees are also required. Since it appears that technology left unchallenged has an enormous potential to frustrate constructive change in the human area, it is necessary

that the factors involved (the product, processes, equipment, facilities, etc.) be understood and controlled as early as possible; for once a routine is established, major degrees of freedom are lost. In order for such understanding and control of the sociotechnical system to occur, a major reeducation for engineers and their management will be required. This is of critical importance, since in reality these people are also acting as inadvertent social engineers in a key sense.

4. The existence of dull and repetitious jobs may be unavoidable in operations involving a large volume of hardware assembly, where the necessity for process operations and equipment disrupts a sequence of hand operations. It is probably easier to implement job design concepts in non-process industries.

5. It is uncertain where the initiative and drive for human innovation in organizations will come from. Lytle noted that if the corporation he studied was at all typical, very little of it could be expected to come from the workforce. Managers who view it with a practical idealism may be the leaders in such change, with other managers becoming interested only when they badly need a reduction in labor costs or more efficient utilization of employees. In any case, the top managements of all operations must be deeply involved and committed to a common goal if such efforts are to be successful.

6. Management's faith in its organization's internal opportunities for upward mobility may lessen its sensitivity to the need for improving its "poorer" jobs.

7. Managers choosing to explore human innovations will need the help of an expert staff to relate conceptual material to organizational realities. If there is to be a major design effort, focusing on changes in the work, the organization, and the people, then consultants from several different disciplines will be needed—engineering, manufacturing, facilities, management, human relations, and so on. It is unrealistic to think one consultant alone could serve as a catalyst and fulfill the needs of a large and complex organization. The consultants and man-

agement must work together to develop some systematic methods of testing for real progress in any change effort.

8. It may not be necessary for a consultant to enter an organization at the top if someone is willing to sponsor him. However, the sponsor must be someone who will remain committed to the effort throughout, and who can arrange for the consultant to have access to the top and to other functions. The views and needs of the sponsor will probably differ from those of other managers, particularly the head of the organization. It is, however, necessary that the latter get involved, for he has a unique perspective of the organization to contribute and a singular responsibility and commitment. He also has the greatest power to involve relevant people and functions, and to effect change if his influence is needed (e.g., to make engineering technology more oriented toward integration with the social and administrative components of the work design *system*).

9. Major innovations in human systems may be easier to bring about in relatively small organizations or those with slow growth rates than in large, complex organizations. With this in mind, perhaps the latter could be restructured into a number of smaller, autonomous, interdependent units that would not necessarily even need to be located in the same building.

10. Getting involved in exploration, design, planning, and promotion of these concepts can provide people with an opportunity for a singularly enriching experience of personal growth. However, they should be in a secure career position before entering into this (that is to say, their reputation should not be on the line), and the organization should be ready to reward them for a competent effort.

Lytle's experiences, especially his problems with job redesign strategies, processes, and already-existing technology, are well worth examination.[19]

[19] See W. Lytle, "Obstacles to Job and Organization Design: A Case." In L. E. Davis & A. B. Cherns (Eds.), *Quality of Working Life* (New York: The Free Press, 1975).

Case Report of a Failure of Job Enrichment in a Bank[20]

Frank and Hackman point out the need to publish systematic accounts and analyses of failures in order to learn from them, which is a position fully shared by the author of this book. The subject of their report is a work redesign project undertaken by the management of the stock transfer department in a large bank. This department had 300 employees performing 16 different functions. The project involved those employees who worked on the six most central jobs in the department. The basic plan for change was to create 10 to 13 "modules" within the department, each of which would be a miniature stock transfer department in its own right. Each module would have its own work coordinator (supervisor) and would function as a semi-autonomous work group. The modules would have complete responsibility for a specific group of corporations whose stock was handled by the bank—in contrast to the previous arrangement, where employees handled whatever work happened to be channeled their way by a supervisor.

Members of each module were to be provided with increased knowledge of the results of their work activities through three new features that were incorporated into the modules. These were: (1) the presence of the corrections clerk in the module on a continuous basis, to show members immediately when they had made a mistake and to help them correct it; (2) the pairing of experienced operators with those less experienced, so the former could verify the latter's work; and (3) programming of the data processing system to provide individualized reports of performance to module members on a weekly basis.

It was expected that the modular operation would produce a general increase in the overall job satisfaction of stock transfer workers. In addition, it was hoped there would be a reduction in workflow delays (because of the increased flexibility of the module) and an increase in the quality of service provided (because of the

[20] Summarized from L. L. Frank & J. R. Hackman, *A Failure of Job Enrichment: The Case of the Change That Wasn't* (Tech. Report No. 8). Yale University School of Organization and Management, March 1975.

additional feedback provided to module members and because of increased employee commitment to the work).

The researchers, who were invited to evaluate the project by the external consultant, collected quantitative and qualitative data on the effects of the change—the latter through interviews and observations. Findings from the data show that the job enrichment project failed to alter significantly either the jobs themselves or the work attitudes and behavior of department employees.

In analyzing the reasons for the failure to achieve meaningful change, Frank and Hackman note:

It is tempting to conclude from the findings reported above that "job enrichment didn't work" in the stock transfer department. Indeed, exactly that conclusion was reached at the end of the project by several managers who had been involved in it. Such a conclusion is severely misleading, however, because the data show that the *jobs themselves* actually changed very little. To ask about the effects of enriched jobs in such circumstances is to ask an empty question. Instead, the critical issues in this project have to do with the reasons *why* the jobs were not substantially changed in the stock transfer department—and why those organizational changes that were carried out had no positive impact on employee attitudes or work behavior.

Some of the implementation factors that affected the outcome were:

Neither the computer-based feedback system nor the planned cross-training of employees was installed when the module was begun.

Shortly after the start of the second module, the data processing system began to malfunction with a frequency that was clearly debilitating to the entire department. A new set of programs for handling stock transfers had recently been installed, and "bugs" in the system were both more frequent and more disruptive to the operation of the department than had been anticipated. The result was that operators often had to remain idle for several hours during the day, and then were required to work overtime to compensate for the lost time.

During the most difficult periods, many part-time employees were brought into the modules to help get the work done. This remedy did provide needed manpower, but also tended to undermine the integrity of the modules as self-contained units.

Shortly after the holiday season, the executive vice-president (who had been instrumental in the initiation and follow-through of the project) left the bank for a several-month executive development program at a distant university. His temporary replacement was skeptical about the basic philosophy of job enrichment, preferring an alternative behavioral science approach to organizational change.

The net effect of these implementation problems was that the introduction of job enrichment features into the program as originally planned was not in fact carried out. As Frank and Hackman put it:

Significant improvements in skill variety, task identity, task significance, autonomy, and feedback from the job . . . were not achieved. . . .

The original plans for the modules included a number of changes in work structure and procedures which, if carried out, should have substantially increased the standing of module jobs on the core job dimensions. For a variety of reasons, most of these plans were either not initiated, or were initiated and not carried through. In effect, the work redesign project was an intervention that affected many aspects of the organizational unit—but not the work itself.

The lessons that Frank and Hackman offer from this study are presented as four prescriptive guides for implementing job enrichment or other organizational change activities that involve the redesign of work:

Guide 1. Work redesign projects should be based on theory—and such theory should be congruent with the kinds of changes that are contemplated.

Guide 2. An explicit diagnosis of the target jobs and of the surrounding social and technical systems should be carried out before the changes are initiated.

Guide 3. Contingency plans should be prepared ahead of time to deal with the inevitable "spin-off" problems and opportunities that emerge from work redesign activities.

Guide 4. Those responsible for redesign projects should anticipate set-backs, and be prepared for continuous evaluation and revision of action-plans throughout the project.

To Frank and Hackman's four prescriptive guides for avoiding some of the pitfalls inherent in attempts to redesign work can be added the more comprehensive guidelines presented in Chapter IV of this book.

Case Report of a Company's Unsuccessful Attempt to Reduce Turnover

A study by the Survey Research Center[21] reports one company's ambitious, expensive, and totally unsuccessful attempt to solve the problem of high turnover rate among its economically dis-advantaged workers. The company instituted a six-week training program, during which the trainees attended classes and were paid $2.50 an hour, to prepare them for the actual job, and to foster their "personal growth." The company assumed that the high turn-over rate was attributable principally to characteristics of these workers rather than to characteristics of their jobs. No specific skills that would later help on the job were included in the program, since the advisers and teachers had no advance knowledge of the particular type of company job each trainee would get.

Yet, a sample interview of 66 workers indicated that the major cause of turnover was the poor quality of their working lives. The heavy-machinery plant where they worked was dirty, noisy, and overcrowded; the work was physically exhausting and dangerous. Of the workers interviewed, 35 percent had been injured on the job during their first six weeks with the company. A newly hired worker was often moved, like a pawn, from job to job, station to station, or supervisor to supervisor because of highly unpredictable fluctuations in company absenteeism and production quotas.

[21] R. P. Quinn, T. Levitin, & D. Eden, *The Multi-Million Dollar Mis-understanding: An Attempt to Reduce Turnover Among Disadvantaged Workers* (Ann Arbor: University of Michigan Survey Research Center, 1971). Used with permission.

The researchers concluded:

These data suggested that turnover was almost exclusively determined by characteristics of the worker's job or by generally immutable properties of the worker's background. Neither of these sources of turnover can be altered by training. That the company's training program failed to reduce turnover was less a function of shortcomings of the program's design or execution than it was a function of the total irrelevance of the program to the social problem it was designed to solve. No amount of employee training can make working conditions objectively less noxious or change a man's history.

If the company did not wish to improve the quality of these jobs or believed it *could* not improve them—another option might have been to seek surer ways of selecting people willing to endure such jobs. Then the degree of early turnover, which still would occur, could be viewed as part of the selection costs. In any case, creative attention to the job conditions could have resulted in some practical solutions for making them less noxious.

Concluding Comments

In this chapter we have described a number of problems and pitfalls that organizations should bear in mind when considering QWL improvement efforts. The key points are: (1) Managers must have (or develop) the attitudes and skills needed to carry through the consultative style of management. This style underlies inviting employees to participate in decisions affecting the structure, design, and organization of jobs. (2) When employees are unionized, the labor union or unions involved must be consulted. (3) Competent diagnosis of each individual situation, including its technology, is needed before job enrichment is undertaken. (4) Time and patience are needed for planning, discussion, respectful working-through of honest differences of opinion, and so forth. (5) Influential internal sponsorship and continuous review are needed to try out ideas, and to monitor results and refine them on the basis of experience. (6) Before naïvely embarking on a QWL improvement program, an organization must consider all the following factors: the length of time required to develop and maintain such programs; the costs involved; where and how to start such programs; the kind of commitment and degree of involvement that will be needed throughout the organization; questions surrounding compensation and unions with respect to job redesign; the problem of individual differences in workers' *desire* for enriched jobs with more responsibility; and problems of technological inertia.

IV. □ Guidelines for Introducing a Job Redesign or Quality of Worklife Program

A number of experts on job enrichment and improving the quality of worklife have suggested guidelines for introducing such programs. Eight of these guidelines are summarized here.

While there are differences in philosophy, emphasis, and strategies, the area of agreement is considerably greater than that of disagreement. Two of the interesting disagreements are: (1) University of Utah Professor Frederick Herzberg argues against inviting direct participation by the employees whose jobs are to be enriched, while most other students and practitioners in the field favor it. (2) Neal Herrick, formerly of the Department of Labor and now at Ohio State University, argues strongly for employees to share in cost savings; a number of others do not consider this essential. The eighth set of guidelines presented here attempts to integrate what has been learned and to present some special emphases.

Perhaps the key question underlying guidelines for introducing a job redesign or QWL improvement program can be phrased as "What are some of the basic considerations and strategies related to introducing and supporting planned change, and what are the common pitfalls?" Some of the problems, pitfalls, and failures already have been discussed. The primary focus in this chapter will be on facilitating strategies, but with some return to the other side of the coin—namely, factors likely to constitute barriers or denigrating forces.

Herrick and Maccoby's Suggestions

Neal Herrick and Michael Maccoby[1] have listed four principles that they believe underlie the humanization of work:

1. *Security*. The worker's freedom from anxiety concerning his health, safety, income, and future employment.

2. *Equity*. The employee receives compensation commensurate to his contribution to the value of the service or product.

3. *Individuation*. Work should stimulate the development of the individual's unique abilities and capacity for craftsmanship rather than force him into a mechanized role. It should include continued learning rather than boredom and stagnation. The principle of individuation, once adopted, can lead to a nonbureaucratic spirit in which workers are encouraged to develop themselves and to learn as much as they wish about the industry as a whole. . . . The desire for craftsmanship is one of the deep strengths of the American character. By weakening it, we have lessened ourselves as a people. Recent studies of worker attitudes have clearly shown workers' concern that their jobs be more interesting, provide more autonomy and allow them to develop their abilities. After a certain level of income is reached, these concerns are more important than receiving money.

4. *Democracy*. The principle of democracy, like that of individuation, is opposed to making the worker into a passive object, a machine part. It implies psychological activeness. Wherever technically possible, workers should manage themselves. Authoritarian, hierarchical control should be replaced by cooperative, self-managed groups.

[1] N. Herrick & M. Maccoby, "Humanizing Work: A Priority Goal of the 1970s." In L. E. Davis & A. B. Cherns (Eds.), *Quality of Working Life* (New York: The Free Press, 1975). Copyright © 1975 by Louis E. Davis and Albert B. Cherns. Reprinted with permission of Macmillan Publishing Co., Inc.

Autonomous work groups should replace pyramidal structures. Where supervisors are necessary, they should be elected directly by the workers.

Herrick and Maccoby contend that a system based on these four principles "would develop in the worker a sense of hope, activeness, and productiveness."

Richard E. Walton's Notations

Harvard University professor Richard E. Walton, who also has served as consultant to many industrial firms and government agencies in the field of applied behavioral science, offers the following observations: *

. . . Employees increasingly want their work to be characterized by challenge, mutual influence patterns, dignity, positive social relevance, balanced attention to emotionality and rationality, and cooperative social patterns. In order to substantially increase these ingredients, the work situation must undergo comprehensive change. Piecemeal reforms, such as job enrichment, management by objectives, and sensitivity training are inadequate.

The organization redesign should be systemic. First, redesign must focus on the division of labor, involving, for example, the formation of self-managing work teams, recreation of whole tasks by reversing the trend toward fractionation of work, and an increase in the flexibility in work assignments by a variety of means.

Second, the redesign must embrace supporting elements, such as a trimming of supervision and more delegation of authority. Also, the information and reward schemes must be tailored to facilitate the delegation of decision making and to reinforce team work.

Third, other elements in the work situation must enhance the status of workers and communicate trust in their exercise of self-control—e.g.,

---

* R. E. Walton, "Innovative Restructuring of Work." In J. M. Rosow (Ed.), *The Worker and the Job: Coping with Change.* © 1974 The American Assembly, Columbia University (Englewood Cliffs, N.J.: Prentice-Hall, Inc., 1974). Reprinted by permission of the publisher.

salaried payroll and no time clock. Similarly, recruitment and/or training are required to ensure the necessary skills.

Obviously, the revisions in these many elements must be coordinated and must result in a new, internally consistent whole.

The impetus for work restructuring experiments of this kind comes from prior philosophical commitment, an interest in the behavioral sciences, and compelling personnel or productivity problems.

A number of conditions are favorable to the introduction of such experiments: new plants with small, nonunionized workforces, located in rural communities geographically separate from other parts of the firm. None of these are necessary conditions, but each facilitates the rapid introduction of the innovative work system.

By design of [our] sample, the experiments reviewed in this study reportedly produced positive results in the first year or two of their existence—in terms of both quality of work life and productivity indexes.

However, several of the experimental units suffered setbacks after an initially successful introduction. A number of factors can threaten termination or create regression in these innovations: a lack of internal consistency in the original design; loss of hierarchical support; loss in internal leadership and skills; heightened stress and crisis; tensions with various parties external to the unit; an unfavorable ratio of psychological costs to benefits for individual participants; and isolation resulting from a failure to diffuse. With foreplanning, sponsors and leaders of innovative work systems can minimize the potential threats listed above.

Hackman, Oldham, Janson, and Purdy's "New Strategy for Job Enrichment"

This section reports on a three-year study,[2] funded jointly by the U.S. Department of Labor and the Office of Naval Research, of a new strategy for going about the redesign of production and clerical work.

The researchers posited three "psychological states" as critical

[2] Technical Report No. 3, Department of Administrative Sciences, Yale University, May 1974.

in determining a person's motivation and satisfaction on the job. They are:

1. *Experienced meaningfulness.* The individual must perceive his work as worthwhile or important by some system of values he accepts.
2. *Experienced responsibility.* He must believe that he personally is accountable for the outcomes of his efforts.
3. *Knowledge of results.* He must be able to determine, on some fairly regular basis, whether or not the outcomes of his work activities are satisfactory.

When all three of these conditions are present to a high degree, then internal work motivation, job satisfaction, and work quality also tend to be high, and absenteeism and turnover are low. When one or more of these three psychological states is low, motivation drops markedly.

The authors identify five core job dimensions that contribute to a job's meaningfulness for the worker. They are:

1. *Skill variety:* the degree to which a job requires the worker to perform activities that challenge his skills and abilities.
2. *Task identity:* the degree to which the job requires completion of a "whole" and identifiable piece of work.
3. *Task significance:* the degree to which the job has a substantial and perceivable impact on the lives of other people.
4. *Increased personal responsibility:* the degree to which the job gives the worker freedom, independence, and discretion in scheduling work and determining how he will carry it out.
5. *Feedback:* the degree to which a worker, in carrying out the work activities required by the job, gets information about the effectiveness of his efforts.

Hackman and Oldham have developed a package of diagnostic instruments called the Job Diagnostic Survey (JDS). The survey includes a test to measure "motivating potential," a single summary index (called the MPS) designating the degree to which the objective characteristics of a job will prompt high internal work motivation. However, as Hackman, et al., point out, "not everyone is able to become internally motivated in his work, even when the Motivating Potential of a job is very high indeed. . . . But . . . we believe that the organization . . . should provide the individual with the chance to reverse that trend whenever it can."

The JDS also provides scores on each of the five core dimensions described above and provides measures of how people feel about other aspects of the work setting, such as pay, supervision, and relations with co-workers. Finally, a score is provided to indicate how strong a need for growth each employee has. As Hackman, et al., have noted:

Employees who have strong growth needs are likely to be more responsive to job enrichment than employees with weak growth needs. Therefore, it is important to know at the outset just what kinds of satisfactions the people who do the job are (and are not) motivated to obtain from their work. This will make it possible to identify which persons are best to start changes with, and which may need help in adapting to the new enriched job.

To translate the diagnostic information gathered by use of the JDS, the authors suggest five "implementing concepts" for job enrichment. Each is a specific action step aimed at improving both the quality of the working experience for the individual and his work productivity. They are:

1. Forming natural work units; autonomy.

2. Combining tasks (for individuals or small teams); task identity.

3. Establishing direct relationships with the "clients" or ultimate users of the work group's product or service; task significance.

4. Vertical loading, or skill variety, through which as many as practicable of the responsibilities and controls that formerly were reserved for higher levels of management are added to the job.

5. Opening feedback channels, by means of which individuals or task teams can learn directly whether their performance is

improving, deteriorating, or remaining at a constant level; feedback from the job itself.

The authors report favorable findings on the question of whether their job enrichment theory really leads to measurable differences when it is applied in actual organizational settings. The full model of the Hackman and Oldham concepts is diagrammed in Figure 7.

Louis Davis's Guidelines

Professor Louis E. Davis of UCLA's Graduate School of Management reviewed six studies "intended to indicate the multi-dimensionality of the job design problem and the pervasiveness of its influence on quantity and quality of output, costs, and job satisfaction." He concluded that performance improves:[3]

1. When job and organization designs lead to responsible, autonomous job behavior. Responsible behavior as defined here implies acceptance of responsibility by the individual for the cycle of activities required to complete the product or service. Autonomous behavior encompasses:
   (a) self-regulation of work content and structure within the job, where the job is an assignment having inputs, facilities and outputs;
   (b) self-evaluation of performance;
   (c) self-adjustment to changes required by technological variability;
   (d) participation in setting up of goals or objectives for job outputs.
2. When there is acceptance of responsibility for rate, quantity or quality of output.
3. When there is recognition of interdependence of the individual or group on others for effective progress of the cycle of activity.

[3] L. E. Davis, *The Design of Jobs* (Reprint No. 163). Los Angeles: UCLA, Institute of Industrial Relations, 1966. Used by permission.

Figure 7

The Full Model: How Use of the Implementing Concepts Can Lead to Positive Outcomes

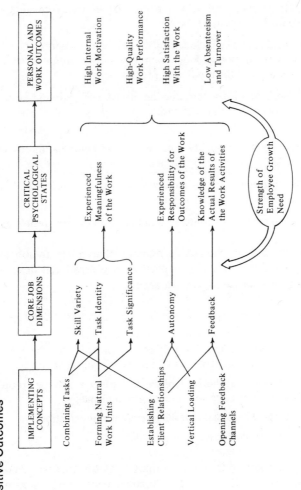

Source: Technical Report No. 3, Department of Administration Sciences, Yale University, May 1974, Figure 4.

4. When the scope of jobs includes all tasks required to complete a part, product or service.

5. When the job content includes all four types of tasks inherent in productive work: (a) auxiliary or service (supply, tooling), (b) preparatory (setup), (c) processing or transformation, and (d) control (inspection).

6. When the tasks included in the job content permit closure of the activity, if not product completion, permitting development of identity with the product or process.

7. When there is the introduction of task variety in the form of larger numbers and kinds of tasks and skills as well as more complex tasks.

8. When product quality acceptance is within the authority of the job holder.

9. When there is social interaction among job holders and communication with peers and supervisors.

10. When there is a reward system that supports responsible autonomy.

In addition to the above items, which relate to job structure, Davis cited the following aspects of organizational design as contributing to improved performance:

1. Group composition that permits self-regulation of the group functioning.

2. Group composition that deliberately provides for the full range of skills required to carry out all the tasks in an activity cycle.

3. Delegation of authority (formal and informal) to the group for self-assignment of tasks and roles to group members.

4. Group structure that permits internal communication.

5. A group reward system for joint output.

Davis points out that one ingredient for success is the proper organizational climate: Top management must support wholeheartedly the development and implementation of the above conditions.

A general caution: In any quality of work program, management cannot delegate its responsibility for successful operation when it gives workers autonomy and the power to regulate and evaluate themselves. To carry out this responsibility properly, top management needs an information system to provide facts on such items as scrap, rework or reject rate, sales trends, expenses, inventories, profits, and whatever else may be necessary for intelligent and timely monitoring. In this way, inquiries and new problem-solving action can be devised if called for.

Frederick Herzberg's Guidelines

Frederick Herzberg suggests the following steps:[4]

1. Select those jobs in which: (a) the investment in industrial engineering does not make change too costly, (b) attitudes are poor, (c) hygiene is becoming very costly, and (d) motivation will make a difference in performance.

2. Approach these jobs with conviction that they can be changed. Years of tradition have led management to believe that the content of the jobs is sacrosanct and that the only scope of action [it has] is in ways of stimulating people.

3. Brainstorm a list of changes that may enrich the job without concern for their practicality.

4. Screen the list to eliminate suggestions that involve "hygiene" rather than actual motivation. [Hygiene refers to job surroundings, motivation to job *content*. See "Guide for Determining Motivation and Hygiene Factors," p. 237.]

5. Screen the list for generalities, such as "give them more responsibility," that are rarely followed in practice. . . .

6. Screen the list to eliminate any horizontal-loading suggestions (that is, suggestions for adding just more of the same kinds of tasks).

7. Avoid direct participation by the employees whose jobs are to be enriched.[5] Ideas they have expressed previously certainly constitute

[4] F. Herzberg, "One More Time: How Do You Motivate Employees?" *Harvard Business Review*, January–February 1968, 53–62. Reprinted by permission.

[5] The author disagrees with Herzberg's advice here. If employees are invited to participate in designing any change in the structure of their jobs,

a valuable source for recommended changes, but their direct involvement contaminates the process with human-relations hygiene and more specifically gives them only a *sense* of making a contribution. Their job is to be changed and it is the content that will produce the motivation, not attitudes about being involved or challenged inherent in setting up the job. That process will be over shortly, and it is what the employees will be doing from then on that will determine their motivation. A sense of participation will result in short-term movement.

8. In the initial attempts at job enrichment, set up a controlled experiment. At least two equivalent groups should be chosen: one an experimental unit in which the motivators are systematically introduced over a period of time, and the other a control group in which no changes are made. For both groups hygiene should be allowed to follow its natural course for the duration of the experiment. Pre- and post-installation tests of performance and job attitudes are needed to evaluate the effectiveness of the job enrichment program.

9. Be prepared for a drop in performance in the experimental group in the first few weeks. The changeover to a new job may lead to a temporary reduction in efficiency.

10. Expect your first-line supervisors to experience some anxiety and hostility over the changes you are making. . . . After a successful experiment, however, the supervisor usually discovers the supervisory and managerial functions he has neglected or which were never his because all his time was given over to checking the work of his subordinates. . . .

T. G. Cummings's "Intervention Strategies for Improving Productivity and the Quality of Work Life"[6]

T. G. Cummings identifies nine "action levers" that were found, in his review of 57 work experiments, to have had a positive effect on productivity and work satisfaction. They are:

---

they not only can make important, reality-based substantive contributions, but are more likely to feel a sense of proprietorship in the new modus operandi, and thus accept/support it.

[6] T. G. Cummings, *et al.*, "Intervention Strategies for Improving Productivity," *Organizational Dynamics, 4,* 1 (Summer 1975), pp. 52–68.

Herzberg's theory of motivation versus hygiene factors can be diagrammed as shown below. The top line represents the hygiene (or maintenance or context) factors surrounding the job. The bottom line represents the motivation inherent in the work itself, or content factors.

Hygiene Items

Perceived fairness of pay
Working conditions
Administrative practices
Job security
Fringe benefits
Satisfaction/dissatisfaction
with interpersonal relations
Status factors
Character of supervision

Motivation Items

Sense of achievement
Recognition for achieve-
ment
Opportunities for advancement
Opportunities for increased
responsibility
Satisfaction with the work
itself
Feeling of continued learning and growth

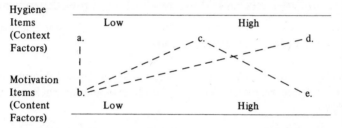

Hygiene Items (Context Factors) — Low — High — a. — c. — d.

Motivation Items (Content Factors) — Low — High — b. — e.

If both are low, as in a.— b., then productivity, morale, and quality of output are likely to be low.

If an organization offers outstanding advantages in the maintenance items but does nothing to upgrade the motivation items (b.— d.), dissatisfactions are likely to be reduced, at least temporarily, but intrinsic satisfactions with the work will not be improved. The likely result is that costs will rise appreciably but there will be no commensurate increase in productivity or sustained improvement in morale. Improvement in hygiene factors indeed can serve to remove or reduce or overcome deficits, and perhaps are needed, but removal of hygiene deficits *alone* is not likely to lead to long-term improvements in productivity, quality, and the like.

If an organization can arrange its modus operandi in a way that optimizes or significantly enhances the motivation or content items, and also sees to it that the hygiene or context items are well above average, as in c.— e., then productivity and morale are likely to rise in a sustained way. Not only will the workforce have dissatisfiers removed or reduced, but, even more important, they will have a rich fare of intrinsic motivators.

1. *Pay/reward systems:* introductions of group bonus.

2. *Antonomy/discretion:* workers were allowed to determine their own work methods.

3. *Support services:* service on demand from technical support groups.

4. *Training:* training all operators for all tasks in the department.

5. *Organization structure:* reduction in the number of hierarchical levels.

6. *Technical/physical:* breakdown of long assembly-line into smaller units.

7. *Task variety:* the inclusion of preparatory and finishing tasks in machining jobs.

8. *Information/feedback:* direct feedback from user departments.

9. *Interpersonal/group process:* increase in the amount and kind of interaction among group members.

Changes in the action levers resulted in positive outcomes for five *criterion variables*. These and an example of each are as follows:

1. *Costs:* direct costs per unit.

2. *Productivity:* increased number of airline bookings.

3. *Quality:* average rate of rejects.

4. *Withdrawal behavior:* decrease in turnover and absenteeism.

5. *Attitudes:* increased job satisfaction.

According to Cummings, manipulation of action levers is more likely to result in positive outcomes when

1. There is sanction for these changes from the highest-involved level in the organization.

2. Workers possess "higher-order" needs.

3. Pay and reward systems are on a group rather than an individual basis.

4. The technological process allows for relatively self-contained task groupings.

5. There is an adequate training program for establishing requisite task skills.

6. Workers are capable of assuming responsibility for a "whole" task.

7. First-level supervisors support the changes.

8. The changes test abilities valued by a worker.

9. The changes do not adversely affect interpersonal relations.

10. Increased participation is perceived as a legitimate part of work.

11. There is no strong resistance to the methods of introducing participation.

12. Participation involves decisions that workers perceive as important.

13. Workers possess a need for independence.

14. Participation involves decisions in those key areas that motivate a worker to enter and remain in the organization.

15. The organizational climate is supportive of innovative behavior.

16. There is a high level of trust between workers and managers.

Eli Ginzberg's Observations

Eli Ginzberg, professor of economics at Columbia University, and four Ford Foundation staff members traveled through the Netherlands, Sweden, Norway, France, Italy, and Israel in 1972 to observe some of the work restructuring experiments in these countries. Ginzberg writes:[7]

[7] E. Ginzberg, "The Humanizing of Europe's Assembly Lines." Chapter 10 of *The Manpower Connection: Education and Work* (Cambridge, Mass.: Harvard University Press, 1975). Reprinted by permission of the author.

As for the workers, why have they been willing to participate in experiments that could not be launched and surely could not be successfully implemented without their cooperation? What have they seen as their own possible gain in all this? To begin with, most factory work in Europe—as in the U.S.—leaves much to be desired. It is characterized by excessive noise, poor ventilation, frequent breakdowns in machinery, poor supervision, infrequent rest periods, and a host of other conditions workers find irksome. As a result, any effort on the part of management to address itself to these problems, provided the workers are convinced that the new approach is not aimed at getting them to produce more without commensurate adjustment in wages, will be seen as a boon. The fact that most experiments require the cooperation of only small numbers of workers—those who volunteer for them—makes it considerably easier to convince them on this point.

The volunteers frequently respond to improved communications and expanded decision-making powers, which are an integral part of many work structuring experiments. They like the idea of having more say about the specifics of the production process: and they enjoy the regularly scheduled conferences at which they learn about how their work fits into the larger picture. They also like the fact that the experiments relieve them of one or more layers of supervision and that they're given more room for initiative. In the case of autonomous work groups —a leading form of experimentation—the members frequently enjoy the camaraderie that develops, and most of them find themselves under less pressure than before, when the pace of work was set by the machine.

Four important principles noted by Ginzberg and others are: (1) the workers—and the unions, in organized situations—need to be convinced that the new approach is not aimed at getting them to produce more just to benefit management. (2) Participation in quality of work improvement should be voluntary, for those who wish to have more voice and take more responsibility in the company. (3) The focus of work structuring experiments should be improvement of conditions that the workers themselves have participated in identifying as unsatisfactory. (4) One clear result should be the opportunity for workers to take more initiative and have more voice in job-related decisions.

Rolf Lindholm's Guidelines

Rolf Lindholm, head of the technical department of the Swedish Employers' Confederation, offers some guidelines for work organization and job reform in his book *Job Reform in Sweden: Conclusions from 500 Shop Floor Projects.*[8] Lindholm notes that since 1969, Swedish industry has been swept up in a job reform movement that has assumed surprisingly broad dimensions. "There is scarcely a Swedish company in which active and intense attention is not being directed to new forms of work, new organizational structures, new wage systems, new working environments and/or new participation practices." The new procedures have consisted of the following:

- Increased emphasis on the objective of enhanced job satisfaction.
- Employees at a work site are given an opportunity, through the agency of various collaborative committees, to make their voices heard and to influence the design of their work.
- Work roles in production are being expanded, and group efforts are being striven for to a greater extent than hitherto.
- The piece-rate system is being replaced by new forms of compensation, usually entailing group incentive wages.
- The technical production apparatus and the physical environment are being developed through, for example, the addition of completely new and different factories.

According to Lindholm, the *driving forces* behind these developments are:

- Difficulties in recruiting staff for production work.
- Employee demands for co-determination and industrial democracy.

[8] R. Lindholm, *Job Reform in Sweden: Conclusions from 500 Shop Floor Projects,* D. Jenkins (Ed. and Trans.) (Stockholm: Swedish Employers' Confederation, 1975). Reprinted by permission.

- Ideas of behavioral scientists regarding autonomous or production groups.
- The need to increase efficiency.

As *criteria for judging the success of an approach to joint collaboration,* Lindholm cites the following:

- The new approaches should lead to *genuine* changes for the better in actual production work.
- Management and the local union branch should regard the results as successful and be prepared to continue and expand.
- There should be spontaneous interest and spontaneous spread to other parts of the company.
- Efficiency trends should be at least comparable to those attainable with conventional models.

In contrast, Lindholm notes *features found in unsuccessful attempts at co-determination.* These include:

- The use of fancy terms borrowed from politics or behavioral science.
- Elaborate written program statements.
- The inclusion of a personnel policy program.
- Collateral status with the works council.
- Imposed organization charts and diagrams.
- Excessive centrally determined rules.
- Quick introduction.
- Overabundant conferencing.
- In discussions, emphasis on trivia and shortcomings.
- Leadership by outsiders with different backgrounds from those of the departemnt's "ordinary staff."
- Advocacy principally by personnel managers, staff representatives, and so on.
- Expectation of public support despite private view of experimental failure.

The *detailed characteristics marking success* in companies that have tried the collaborative approach are noted by Lindholm as follows:

1. The objectives were almost always specified in terms of increased productivity, increased job satisfaction, and a better working environment.

2. The programs were designated by a simple pragmatic approach in which only a few initial measures were staked out, and were described in concrete, everyday terms.

3. All the expansion in collaboration took place within the work organization itself, and was supported and monitored by the works council, whose activities generally remained unchanged. Nonetheless, considerable efforts were made to incorporate new work procedures and collaborative routines, and line managers and skilled professionals from the production side played leading roles in the program.

4. Efforts began on a small scale; they encompassed the departments of one or two foremen in which the workers were interested in and willing to try out new ideas.

5. The program was usually guided and supported by a central group especially established for these matters. Considerable efforts were made to prepare participants for the new approach.

6. There were no written rules for collaborative procedures, but central efforts were made to supply the program with ideas.

7. Running production matters and change attempts were under continuous discussion, concrete changes in production occurred, and shortcomings in the work environment and in work planning were removed. Major contributions were made toward improved and more efficient production.

8. Collaboration in the conference room (or the foreman's booth) bore fruit in the form of new and more stimulating work roles.

9. There was a gradual and accelerating spread of new forms for collaboration and a new organization from the first few experimental departments.

10. Departmental production matters and questions on procedure and possible improvements provided nourishment for a constructive process of collaboration, free of organizational gimmicks.

11. Gradual liquidation of the "reference groups" and the other strictly formal arrangements as new ways of working became completely natural, and were integrated fully into the company's organization and day-to-day operations.

To facilitate job redesign efforts, Lindholm emphasizes the importance of the *special project group,* especially in situations that demand an unusual concentration of knowledge and resources to make the necessary studies and reach the right decisions. He explains:

It is in such situations that the project group has been found to be useful—a committee, a working group or, if the circumstances warrant, a project organization with many subgroups. Persons whose jobs will be affected by the planned change, along with union representatives, take part in the work. Some of the members of the group are selected because their skills are needed, others because they represent a particular "territory." The task to be done, its size, the objectives, resources and other details are set out in advance, and the group sets to work. When the job is finished the group is dissolved.

The project organization can be said to float somewhat above the basic organization. It is a device for assembling and organizing resources, on a temporary basis in a completely different dimension, but, for the purpose, a more practical one. Such groups have long been used by large companies, and to great effect.

Lindholm goes on to say that project groups "must be organized in such a way that genuine teamwork takes place, and not merely fruitless committee meetings. Such groups should be used only for the most important projects, so as to avoid the creation of a 'jungle' of committees."

There are difficulites that project groups are likely to face, such as constant competition with the regular work organization for the members' time and difficulty in communication because of the participants' diversity of backgrounds, abilities, and areas of expertise. However, according to Lindholm, the project groups will function well if they meet these five major criteria for success:

- The individual project groups should be small—preferably no more than six members—consisting only of those persons who are absolutely essential.
- All participation should be voluntary.
- Low-level employees experienced in the operations under study should be invited to participate and share their first-hand knowledge.
- Best results are achieved when working in groups is a normal activity and when communication and cooperation skills are highly developed.
- The project groups and the "work environment" should be coordinated along the following lines: narrow at the top and bottom, wide at the middle. At the top there is a project management that coordinates the work. In the broad middle range are the various specialist groups, each of which concentrates on specific, limited areas. At the bottom, there should be one group whose job it is to see that working conditions and the work organization are as favorable as possible. This group should be headed by someone from the project management group at the top, and ordinary workers must be represented. This group should be kept well-informed on the work of the middle groups.

In his book, Lindholm also discusses the manner in which work should be conducted in the light of criticisms leveled at work on the factory floor by the press and by trade unions. Several of his suggestions for meeting these criticisms are given below:

- Extension of the work cycle by including a longer sequence of cyclical, repetitive production steps in a given work task.
- Integration of production and auxiliary tasks by including occasional collateral duties such as lubrication, maintenance, transport, and so on.

- Decentralization of authority and responsibility down to the individual and group level in, for example, planning matters and quality control.

- Job rotation, either by means of a limited, multi-skill training program meant to increase the workers' familiarity with jobs adjacent to their own but not intended to be permanent, or through spontaneous, continuous rotation because the job demands it ("group work"). Job rotation programs that entail a circulation schedule or arrangements for the worker to follow the product through the production system have proved unsuccessful.

- A matrix organization in production and maintenance.

- Organization of production-line work stations so that good communications and movements of personnel are maintained—without, however, inhibiting the individual's ability to carry out certain hand movements or make certain observations.

- Attention given to sound-level factors on the factory floor.

- The building of completely new production systems and factories in order to facilitate the introduction of the new organizational ideas.

The role of the new leader under the autonomous group program is next discussed. In the spring of 1974, SALF (the Swedish Confederation of Supervisory Employees) and the Swedish Metalworkers' Union (the largest union in the LO group) met and published a declaration which suggests that the development of new organizational forms on the shop floor is considered highly important. Regarding the role of the supervisor, the statement indicates that the Metalworkers' Union believes the position of supervisor not only should not disappear but should be strengthened:

. . . the Confederation of Supervisory Employees and the Metalworkers' Union believe that they have a joint responsibility to work for changes in company organizations in the direction of a decentralization of decisions, and that the prevailing division of functions should be changed so that the decision-making process, which is now concentrated on staff and specialist levels, [would] be moved closer to production departments.

We believe it is urgent that groups of employees, together with supervisors, be granted greater authority and responsibility so that they can jointly plan, organize, and check their own production work.

The present system, in which the organization of production is decided far from the shop floor and over the heads of production workers, must be broken. It must be replaced by a democratic order in which workers have the guaranteed right to participate in matters that concern them. Although this demand rests essentially on the wish for an enrichment of job content and a higher quality of life, we are convinced that company efficiency will increase if this overall view is put into practice. . . .

Lindholm comments that these groups' ideal picture of a work organization corresponds to what he calls a "product shop" rather than an autonomous group without a leader. He further notes that

supervisors in Sweden have played a key role in the process [of job redesign] and have made some valuable contributions. Their own duties have developed in a direction that they themselves have judged to be desirable and worthwhile. They have also participated in the remolding of workers' roles so that both sides can get more out of their work. Finally, the overall result has been beneficial for companies' financial results.

Lines of development for the role of supervisor can be summarized as follows:

- Every employee, and every group of employees—including those who are technically designated as "autonomous"—will always need a leader. Absolute autonomy in a work organization, whether with respect to individuals or entire groups, is a utopia.

- Supervisory roles in production are steadily changing. The people in these positions will find it necessary to meet new demands placed on them.

- Production groups in which the members are responsible for meeting day-to-day problems will become a common organizational form. Because they operate with a great deal of independence, this will eliminate a considerable amount of the supervisors' involvement in "putting out fires."

- The concept of "team leaders" and similar persons, which has increasingly come to the fore in Sweden and elsewhere, will doubtless continue in importance. This trend will also result in relieving supervisors of many of their routine chores, but it will not eliminate the need for supervisors.

- The increasing desire of workers to have something to say about their own work will create new and difficult demands on supervisors, who will have to learn to discuss, not order; to present workers with problems, not ready-made solutions.

- Handling coordination between groups and relations with other entities in the company will become an increasingly important part of the work of supervisors.

- To be eager to use the knowledge of others, to delegate responsibility, to carry responsibility for the *development* of an operation, to think in terms of the future—all of this will become necessary for supervisors and managers on all levels.

- An evolution of the present supervisory role—from a situation of being rigidly tied to numerous small tasks to an arrangement including responsibility for the steady development of an operation—means that there will be new and stimulating jobs for supervisors, but also a demand for new ways of thinking and for greater knowledge.

- This greater knowledge can be acquired only partly through participation in seminars and conferences. It is also important to learn more about the activities and financial position of one's own company, about methods of attaining greater efficiency, about the possibilities of developing one's own activities, and about contributions that supervisors can make to increased involvement in company activities.

- The "in-between" position experienced by many supervisors today, consisting of feelings of isolation from higher and lower levels, will be changed to an active supervisory role that will command confidence and respect.

- The role of first-line supervisors in production cannot be broadened and developed without a considerable degree of responsibility, authority, and whole-hearted support from top management.

- Supervisors will have the roles they deserve in the future. Those who have the interest, will, and capacity to develop themselves and their jobs will unquestionably achieve new and rewarding positions in the companies of the future. Developments are already in motion, and so far, supervisors have not needed to be pushed—they have been eager to take part.

In his final comments, Lindholm refers again to two of the driving forces for change in Sweden: the desire for more attractive jobs and the desire for increased efficiency. The two objectives are at times found to be in conflict. There are other potential limitations on progress, such as conditions imposed by competition with other countries, by existing and not readily changed production equipment, and by the absence of an organized theory regarding the renewal of production technology. Lindholm believes, however, that there are positive factors involved. For example, the Swedish predilection for cooperation can help bridge the gap between the desire for better working conditions and increased production efficiency.

Integration and Recommendations—Edward Glaser & Associates (EGA)[9]

Among the researchers, consultants, and experienced practitioners who have been involved with efforts to improve quality of

[9] Edward Glaser & Associates is a firm of psychological consultants to organizations, established in 1952 and with headquarters in Los Angeles. The industrial-social-clinical psychologists in the group have had experience with a considerable number of companies in connection with organization development and other relevant efforts to improve the quality of worklife and, in the process, productivity.

worklife and productivity, there is general agreement that attention needs to be focused on:

1. Trying to elicit the understanding, commitment, and support of the concept at the highest management level of the organization (or *at least* the highest level in the division, department, or plant where such a program is to be tried).

2. Arranging for a company interested in undertaking such an effort to visit some other companies that have worked out successful, sustained programs of this type; also, encouraging some relevant reading.

3. Developing practicable ways of arranging for the members of given functional work groups to participate in task review, problem identification, problem solving, and goal setting; and in unionized situations, working out a modus operandi that is likely to elicit union support and participation.

4. Structuring the work—where practicable and desirable—into relatively small (5–25-person) task-group teams *if* that evolves from step three.

5. Providing open channels for communication and systematic feedback of progress (from baseline measures) to all concerned.

6. Obtaining assessment data at periodic intervals regarding the organization's effectiveness—data on productivity, return on investment, perceptions of management style, intergroup relations, problems, opportunities, suggestions; inviting any who feel concerned to volunteer for service on ad hoc problem-solving committees or temporary task forces.

7. Offering the special resources of a knowledgeable and experienced consultant, whether from in-house staff or from outside, to the organization and the task teams wherever wanted or needed; at the same time, making sure that the planning and implementation of the improvement effort belongs to the company—that it is the *company's* program, not the consultant's.

8. Studying the pros and cons of providing incentives, perhaps through a share in cost savings resulting from workforce-derived productivity improvement.

9. Keeping the organization's "eye on the ball," the ball or end result being to enhance the organization's effectiveness and efficiency in task performance as well as to manifest creative concern for the quality of working life rather than ritualistically following any prescribed management style in all cases.

10. Keeping in mind an objective whereby all constituencies can "win" simultaneously: customers, company, work group, individuals, unions if the work site is unionized, investors, and public without the gains to any one group being at the expense of others.

The author—from his own experience, a review of the experiences of others, and a study of the literature—has drawn the following conclusions, which can constitute guidelines for introducing a job redesign or quality of work improvement program:

1. If long-term gains are to be made and maintained, the top manager of the company (or of whatever division, department, or subsidiary that is interested in a quality of work program) needs to understand and give sustained commitment to the philosophy and practice of that program. Personal role modeling of any espoused modus operandi is a good way to demonstrate it.

2. Once the high-level decision is made to explore ways of operating under a philosophy of invited employee participation in job design, work structure, or whatever aspects of the operation seem appropriate, then all concerned, from the top down, need to understand the concept and become colleagues in planning the implementation program.

    The concept and implementation programs, however, are not ends in themselves. They are *means* for achieving more effective and efficient task performance, plus enhanced job satisfaction. It often is better to avoid labels such as "participative management" or "job enrichment"; instead, just figure out how to distribute influence from a top power center to all levels of the organization in ways that are likely to tap the creativity and resources of all employees. Review cases such as Donnelly Mirrors, Volvo, and the others in this book for ideas or *modus operandi* that may seem suitable for your organization. The main purpose of the program should be to encourage the members of task groups to become ego-involved and participate in helping to improve the quality of their worklife (thereby improving the effectiveness, efficiency, and productivity of the organization so that it can survive, be in a good position to share its success with the workforce, and better serve its customers and society). The attitudinal component of this is nondefensive encouragement and reinforcement from top management downward for constructive challenge of standard procedures, in a continual quest for improvement and excellence in every aspect of organizational or operational performance.

A company's readiness to embark on a worklife improvement program should be carefully assessed before deciding what steps may be appropriate to initiate. In some situations, a survey of employee perceptions and their suggestions for improvement, along with the setting up of some program for constructive follow-through, would be a simple way to invite broader employee participation. At other companies there may be readiness to try more comprehensive experiments in job enrichment—such as forming modular work units or combining tasks. In still other situations it may be desirable to invite employees to review standard practices, such as work rules, discipline specifications, fringe-benefit arrangements, and so on. The objective, with economic and technical factors kept in clear view, should be improvement in both mission performance and job satisfaction.

A survey, if undertaken, could be part of an overall organizational development effort. It might include a small task force or council or steering committee, often best set up with membership from various levels, to: (a) review (become familiar with) objectives, plans, and programs of the organization or segment of the organization being studied; (b) interview administrators and staff at all levels to identify problems, determine probable causes of the problems, and make recommendations for improvement; (c) supplement personal interviews with a carefully constructed, brief questionnaire to a broader sample—or to anyone in the organization who wishes to respond; (d) feedback the findings in coherent form to management and then to others who might appropriately be involved; (e) implement "breakthrough" projects, pilot efforts, or new policies and procedures to meet important identified problems—again involving interested persons from various levels; (f) monitor, ascertain, evaluate, and feed back results from any changes made; (g) repeat the process of organizational assessment from time to time in a never-ending nurture of development, improvement, and renewal.

3. For a company interested in pursuing quality of worklife improvement through work restructuring, one of the best ways to begin is by having some personal contact and interaction with respected kindred organizations that have successful "living demonstrations" of such programs. A special study team of interested personnel (rather than any single individual) should be invited to volunteer to visit such other companies. Background reading[10] will then be more meaningful.

4. The entire task group with which a quality of worklife program is to be implemented, not just the volunteer study team, should be invited to develop criteria for effective group performance. They also should have a voice in establishing ways to get baseline evaluation of existing performance, and ways to measure periodic progress. Consultants who are skillful in

[10] The author particularly recommends Alfred Marrow's *The Failure of Success*; the HEW 1972 task force report on *Work in America*; Robert Ford's *Motivation Through the Work Itself*; the American Assembly's *The Worker and the Job;* Hackman *et al.*'s *A New Strategy for Job Enrichment;* and David Jenkins's *Job Power.* See the bibliography for complete publication information.

group process, problem solving, and the introduction of change and evaluation—whether they are internal or external to the organization—can be helpful here. In a company where the workers are union members, a sincere effort should be made to invite the union's collaboration.

5. The greatest productivity gains over time have often come through improvements in product design and production methods. Such improvements are likely to be boosted appreciably when the workforce members (not just the engineers) are invited to participate in those efforts. The case report on quality control circles in Japan cited in Chapter II outlined one method (and the requisite training needed) for involving nonmanagement personnel in quality improvement efforts. Be careful, however, to avoid asking people to do what they really are not capable of doing, thereby inviting a sense of failure. At the same time, do provide the opportunity to learn, stretch, and grow; to experience a sense of successful achievement. Competence in the staffing for given task-performance responsibilities, particularly managerial and supervisory competence, is a *sine qua non* for excellence, as is workforce potential for learning what is truly required.

6. In the early stages of change from an authoritative to a consultative or participative work structure, a task team should have available all the resource-person help or guidance it may want. Either a resource person or a specially designated ombudsman should be readily available to the group in this transition stage.

It is important that some appropriate structure be set up in the organization to assure sustained commitment to the team approach and to other concomitants of a QWL improvement program. One way to achieve this might be to invite each major segment of the organization, such as sales, the key production components, accounting, and quality assurance, to nominate two volunteers to participate in a steering committee. One person from each major department might be a supervisor and one a nonsupervisor. Such an arrangement might add up to a group of about 10–14 persons who would constitute an internal steering committee or council to provide thrust, support, and nurture to the program as well as to monitor it. This group would develop its own knowledge about quality of worklife improvement and would also bring in new ideas from the outside. For example, the group might make contact with other companies in the region operating in a similar management style, or attend occasional workshops or courses related to QWL and productivity improvement.

A related requirement is to provide an excellent, ongoing internal training or organizational development (OD) program, both for refresher purposes and to orient groups of new employees in the philosophy and practice of this style of management. Such training (which was referred to in point 5) can be led by a competent internal training officer or by a knowledgeable consultant working in tandem with the inside staff. This training is needed to support the efforts of the steering committee referred to above. Its emphasis, however, might well be on how to carry out the role-modeling, learn-by-doing approach discussed in point 2 above rather than on abstract conceptual material. Training in listening skills, problem solving, conflict resolution, and techniques for developing group agreement on performance goals plus appropriate assessment and feedback regarding goal attainment can sharpen the management and supervisory skills needed for successful modeling of the desired roles.

The nontraditional QWL program requires systematic support in order for the change to last long enough in its original (and enthusiasm-generating) form to become internalized and hence self-maintaining.

A word of warning to any outside consultant: He should minimize possible credit ascribed to him by management if the program progresses successfully. His stance should never imply that his help was anything more than that of facilitator, catalyst, resource person, or perhaps occasionally gadfly for getting the organization's personnel to work more effectively together in identification and constructive resolution of their problems and opportunities.

7. Time should be set aside for a periodic (and fairly frequent) review by all concerned. Some questions that should be discussed are: "How are we doing?" and "What changes or modifications in policy or procedure might we like to try in order to overcome problems or make further improvement?" The general thrust here is "What can we learn from the events of the yesterdays and today to shape better tomorrows?"

8. Top management of the organization—or at least of the division involved—should give recognition and reward (positive reinforcement) for any unusual, noteworthy accomplishment by a task group. This is in addition to the day-by-day recognition for noteworthy achievements or tasks well done.

9. Any persistent problems in the operation should be studied by all concerned. The atmosphere should be problem solving and not culprit seeking.

10. After the change has been in operation for a year or two, surveys should be made at regular intervals to find any problems or suggestions which have not come to light through the everyday communication channels provided. Such surveys are best made through confidential, open-ended interviews conducted by someone the members trust—perhaps (but not necessarily) an outside consultant.

11. If the group improves productivity, all members should share in these gains. Cost-savings-sharing arrangements, such as adaptations of the Scanlon Plan, might be examined in depth. (See the Donnelly Mirrors case in Chapter II.)

    As noted earlier, jealousy and dissension may result among workers who are not participating in the experiment if one segment of the organization—an experimental group—is drawing higher pay in any form, whether from the productivity gains or from some different way of evaluating their pay grades. When success has been demonstrated and if the principles can be extended to the entire operation, this may be the ripe time to introduce cost-savings-sharing for the entire workforce.

12. The decision to move a traditionally structured organization toward a more open, participative style of operation can lead to various problems attendant on the introduction of a major

change. The management of change is a closely related subject which has its own voluminous literature.[11]

If a summary of a summary might be of value, five of the most important conditions for the sustained success of quality of work-life improvement programs, from which there is likelihood that productivity gains also may emerge, are:

- Giving all employees in an organization or whole segment thereof an opportunity to have a meaningful voice in decisions about the design and structure of their work.
- Providing sustained support of the quality of worklife efforts by the organization's leaders.
- Involving the line organization in designing and then assuming responsibility for the program as (rather than the staff's or consultant's), so that it can be perceived essentially as a better *modus operandi* for human-resource management, which in turn is likely to result in better mission performance.
- Working out specific, difficult, but definitely attainable goals with task groups or individuals wherever feasible, with a system of rewards for goal attainment and an adequate training program, providing structure and frequent timely feedback to let all concerned know about progress and problems.
- Monitoring or auditing in helpful, rather than "snoopervisory," ways to assist in problem solving and to assure high standards of performance.

Some General Ways of Getting Started on a Program: A Recap

A vital question in planning a successful QWL program is how to win the sustained support of top management. The following suggestions recapitulate comments made in other sections of this book.

---

[11] A practical start on that subject is offered by G. Watson and E. Glaser in an article entitled "What We Have Learned About Planning for Change," *Management Review*, November 1965, *54*, 34–46.

One helpful method is for the advocate of change—the personnel manager, plant supervisor, or whoever—to summarize what is being proposed, together with an honest assessment of the anticipated benefits, the costs, and the possible risks. The report should then be submitted to the executives whose sponsorship is vital to the program's success. If the situation permits, discuss the matter beforehand, then ask for another meeting after the proposal has been read. This works better than trying to resolve questions and make decisions on pieces of paper going back and forth.

The advocate's report should not be presented as a finished recommendation, but as a draft inviting serious critique by the executives and, where appropriate, any union officials whose sponsorship and participation are needed. The second draft should reflect questions or criticisms offered and presumably discussed in the first round. It is obviously helpful if there is a company where a similar program is in operation, to which a visit can be arranged.

Another approach is to have the interested supervisor or manager simply discuss his idea first with his immediate boss. The program can be presented as an experiment in better management that he would like to try, with the expectation that it will lead to better task performance as well as increased job satisfaction. The manager or supervisor then might outline the plan to the personnel who would be involved, explain the reasons and objectives, and invite a free airing of questions and criticisms. If the consensus is that the idea is worth trying, the next steps are to set up a planning committee and consider engaging a consultant with successful experience in facilitating quality of work improvement programs.

No matter how the program gets started, it is desirable to agree on criteria of effectiveness and, if feasible, get some measures of present performance so that progress from baseline can be calculated and periodic reports on progress provided. The Hackman and Oldham Job Diagnostic Survey (JDS) can be of real value in this connection.

Nothing should be done in one part of an organization which cannot in due time be spread to other parts if the results seem favorable to all concerned. Resentments can build up if one segment is seen by others as receiving advantages that cannot be made generally available to the rest of the workers. At the same time it usually is best to start slowly, with a segment of the organization or a pilot program, and "debug" it before installing it on a large scale.

Reif and Monczka,[12] in a paper that discusses conditions that are most and least favorable to the eventual outcome of any job enrichment or job redesign project, offer the following 24 sets of bipolar statements. These statements can constitute an organizational audit or a situational analysis of whether the organizational climate appears ready and able to support what we would term quality of worklife improvement projects:

An Organizational-Audit Format for Job Enrichment

	MOST FAVORABLE CONDITIONS FOR IMPLEMENTATION	LEAST FAVORABLE CONDITIONS FOR IMPLEMENTATION
A. Job design		
1. Variety	Little variety exists because of the way jobs are presently structured, but there is potential for variety because there are a large number of parts, tools, and controls that can be manipulated, and the work pace, physical location, and prescribed physical operation of work can be modified to meet individual requirements.	The work environment is such that little potential for increasing variety exists (for example, a toll booth attendant on a highway).

[12] W. E. Reif and R. M. Monczka, "Job Redesign: A Contingency Approach to Implementation," *Personnel*, May–June 1974. © 1974 by AMACOM, a division of American Management Associations. Reprinted by permission of the publisher.

An Organizational-Audit Format for Job Enrichment (*continued*)

	MOST FAVORABLE CONDITIONS FOR IMPLEMENTATION	LEAST FAVORABLE CONDITIONS FOR IMPLEMENTATION
2. Autonomy	Inputs to the job and methods of doing the job (procedures, sequence, pace, etc.) do not have to be totally dictated to the worker by the production/operation system.	The production/operation system defines work flow, methods, pace, and sequence, and changes cannot be made without seriously affecting scheduling, line balance, worker efficiency, and output levels.
3. Interaction	The opportunity exists for people to work together as a team—that is, the job naturally requires the coordination of tasks or activities among several workers.	The job can be performed best by an individual working alone.
4. Knowledge and skill	The job can be made more challenging by adding additional or more complex tasks, and workers are capable of meeting more demanding job requirements.	It would be inefficient to incorporate new tasks into the existing job structure, and/or increasing worker proficiency would be difficult to achieve.
5. Responsibility	It is feasible to reduce reliance on the "only one way to do the job" approach to performing work and making work-related decisions.	It would be economically or technically unrealistic to allow variability in the way job situations are handled.

	MOST FAVORABLE CONDITIONS FOR IMPLEMENTATION	LEAST FAVORABLE CONDITIONS FOR IMPLEMENTATION
6. Task identity	The job can be redesigned so that the worker can see the value of his work in terms of its contribution to the total work effort.	An increase in the scope of the job would reduce the likelihood that the individual could successfully complete his task efficiently.
7. Feedback	It would not be difficult to redesign the control system to provide workers on a regular basis with information about their job performance.	Information cannot be readily provided workers because of cost and data collection problems.
8. Pay	The wage payment plan is not based solely on output.	Workers are paid under a straight piece-work wage plan.
9. Working conditions	Working conditions, along with other hygiene factors, are perceived as satisfactory by most workers.	Working conditions are considered to be unsatisfactory by most workers.
10. Cycle time	Short, with potential for expansion.	Longer cycle times would interfere with other, interrelated work activities.

B. *Psychosocial environment*

1. Personality	Workers are self-confident and achievement-oriented.	Workers lack self-confidence and have low achievement drives.

An Organizational-Audit Format for Job Enrichment (*continued*)

	MOST FAVORABLE CONDITIONS FOR IMPLEMENTATION	LEAST FAVORABLE CONDITIONS FOR IMPLEMENTATION
2. Work attitudes, values, and beliefs	Workers are positively oriented toward the work ethic and willingly accept change.	Workers do not readily identify with the work ethic and fear change.
3. Position in need hierarchy	Workers are primarily concerned with fulfilling higher-level needs (esteem, autonomy, and self-actualization).	Workers are primarily concerned with fulfilling lower-level needs (physiological and security).
4. Knowledge and skills	Workers are capable of developing their talents to the fullest and motivated to do so.	Workers have little interest in developing new knowledge and skills, or lack the capacity to do so.
5. Work-group characteristics	Younger, more highly educated.	Little education, unsatisfying work experiences.
C. *Technology*		
1. Dominance	Workers, not technology, are primarily responsible for output and quality levels.	Emphasis on equipment, machines, and systems in job design; technology primarily dictates the quantity and quality of work.
2. Cost	Low dollar investment in technology.	High dollar investment in technology.
3. State of technology	Technology is available to improve the quality of working life.	Technology is not capable of dealing with problems of worker dissatisfaction.

D. Management

	MOST FAVORABLE CONDITIONS FOR IMPLEMENTATION	LEAST FAVORABLE CONDITIONS FOR IMPLEMENTATION
4. Organization's ability to apply technology	High, in both a technical and managerial sense.	Low.
1. Management philosophy	Concerned with the utilization of human resources to the mutual benefit of the individual and the organization.	Primarily concerned with production; view job enrichment only as a means of increasing output.
2. Attitude toward change	Positive.	Negative.
3. Leadership style	Democratic, employee-centered.	Authoritarian, task-centered.
4. Super-subordinate relationships	Built on Theory Y set of assumptions about work behavior.	Built on Theory X set of assumptions about work behavior.
5. Union-management relationships	Open, supportive.	Closed, antagonistic.

V □ Some Questions Answered – and Others Still Unanswered

Here are eleven questions frequently raised in companies in the process of deciding whether or not to embark on quality of worklife and productivity improvement programs.

1. Is any company capable of undertaking a quality of work program?

No. The top management and the supporting cast need to clarify for themselves what they mean—what is involved in a quality of work program. They need to understand that at the least it is concerned with the structure and processes of the work itself, and of the organizational context within which the work occurs. Further, they have to "give a damn"—even if they do so only to reduce labor problems and increase profits. Beyond a willing spirit, there must also be the patience and readiness to sustain a deep commitment. If a QWL activity is not painstakingly planned, based on careful diagnosis of problems and an assessment of the *learning readiness* of the various parts of the organization that would have to be involved in the program, it probably will fail.

2. If a company seems incapable of undertaking what might be termed a humanization of work program, what changes are needed to gain such capability?

This depends on the reasons for the company's unwillingness, inability, or nonreadiness. In some cases management and/or union attitudes and practices need attention first. In other cases, the main obstacle may be the technology itself; a negligible labor involvement in a highly automated production process; management's fear of losing control or "stirring up the natives"; or concerns about having to revamp the reward system, such as by instituting cost-savings sharing.

Before an enterprise tries to make the necessary changes, it should first find leadership that wants to explore the new directions. Next comes personal contact with one or more somewhat similar companies that have had successful experience with such programs and a study of the conditions that seem essential for the observed success. This should be followed by collaborative planning by all the people necessary for successful implementation, and a pilot tryout.

Qualified consultants may be able to help in the role of resource persons, catalysts, facilitators of learning readiness, and (if readiness is present) trainers.

3. Have worklife improvement programs to date been limited to small companies in the Western world using mainly middle-class employees?

No. Large companies in both Japan and India, as well as large and small companies in the United States and Europe, have tested and are still experimenting with ways to improve the quality of work and increase productivity. Many U.S. companies are doing so with workforces in which a large percentage are classified as disadvantaged.

It is interesting to note here, however, that most of the very large corporations reporting noteworthy success with job enrichment or efforts to improve the quality of worklife in some division of their company (AT&T, General Electric, General Foods, Imperial Chemical, Motorola, Procter & Gamble) have not yet introduced these successful programs throughout the firm, whereas some smaller companies, like Donnelly Mirrors, have carried the principles into all segments of their operation.

4. Is there any evidence that good results from the experimental programs are sustained?

Yes, but not always. Few cases reported in the literature evaluate change over time, but there are several longitudinal studies. Some companies have been operating cost-savings-sharing or productivity-sharing plans (which include worker participation in job design) for up to 35 years, with continued good results as measured by reduction in labor costs, grievances, turnover, absenteeism, and machine downtime. Other companies not using group financial incentives (AT&T, Motorola, Polaroid, Procter & Gamble, Texas Instruments) have sustained desirable results from job enrichment efforts for lengths of time varying from three to nine years.

5. Should it be assumed that most workers today are alienated, and that nearly all workers would respond favorably to a job-enrichment program?

No. Available survey evidence suggests that, on the whole, most workers do not now feel alienated, although they do evince some *degree* of alienation in many situations. An overall approach to the humanization of work seems to be desired by most but not all workers, according to reports from companies with well-planned programs of employee involvement in job design and other matters that affect them. Those who do not want increased responsibility or do not want to learn new skills will need a specially tailored approach to cope with their feelings. This minority should be permitted to continue in their still-needed and familiar tasks so long as they perform satisfactorily. As Sam Zagoria, director of the Labor-Management Relations Service of the National League of Cities has observed,

All workers are not alike; they are not cast from the same mold. They come in assorted shapes, sizes, education and experience, attitudes and ambitions. Some work for a living; for others working is living. Some think of work as their central purpose in life; others consider work as a way of providing the necessities and look to the time away from work as the real joy of living. The net of this is that while many workers look on their jobs as unexciting, boring, repetitive exercises that require only part of their potential capability, others enjoy the regularity, repetition, and steadiness of a job. They are delighted to leave to a management all the headaches and heartaches of a competitive, high risk economy. Truly, one man's straitjacket may be another's security blanket. . . . In sum, workers vary in their job objectives. For most, whether by conscious choice or unconscious acceptance of life as they find it, a job which provides a living is enough. For others, and in increasing numbers I suspect, taking home a paycheck is not enough— they want a chance for self-fulfillment in the many years they spend in the workplace.

6. **We read a lot about firms such as AT&T, Donnelly Mirrors, General Foods, Motorola, Polaroid, and Texas Instruments in which efforts to improve organizational effectiveness and efficiency through quality of work programs have been successful. Have there been many failures or disappointments following such efforts?**

Yes. Indeed there have been failures and disappointments, some of them examined in this book. To borrow a concept from the psychology of learning, quality of work programs do not present a simple stimulus/response situation. If you apply a burning match to any normal person's skin, you will get an "ouch," or pain response. Instead, the learning principle here can be diagrammed:

$$S \rightarrow C \rightarrow O \rightarrow R$$

S, the stimulus (i.e., the quality of work program) is applied under *C,* certain conditions—including given qualities of appropriate planning, skill, and timing—to *O,* an organization having its own history, readiness for change, and feelings of commitment (or lack thereof). All of this then leads to *R,* certain responses and results.

In other words, the same fire can melt the butter or harden the egg. It would seem that when a program has been successful in many organizations with different sorts of people and under different conditions, something can be generalized about the principles involved. The fact remains, however, that in a number of cases job enrichment efforts have not worked out well and have been discontinued. There may be things that can be generalized from those experiences too, such as the common problems and pitfalls summarized in Chapter III. Perhaps job enrichment efforts can be compared with medical or surgical procedures: Although helpful in many cases, they haven't worked out well in others. It may be in the variables: the condition of the patient at the time of treatment, the diagnosis, the appropriateness of the intervention, the skill of the physician, the degree of intelligent cooperation of the patient, the care in preparation for the surgery, and the treatment following it.

7. Is it possible to identify the factors (i.e., the dimensions of the person, organization, environment, or task) that seem essential to successful outcomes?

Yes, to a degree, but not with certainty. This question was discussed in some detail in Chapter IV. *Some* of the dimensions that make a difference seem to be: (1) sustained commitment from management to the open, nondefensive modus operandi of sincerely inviting the workforce to help identify problems and suggest improvements, with incentives provided for such participation; (2) invited involvement of task groups in recommending solutions for identified problems; (3) training of supervisors to equip them to function effectively in this less directive style; (4) implementation of practicable suggestions, and explanations of reasons for ideas being rejected; (5) feedback, and recognition for good results achieved; (6) selection of personnel who can be motivated, under appropriate conditions, to "give a damn" about striving for excellence in task performance; (7) evaluation and analysis of results, including failures, leading to revised efforts toward continual improvement in modus operandi.

8. Why, despite clear evidence of significant gains in productivity following the establishment of job enrichment programs in certain companies, has there been no follow-through? Why, in some cases, has the program been scuttled when compelling evidence points to success?

We think we have some partial answers. Job enrichment programs pose a psychological threat to certain managers, union leaders, and the bureaucracy. They tend to challenge or at least depart from traditional values and structures. The concept of inviting workers to have a voice and influence in all aspects of a task, and of providing open channels of communication at all levels, does mean giving up some of the conventional authority exercised by the company or union bosses. If commitment is dubious at the start, relatively minor problems or costs can readily be exaggerated, followed by reversion to traditional, more comfortable ways of operating. Furthermore, in some cases the initial good results do not in fact continue. This may occur for a variety of reasons—loss of initial internal leadership, commitment, and skills; new technical problems; equity issues; collective bargaining dynamics; unforeseen stress and crisis, such as a serious shrinkage in sales (and thus personnel layoffs) resulting from bad economic conditions; and so on.

Richard Walton conducted a study of the reasons for the limited diffusion in seven out of eight successful experiments in work restructuring. The barriers he identified were:[1]

- Emergent weaknesses or lack of sustained success in the pilot projects, which in turn may be caused by: (1) internal inconsistencies in the original design; (2) loss of support from levels of management above the experimental unit; (3) premature turnover of leaders, operators, or consultants directly associated with a project; (4) stress and crises that lead to more authoritarian management, which in turn demoralizes the innovative unit; (5) tension in the innovative unit's relations with other parties—peer units, staff groups, superiors, labor unions; (6) letdown in participants' involvement after initial success with its attendant publicity; (7) lack of diffusion to other parts of the organization, which isolates the original experiment and its leaders.

- Atypical character of the pilot project in relation to the rest of the system, causing it to lack credibility as a viable demonstration.

[1] R. E. Walton, "The Diffusion of New Work Structures," *Organizational Dynamics,* Winter 1975, *3,* 3–22. © 1975 by AMACOM, a division of American Management Associations. Reprinted by permission of the publisher.

- Confusion over what is to be diffused; failure to make clear that the policy was for managers to pursue certain *aims* rather than to employ particular *techniques*.

- Inappropriateness or lack of realism of the concepts employed.

- Deficient implementation or inadequate follow-through in terms of locating accountability for the change and providing "how-to" knowledge.

- Lack of manifest, sustained top management commitment to the effort, and [lack of] continuing interest.

- Union opposition—lack of union support or acceptance in situations where the workforce is unionized.

- Bureaucratic barriers, vested interests, and existing organizational routines that limit local autonomy.

- Threatened obsolescence of people's established roles, skills, knowledge, and patterns of functioning which may be required by a restructured work situation.

- Self-limiting dynamics such as a "star envy" phenomenon, where the attention given to the experimental project engenders resentment and envy among other persons asked to adopt the innovation in their own operations.

9. Why have so few companies tried upgrading the quality of life at work when evidence of promising results and descriptions of methodology have frequently appeared in the management, personnel, and behavioral science literature since the early 1960s?

Again, it is possible to supply an opinion but not a definite answer to this important question. As above, management fears play a part. Inviting participation in decision making from persons "down the line" (and perhaps their union representatives) implies to some people a loss of control and an attenuation of management prerogatives, responsibility, and authority. Further, job enrichment efforts require a willingness to engage in considerable planning *with* the workforce, and the concomitant patience involved, before making decisions that affect them. Many organizations feel uncomfortable with this style of management. In addition, if the workforce below them in the hierarchy is invited to identify things that need improvement, some managers consciously or unconsciously fear that *their* boss will wonder why they seemingly hadn't been aware of those problems or opportunities before and thus perhaps wonder about their capability or whether they are "on top of things."

Finally, unions may fear losing status with their members if individual workers' ideas and suggestions can be discussed directly with a receptive management in a "non-adversary" climate.

10. If you asked all personnel in organizations reporting success with their quality of work programs if they wished to continue to organize and structure the work the way it is now, or change it, what would the probable answer be?

Continue, but with regular review and openness to refinement based on experience. In the few situations where this questioning has been tried (on an informal basis), some 80 percent of the personnel expressed a desire to continue the consultative format.

11. What seem to be the major areas of new knowledge needed to facilitate the introduction and successful carrying through of QWL improvement programs?

A succinct summary follows. It is a review of further R&D needs as perceived by an organization that has funded several studies in this field, and with which the author concurs from his experience and review of the literature:[2]

Knowledge is presently limited or inadequate in four areas: first, the process of intervention in existing organizations in order to reorient values, attitudes, and the structures of jobs and organizations on QWL principles; second, the process of designing *new* work organizations on those principles; third, the process of spreading innovations from small experimental beginnings to larger portions of workplaces; and fourth, the process of managing sizable organizations composed of work units based on these approaches.

Three other needs could be added—namely, to survey what business schools and graduate-level management training programs

[2] From personal correspondence.

offer regarding the theory and practice of QWL programs; to survey student reactions to the programs offered and students' degree of interest in using QWL improvement programs in their own job situations; and to explore further the frequent resistance of organized labor to such programs and way of meeting understandable suspicions.

VI.☐ Outline of an Evaluation Procedure

An organization about to embark on a quality of work program that it hopes will also improve productivity needs to devise ways of measuring the results of its efforts. It should also assess systematically the "readiness" of the organization to make such a change and carry it through successfully.

Howard R. Davis, chief of the Mental Health Services Development Branch, National Institute of Mental Health (NIMH), Rockville, Maryland, has developed a model for understanding what appear to be the principal factors underlying change in human systems, using the acronym A VICTORY. The model is based on the principle of synergism—the force of relevant factors working together. Among the several uses to which the model may be put are: (1) determining the readiness of a given system or organization to adopt a specified change; and (2) identifying the "weak links"

[1] Portions of this brief summary were excerpted from H. R. Davis & S. E. Salasin, "The Utilization of Evaluation." In B. Struening & M. Guttentag (Eds.), *Handbook of Evaluation Research*, Vol. I (Beverly Hills, Calif.: Sage Publications, 1975).

among the eight factors that may need strengthening before the change efforts per se are launched into.

Davis evolved the A VICTORY formulation from a behavioral model of change adapted from learning theory, embracing such considerations as drive or motivation, the ability or capacity of the learner, and circumstances or stimulus conditions. Results from a number of experiments on adoption of innovations, as well as from literature surveys, have been matched with the behavioral factors.

The factors, or elements, of this model are defined briefly as follows:

1. *Ability*—the capability required to adopt the innovation. Includes freedom from sanctions; sufficient fiscal, manpower, and physical resources; freedom from overweening competing demands.

2. *Values*—the nature of the innovation. Refers to values implicit in its adoption, both generally and from the standpoint of organizational attributes relevant to its success, such as compatibility with the value system of particular decision makers.

3. *Information*—the clarity and communication qualities of the innovation; information relevant to understanding how the innovation will help solve a problem.

4. *Circumstances*—stimulus conditions or environmental features or events relevant to the success of the project; prevailing factors pressing for or detracting from certain actions.

5. *Timing*—of critical phases or events relevant to the innovation; synchrony with other significant events.

6. *Obligation*—awareness and felt need to do something about a problem that the innovation seems likely to solve.

7. *Resistances*—inhibitors of the change, rational and irrational; perceived risks if the specific action is taken.

8. *Yield*—the benefits or payoff from the innovation as perceived by potential adopters and by program participants.

The definition of the above factors, and the profile rating to follow, are based on distillations of much of the literature on knowledge utilization and organizational change as deemed to pertain to human services. The development of the A VICTORY model also has been dependent on a series of conferences and experimental studies over the past ten years, supported largely through NIMH in-house resources, contracts, and collaborative grants. Extensive help has been provided by consultants working in the field of change outside the topical area of mental health. The A VICTORY technique, in its several developing stages, has been applied in technical assistance and in research consultation and administration within the Services Program at NIMH. It also has had continual use as an internal management approach within that program.

On the basis of a series of collaborative studies under way and sponsored by NIMH, it seems fair to conclude at this point that the A VICTORY technique may at least offer a beginning framework for planning the adoption of new policies or practices.

To determine the readiness of an organization or system to adopt a particular change, interested persons may employ the rating scheme given in Figure 8.

Assuming that the organization seems ready for tryout of the program, a necessary early step is to identify criteria for effective performance and for a generally satisfying work situation. Of course, different types of organizations have different criteria. To illustrate, Table 6 lists samples of "hard-data" and "soft-data" criteria for three different types of organizations. The table is presented only as an example; each organization has its own set of criteria for effectiveness, efficiency, and goal attainment that it needs to think through and make explicit.

Another step is to determine whether significant and reliable information on each of the identified factors can be collected in the organization. It also is necessary to explicate what kinds of data-gathering techniques would be required for this kind of management information system. If data are collected from more than one site, special care and effort are needed to ensure comparability of information.

Figure 8

A VICTORY Profile

	FACTOR	RATING OF FACTORS*
		0 1 2 3 4 5 6 7 8 9 10
	Are staff skills and knowledge appropriate to accommodate the change?	. . . .
	Are fiscal resources adequate for the desired change?	. . . .
ABILITY	Are physical resources appropriate and adequate for the change?	. . . .
	Are the necessary managerial skills available to accomplish the change?	. . . .
	Is the change consonant with relevant values of clients, such as social, religious, ethnic, or political values?	. . . .
	Is the change consonant with the philosophies and policies of program supporters?	. . . .
VALUES	Is the change consonant with the personal and professional values of the staff?	. . . .
	Is the change consonant with the personal and professional values of the top person?	. . . .
	Are the characteristics of the organization such as to render change likely?	. . . .

* KEY TO RATINGS
 0 = An exceedingly negative answer to the question
 5 = A midpoint rating
 10 = An exceedingly positive answer, or "resounding yes," to the question raised under the particular factor
Ratings intermediate between the above points may be assigned according to the rater's judgment as to where the organization falls with respect to each factor.

FACTOR		RATING OF FACTORS
		0 1 2 3 4 5 6 7 8 9 10
INFORMA-TION	Is information regarding the desired change adequate and clear?	. . . .
	Does available information about the idea bear relevance to the seemingly needed improvement?	. . . .
	Does available information indicate that the idea behind the desired change is "tryable"; can its alleged advantages be demonstrated and observed?	. . . .
	Have the possible negative side effects been surfaced with appropriate *conditions* of optimal use specified?	. . . .
CIRCUM-STANCES	Are conditions in the potential adopter's situation similar to those where the idea was demonstrated to be effective?	. . . .
	Does the organization appear to be in a condition or mood of "readiness" for the given change?	. . . .
	Is the organization located near facilities or community services that may be needed to help implement the change?	. . . .
TIMING	Should the change be implemented now or will the organization be in a better position to do this successfully sometime in the future?	. . . .
	Is the suggested improvement likely to continue to be of value or might it become outdated in the near future?	. . . .
	Are other events occurring at this time that could bear on the response to this change?	. . . .

Figure 8 (continued)

FACTOR	RATING OF FACTORS
	0 1 2 3 4 5 6 7 8 9 10

OBLIGATIONS	Has the need for this change been ascertained through sound evaluation? · · · · · · · · · ·
	Has the need for this change been compared with other needs in the program? · · · · · · · · · ·
	Are there other strong reasons—political, administrative, fiscal or powerful/influential advocacy—pushing for the change? · · · · · · · · · ·
RESISTANCES	Have all the reasons for *not* adopting this change been considered at least by all key persons concerned? · · · · · · · · · ·
	Has consideration been given to what may have to be abandoned if the plan is implemented? · · · · · · · · · ·
	Has consideration been given to who will lose in this change? · · · · · · · · · ·
	Has consideration been given to possible unrealistic staff resistances to the change; can these be overcome satisfactorily? · · · · · · · · · ·
YIELD	Has the soundness of evidence about the potential benefits of the plan in comparison with present or alternative plans been carefully assessed and made available to those concerned? · · · · · · · · · ·
	Have possible indirect rewards for this change been examined and communicated appropriately? · · · · · · · · · ·

TABLE 6

Sample Criteria for Outcome Measurements

| | OBJECTIVE FACTORS | |
Manufacturing	*Social Service*	*Local Government*
Direct labor cost in relation to units produced (or percent of yield from so much input of raw material)	Volume of cases handled Percent of successful outcomes	Financial solvency. Costs of manpower and equipment for particular services Cost-of-living statistics and tax rate as compared with other, similar cities
Reject rate or process losses Machine downtime due to equipment malfunction	Average time required for satisfactory closure of a case Cost of services per case	Periodic ratings by citizenry regarding quality of services to the community, broken down by categories such as crime statistics, compared with comparable cities Range and adequacy of services provided, as compared with similar cities
Number, type, and disposition of labor grievances per month	Number, type, and disposition of labor grievances per month	Number, type, and disposition of labor grievances per month
Employee absenteeism rate	Staff absenteeism rate	Employee absenteeism rate
Employee turnover rate	Staff turnover rate	Employee turnover rate
Tardiness rate	Tardiness rate	Tardiness rate
Safety performance	Safety performance	Safety performance
Ability to adhere to a schedule	Ability to adhere to a schedule	Ability to adhere to a schedule
Index of employee satisfaction with the work situation	Index of staff satisfaction	Index of staff satisfaction

TABLE 6 (*continued*)

SUBJECTIVE FACTORS		
Manufacturing	*Social Service*	*Local Government*
Index of customer satisfaction with goods or services	Index of client satisfaction	Index of city council or board of supervisors' satisfaction
Index of board of directors' satisfaction	Index of board of directors' satisfaction	Index of constituents' satisfaction
	Community satisfaction	

The list of criteria finally arrived at should be those regarded as: (1) the best indicators of organizational effectiveness, efficiency, and general satisfaction to all those concerned with the evaluation; and (2) variables susceptible to being measured by the organization without undue effort.

To sum it up, evaluation methodology requires four key steps: (a) deciding which variables to include in a data-collection system; (b) obtaining baseline data regarding the relevant variables; (c) developing a system that permits evaluation of results in comparison with baseline data; (d) developing reliable and valid data-collection procedures. With regard to the latter, methods for data collection include gathering of accounting or statistical data from company records; pencil-and-paper survey questionnaires; structured individual or small-group interviews; and on-the-job standardized observations.

Analysis might focus on the individual, on various task groups, on the organization as a whole, or on all of these. Obviously, what to look for must be thought through in each situation, depending on what is important and what is susceptible to measurement.

A sample questionnaire for measuring organizational climate, adapted with permission from one used by General Electric, is presented in Figure 9. Also presented (Figure 10) is a questionnaire developed by Rensis Likert and his colleagues at the Institute for Social Research, University of Michigan, which graphically portrays what Likert calls the management system—a cluster of factors that bear on how the respondent perceives the management system with regard to leadership, motivation, communication, decision making, organizational goals, and control functions. Both questionnaires can be used either on a before-and-after basis or at periodic intervals. The remaining two questionnaires in this chapter (Figures 11 and 12) were developed by Arthur Associates, a consulting firm in Holland, Michigan, and are based on Likert's work.

A number of data-collection instruments to measure employee satisfaction and individual perceptions of an organization and its management are available commercially. An organization should select those measures which best mesh with its special needs. Also, it is often necessary to tailor a measure to the particulars of a given organization and situation.

Figure 9

General Electric Questionnaire for a Study of
Climate in Organizations[2]

THE QUESTIONNAIRE

This questionnaire is part of a study being conducted to gain better understanding of the kind of work climates or environments in which managers and specialists in an organization find themselves, how these climates are created, and how they affect the individual's performance and satisfaction.

We hope you will be as frank and honest as you can in answering these questions and that you will spend enough time on each to put down what you really feel. This research will be of little or no value unless you provide us with a *truly accurate* description of the climate in your Section. (The word "Section" refers to your department or

[2] Adapted with permission from a General Electric personnel research study.

branch or whatever would be an appropriate designation of your work group.)

The information you provide herein will be used for research purposes only, and your answers will be kept *strictly confidential.*

In Part I you will be asked to indicate how you feel about a number of subjects in terms of agreement or disagreement. The statements at the top of the four columns may be described as follows:

Column 1, Definitely Agree: that is, the statement definitely expresses how you feel about the matter.

Column 2, Inclined to Agree: that is, you are not definite, but think that the statement tends to express how you feel about the matter.

Column 3, Inclined to Disagree: that is, you are not definite, but think that the statement does *not* tend to express how you feel about the matter.

Column 4, Definitely Disagree: that is, the statement definitely does *not* express how you feel about the matter.

PART I For each of the statements below, please place an (X) in the column that most nearly expresses how you feel about the matter.	Definitely Agree	Inclined to Agree	Inclined to Disagree	Definitely Disagree
	1	2	3	4
1. The assignments in this Section are clearly defined and logically structured.				
2. Our management isn't so concerned about formal organization and authority, but concentrates instead on getting the right people together to do the job.				

3. In this Section there are very high standards for performance.				
4. We don't rely too heavily on individual judgment in this Section; almost everything is double-checked.				
5. If a mistake is made in this Section, punishment follows.				
6. People are proud of belonging to this Section.				
7. The policies and organization structure of the Department have been clearly explained.				
8. Ordinarily we don't deviate from standard policies and procedures in this organization.				
9. Around here there is a feeling of pressure to continually improve personal and group performance.				
10. Our philosophy emphasizes that people should solve their problems by themselves.				
11. There is not enough reward and recognition given in this Section for doing good work.				
12. People in this Section don't really trust each other enough.				
13. Things seem to be pretty disorganized around here.				
14. Excessive rules, administrative details, and red tape make it difficult for new and original ideas to receive consideration.				
15. In this organization people don't seem to take much pride in the excellence of their performance.				

For each of the statements below, please place an (X) in the column that most nearly expresses how you feel about the matter.	Definitely Agree	Inclined to Agree	Inclined to Disagree	Definitely Disagree
	1	2	3	4
16. Around here management resents having everything checked with it; if you think you've got the right approach, you just go ahead.				
17. We have a promotion system here that helps the best person to rise to the top.				
18. People in this Section tend to be cool and aloof toward each other.				
19. Our productivity sometimes suffers because of lack of organization and planning.				
20. If you want to stay out of trouble around here, you have to conform to standard practice.				
21. Management sets difficult, challenging goals in this organization.				
22. The best way to get ahead in this organization is not to stick your neck out.				
23. In this Section people are rewarded in proportion to the excellence of their job performance.				
24. A friendly atmosphere prevails among the people in this Section.				
25. I feel that I am a member of a well-functioning team.				
26. There are a lot of rules, policies, procedures, and standard practices one has to know to get along in this organization.				

27.	Our agency has grown because people are encouraged to take calculated risks at the right time.			
28.	In this Section the rewards and encouragements you get usually outweigh the threats and the criticism.			
29.	There is a lot of warmth in the relationships between management and other personnel in this Section.			
30.	Management doesn't put much emphasis on improving performance.			
31.	Unnecessary procedures are kept to a minimum in this Section.			
32.	There is a great deal of criticism in this Section.			
33.	As far as I can see, there doesn't seem to be very much personal loyalty to the organization.			

PART II

1. How would you describe to a friend, who had never been in your office, the climate and the pressures of your day-to-day work situation?

2. Describe the situation in this Section regarding rewards (for accomplishments) and what is liable to happen if someone makes a mistake (and fails). Are significant accomplishments encouraged and well-rewarded, or are you better off if you just keep your nose clean and avoid any mistakes?

PART III

We would like the following information for research comparisons only.

What is your age?

       Under 30 _____

       30 to 49 _____

       Over 50 _____

How long have you worked for this organization?

       Less than one year _____

       1 to 10 years   _____

       Over 10 years   _____

How long have you worked for the Section in which you now are employed?

       Less than 1 year _____

       1 to 10 years   _____

       Over 10 years   _____

Male _____ ; Female _____ .

DEFINITIONS OF CLIMATE DIMENSIONS

Constraining Conformity

The feeling employees have about the constraints in the office—e.g., degree to which they feel there are many rules, procedures, policies, and practices to which people have to conform, rather than being able to do their work as they see fit. Too much "structure" in the form of rules, policies, and standard procedures tends to stifle achievement motivation. Therefore, high scores on this dimension are generally considered undesirable.

Responsibility

The feeling that employees have a lot of individual responsibility delegated to them—they can run their jobs pretty much on their own without having to check with the boss every time a decision must be made. This dimension also includes the feeling that management is willing to take some risks in operating the business. Achievement-oriented workers like a lot of individual responsibility and are challenged by moderate risks, whereas the more security-oriented worker seeks to avoid risks and likes a climate where double-checking is stressed.

Standards

The emphasis that employees feel is being placed on doing a good job. Includes the degree to which people feel that challenging goals are set and that there is some pressure to continually improve personal and group performance. Achievement-oriented people usually respond enthusiastically to high but reasonable standards. Security-oriented people may find standards threatening.

Reward

The degree to which employees feel that they are fairly rewarded for good work, rather than only being punished when something goes wrong. A climate where stress is primarily on punishment for deviations tends to cultivate a fear-of-failure orientation and is de-motivating to the individual who might otherwise be an enthusiastic, success-oriented worker. Furthermore, punishment has been found to have little effect in correcting undesired performance if it is not balanced off by some commensurate rewards for good performance.

Organizational Clarity

The feeling that things are pretty well organized rather than being disorderly, confused, or chaotic. While too much organization leads to feelings of constraint, too little organization does not permit people to achieve group goals effectively. This should be considered as a *supportive* dimension, since organization as such does not engender achievement motivation, but the lack of it may be frustrating to the achievement-oriented individual.

Friendly Team Spirit

The feeling that general "good fellowship" prevails in the atmosphere—that management and fellow employees are warm and trusting, and that the organization is one with which people identify and are proud to belong. This dimension may also be considered as *supporting* in character, since a friendly atmosphere won't necessarily lead to achievements, but a cold, untrusting climate will usually stifle achievement motivation.

KEY[3]

Constraining Conformity

+   8. Ordinarily we don't deviate from standard policies and procedures in this organization.

+   14. Excessive rules, administrative details, and red tape make it difficult for new and original ideas to receive consideration.

+   20. If you want to stay out of trouble around here, you have to conform to standard practice.

[3] The 33 items in Part I have been regrouped here into six categories. To obtain a score for *Constraining Conformity*, if a "+ item" (8, 14, 20, 26) is marked "Definitely Agree," score 2 points; if it is marked "Inclined to Agree," score 1 point. If a "– item" (2, 31) is marked "Definitely Disagree," score 2 points; if it is marked "Inclined to Disagree," score 1 point. Thus, the maximum score for *Constraining Conformity* is 12 (2 × 6 items). The other five categories are scored similarly.

+   26.   There are a lot of rules, policies, procedures, and standard practices one has to know to get along in this organization.

−   2.   Our management isn't so concerned about formal organization and authority, but concentrates instead on getting the right people together to do the job.

−   31.   Unnecessary procedures are kept to a minimum in this Section.

Responsibility

+   10.   Our philosophy emphasizes that people should solve their problems by themselves.

+   16.   Around here management resents your checking everything with them; if you think you've got the right approach, you just go ahead.

+   27.   Our agency has grown because people are encouraged to take calculated risks at the right time.

−   4.   We don't rely too heavily on individual judgment in this Section; almost everything is double-checked.

−   22.   The best way to get ahead in this organization is not to stick your neck out.

Standards

+   3.   In this Section there are very high standards for performance.

+   9.   Around here there is a feeling of pressure to continually improve personal and group performance.

+   21.   Management sets difficult, challenging goals in this organization.

−   15.   In this organization people don't seem to take much pride in the excellence of their performance.

−   30.   Management doesn't put much emphasis on improving performance.

Reward

+   17.   We have a promotion system here that helps the best person to rise to the top.

+   23.   In this Section people are rewarded in proportion to the excellence of their job performance.

+   28.   In this Section the rewards and encouragements you get usually outweigh the threats and the criticism.

−   5.   If a mistake is made in this Section, punishment usually follows.

−   11.   There is not enough reward and recognition given in this Section for doing good work.

−   32.   There is a great deal of criticism in this Section.

Organizational Clarity

+   1.   The assignments in this Section are clearly defined and logically structured.

+   7.   The policies and organization structure of the Department have been clearly explained.

+   25.   I feel that I am a member of a well-functioning team.

−   13.   Things seem to be pretty disorganized around here.

−   19.   Our productivity sometimes suffers because of lack of organization and planning.

Friendly, Team Spirit

+   6.   People are proud of belonging to this Section.

+   24.   A friendly atmosphere prevails among the people in this Section.

+   29.   There is a lot of warmth in the relationships between management and other personnel in this Section.

−   12.   People in this Section don't really trust each other enough.

−   18.   People in this Section tend to be cool and aloof toward each other.

−   33.   As far as I can see, there isn't very much personal loyalty to the organization.

Figure 10

Organizational and Performance Characteristics of
Different Management Systems—Rensis Likert[4]

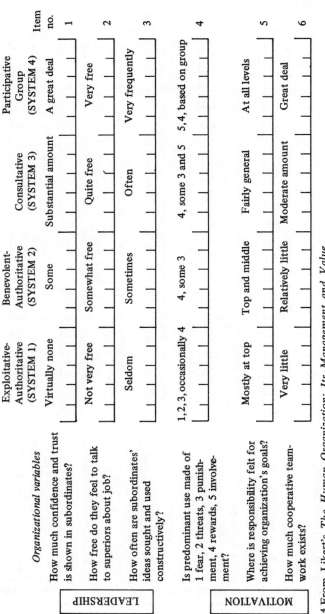

Organizational variables	Exploitative-Authoritative (SYSTEM 1)	Benevolent-Authoritative (SYSTEM 2)	Consultative (SYSTEM 3)	Participative Group (SYSTEM 4)	Item no.
LEADERSHIP How much confidence and trust is shown in subordinates?	Virtually none	Some	Substantial amount	A great deal	1
How free do they feel to talk to superiors about job?	Not very free	Somewhat free	Quite free	Very free	2
How often are subordinates' ideas sought and used constructively?	Seldom	Sometimes	Often	Very frequently	3
MOTIVATION Is predominant use made of 1 fear, 2 threats, 3 punishment, 4 rewards, 5 involvement?	1, 2, 3, occasionally 4	4, some 3	4, some 3 and 5	5, 4, based on group	4
Where is responsibility felt for achieving organization's goals?	Mostly at top	Top and middle	Fairly general	At all levels	5
How much cooperative teamwork exists?	Very little	Relatively little	Moderate amount	Great deal	6

[4] From Likert's *The Human Organization: Its Management and Value.*
(New York: McGraw-Hill, Inc., 1967). Copyright © 1967 by McGraw-Hill, Inc.
Used with permission of McGraw-Hill Book Company.

Figure 10 (continued)

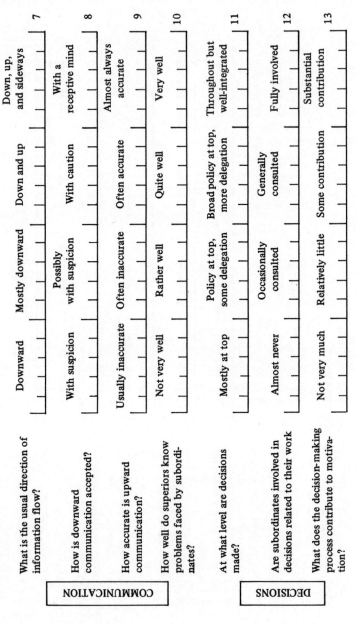

Figure 10 (continued)

		Orders issued	Orders, some comments invited	After discussion, by orders	By group action (except in crisis)	
GOALS	How are organizational goals established?	Orders issued	Orders, some comments invited	After discussion, by orders	By group action (except in crisis)	14
	How much covert resistance to goals is present?	Strong resistance	Moderate resistance	Some resistance at times	Little or none	15
CONTROL	How concentrated are review and control functions?	Very highly at top	Quite highly at top	Moderate delegation to lower levels	Widely shared	16
	Is there an informal organization resisting the formal one?	Yes	Usually	Sometimes	No—same goals as formal	17
	What are cost, productivity, and other control data used for?	Policing, punishment	Reward and punishment	Reward, some self-guidance	Self-guidance, problem-solving	18

Figure 11

Questionnaire for Evaluating Degree of Participative
Management in Work Teams

THE QUESTIONNAIRE

Circle the appropriate number

1. Degree of mutual trust:
   High suspicion . . . . High trust

   | 1 | 2 | 3 | 4 | 5 | 6 | 7 | 8 | 9 | 10 |

2. Degree of mutual support:
   Every man for himself . . . . Genuine concern for each other

   | 1 | 2 | 3 | 4 | 5 | 6 | 7 | 8 | 9 | 10 |

3. Communications:
   Guarded, cautious . . . . Open, honest

   | 1 | 2 | 3 | 4 | 5 | 6 | 7 | 8 | 9 | 10 |

4. Communications:
   We don't listen to each other . . . . We listen; we understand and
   are understood

   | 1 | 2 | 3 | 4 | 5 | 6 | 7 | 8 | 9 | 10 |

5. Team objectives:
   Not understood by team . . . . Clearly understood by team

   | 1 | 2 | 3 | 4 | 5 | 6 | 7 | 8 | 9 | 10 |

6. Team objectives:
   Team is negative toward objectives . . . . . Team is committed to objectives

   | 1 | 2 | 3 | 4 | 5 | 6 | 7 | 8 | 9 | 10 |

7. Handling conflicts within team:
   We deny, avoid, or suppress conflicts . . . . We accept conflicts and "work
   them through"

   | 1 | 2 | 3 | 4 | 5 | 6 | 7 | 8 | 9 | 10 |

8. Utilization of member resources:
   Our abilities, knowledge, and experience
   aren't utilized by the team . . . . Our abilities, knowledge, and
   experience are fully utilized
   by the team

   | 1 | 2 | 3 | 4 | 5 | 6 | 7 | 8 | 9 | 10 |

9. Control methods:

Control is imposed on us .... We control ourselves

| 1 | 2 | 3 | 4 | 5 | 6 | 7 | 8 | 9 | 0 |

10. Organizational environment:

Restrictive; pressure toward conformity .   Free; supportive; respect for individual differences

| 1 | 2 | 3 | 4 | 5 | 6 | 7 | 8 | 9 | 10 |

Total Points . . . .

SCORING KEY

Score 10 points if this definition fits your work team; if not, score your team lower.

1. *Mutual trust:* There is a high degree of mutual trust that encourages teamwork. There are no suspicions inhibiting teamwork. The leader trusts the team members. The team members trust the leader. Each member trusts all other members of the team.

2. *Mutual support:* There is a high degree of mutual support and genuine concern shown by all members for one another. The leader is concerned for and supports the team and each member on it. The team is concerned about the effectiveness of the leader and supports him and his objectives. Each team member supports all other team members in pursuit of their own and the team's objectives.

3. *Candor:* Communications within the team are open and candid. No one needs to be cautious in communicating. No one on the team is afraid of being misunderstood or misinterpreted. The leader is candid with the team and each of its members. The team is candid with the leader. There is complete candor among the various members of the work team.

4. *Listening:* Whenever a team member speaks he is heard and thoroughly understood by all. The leader listens to the group and the individual members of the team. The team listens to the leader. Individual members of the team listen to one another. No one's contribution is thought to be unimportant.

5. *Objectives:* The team has a plan of challenging, meaningful objectives that are clearly understood by all members of the team. The objectives do exist as the team's long- and short-range plan and have been thoroughly communicated to all members of the team, by written means or otherwise.

6. *Commitment:* Because team objectives are clearly compatible with those of each individual, there is aggressive commitment to team objectives. Objectives are in fact compatible. Commitment to objectives is total, with no reservations. All team members show enthusiastic and wholehearted support of objectives. The team is aggressive in achieving objectives.

7. *Conflict:* Conflict is expected in the dynamic team. It is accepted without prejudice or anxiety and worked through to a solution. Conflict in fact does exist—it is not suppressed. When it arises, conflict is accepted by the leader and all members of the team. The team is not afraid of conflict when it occurs. When it happens, conflict is worked through to a thoroughly satisfactory solution to all parties. The team is developing strength as it resolves conflict.

8. *Utilization of resources:* The team is aware of its individual and collective resources. They are fully utilized. The leader and each member of the team are aware of the outstanding strengths of each member of the team. The strengths are then used in such a way as to make any weaknesses that exist irrelevant. No one on the team is considered unimportant.

9. *Control:* Control has been completely internalized by individual team members. The team does not have to police its members for performance because each member does this himself. Division and corporate policies and controls are accepted as legitimate boundaries within which team members have complete freedom.

10. *Environment:* The environment within the team is free and supportive, respects individual differences, facilitates work, and is challenging. Team members feel comfortable working with each other. There are no fears or suspicions inhibiting performance.

Figure 12

Arthur Associates' Questionnaire for Evaluating

YOU AND THE COMPANY *Directions*: For each question, please check the category that you feel best applies to you and your company.	To a very little extent	To a little extent	To some extent	To a great extent	To a very great extent
1. In general, to what extent are there mutual trust and support in the company?	( )	( )	( )	( )	( )
2. To what extent do you feel a real responsibility to help the company be successful?	( )	( )	( )	( )	( )
3. To what extent are there things about working here (people, policies, or conditions) that encourage you to work hard?	( )	( )	( )	( )	( )
4. To what extent does your company have clear-cut, reasonable goals and objectives?	( )	( )	( )	( )	( )
5. To what extent does the company have a real interest in the welfare and happiness of those who work here?	( )	( )	( )	( )	( )
6. When decisions are being made, to what extent are the persons affected asked for their ideas?	( )	( )	( )	( )	( )
7. To what extent are the persons who make decisions aware of problems at lower levels in the company?	( )	( )	( )	( )	( )
8. How receptive are those above you to your ideas and suggestions?	( )	( )	( )	( )	( )

YOU AND THE COMPANY *Directions*: For each question, please check the category that you feel best applies to you and your company.	To a very little extent	To a little extent	To some extent	To a great extent	To a very great extent
9. In general, how satisfied are you with your job?	( )	( )	( )	( )	( )
10. All in all, how satisfied are you with this company, compared to others?	( )	( )	( )	( )	( )

COMMENTS: Please include here any comments that you feel you would like to add to the data you have already provided.

A. Appendix
Proposed Outline for a Two-Day Workshop on Improving the Quality of Worklife

The participants usually are all those supervisors who would be involved in a QWL program within a given organization. If appropriate, union representatives and all members of a given task team might well be included, so long as the total number of participants at one time is not greater than approximately 25. Such a workshop can also be adapted to persons from different organizations who simply wish to learn more about QWL programs. All the instructions given below are addressed to the workshop leader.

First Day

8:30–10:30 A.M.   Start by passing out reading materials, because most participants in conferences, seminars, and workshops don't have the time—or take the time—to do much pre-conference reading. We will assume that the only preliminary material distributed in preparation for the workshop was some journal article reprints. Since *Productivity Gains Through Worklife Improvement*[1] does provide carefully selected case reports and an orientation to the subject, the first 1–2 hours might be used to read the main body of that book. This can be followed by a brief (10-minute) self-scored test on quality of worklife concepts (see pp. 304–308) to see if any key concepts need discussion, so that all participants can start from a common information base.

Coffee Break (10:30 A.M.–10:45 A.M.)

10:45–11:00 A.M. Make the point that QWL improvement refers essentially to a style of management that seems to facilitate organizational effectiveness *plus* job satisfaction. Among the key elements that characterize QWL are: (1) creating an open communication climate and structure in which members of a task group are encouraged to present ideas for improving the design of their jobs or the organizational functioning, if they have any such thoughts or feelings; and (2) providing opportunity for workers to find a sense of achievement in their work, receive recognition for that achievement, handle larger responsibilities when ready for them, and be considered for advancement opportunities when they occur. To repeat, the focus is on more effective performance and, at the same time, on the conditions of work that make for greater job satisfaction. QWL improvement is a systems approach that seeks to benefit all parties concerned and takes into account the technical, social, administrative, and economic factors bearing on an organization's health, viability, effectiveness, and efficiency. In short, it is simply intelligent management that is thoughtfully considerate of people while seeking to achieve legitimate organizational objectives. It requires competence in the handling of the usual managerial functions—namely: planning, organizing, staffing, coordinating, motivating, and controlling. It is not a programmatic panacea for anything; it is, however, a determined thrust toward ex-

[1] Other books (cited in the bibliography) that might be used in this context are: Davis and Taylor, *Job Design in a Wider Context;* Jenkins, *Job Power;* Marrow, *The Failure of Success;* Rosow, *The Worker and the Job;* or U.S. Department of Health, Education and Welfare, *Work in America.*

cellence, pride, and pleasure in the integration of human effort at work.

In a participative management style, there is commitment to invite and respectfully consider ideas, suggestions, and criticisms from all concerned, so that decisions can be better-informed and those affected can become more ego-involved by virtue of their participation. However, it should be made clear that participative management is not permissive management. The persons responsible for given types of decisions continue to have the authority to make them, and those who might have made a different decision if they were "the boss" are nevertheless expected to support the decision made until and unless it can be changed. Otherwise there is inadequate organizational discipline, and, as Abraham Lincoln observed, "A house divided against itself cannot long stand."

11:00 A.M.–12:00 noon Show film *Motivation Through Job Enrichment*,[2] through the engineer vignette. Stop film after the words "We're talking about two different things" and ask the group what's wrong with the engineer's job. After discussion, finish the vignette and the remainder of the film. Invite further discussion and summarize Herzberg's motivation–hygiene theory, using the guide on page 235.

Lunch (12:00 Noon–1:30 P.M.)

1:30–2:30 P.M. Invite each member of the group to take ten minutes to complete a questionnaire on understanding work motivation (see pages 308–312). Break the total group into subgroups of three to seven persons to discuss their answers, and then have each subgroup report its results to the total group. Spark debate. Sit in with each subgroup for sufficient time to offer group process observations, if appropriate.

2:30–3:15 P.M. Next, present the case of an electronics assembly plant (see page 312). Ask each person to serve as a consultant to this hypothetical company. How would he cope with the

[2] Obtainable from BNA Communications, Inc., Division of the Bureau of National Affairs, Inc., 5615 Fishers Lane, Rockville, Md. 20852.

problem using the Herzberg concepts, using other material from the reading, or using any other relevant ideas? Write all suggestions on the board. Has anyone proposed taking the problem to the employees for their ideas? Discuss, see if a consensus can be reached, and explicate the principles involved in the proposed approach or recommended resolution. This exercise can be carried out either with the total group or by breaking into subgroups and then reassembling to hear each subgroup's ideas.

Break (3:15 P.M.–3:30 P.M.)

3:30–5:30 P.M. Pass out the sheets on "Steps in Improving a Job" and "Factors Which Appear as Dissatisfiers and Satisfiers" (see pages 313–314). Explain the steps briefly, then have each participant who wishes to do so describe a real situation for which he would like to work out steps for improving the quality of work-life—through job enrichment or other means. From the case situations presented, have the group select two which they would most like to discuss and develop.

Again, break the group into small groups of three to five people to tackle the first case. Instruct each group to list or diagram its proposed steps sequentially. The small teams should also be prepared to present their reasoning when they report to the total group.

Before reassembling as a total group, allow about 10 minutes for each subgroup to critique its own group processes and see what can be learned for more effective functioning as a problem-solving group.

Summarize each small group proposal on the board. Organize the material in a way that will permit comparisons. For example:

	GROUP A	GROUP B	GROUP C
PROPOSED STEPS:	1.	1.	1. ....
	2.	2.	2. ....
	3.	3.	3. ....
	etc.	etc.	etc.

Since the exercise in which the group has been involved is realistic and affords an opportunity for clarification of principles and procedures, give it as much time as seems fruitful. Discuss any differences among the proposals of the small groups. Consensus or agreement is not necessary, since there is no one best way, but reasons should be clarified and an effort should be made to foresee probable consequences and problems. There should be an attempt to profit from the case material distributed.

5:30–5:45 P.M. Reassemble as a group, and have the participants read some selected cases from Chapter II of *Productivity Gains Through Worklife Improvement* as preparation for the next day's meeting. Invite a critique of the day's meeting and any suggestions for making the second day optimally valuable for the participants. Then adjourn for refreshments and dinner.

Second Day

8:30–10:30 A.M. Convene the entire group. Call for questions about the case material in *Productivity Gains Through Worklife Improvement* or about anything else before breaking into (differently constituted) small groups to tackle the second real-problem case. Proceed in the same manner as on the preceding afternoon. When ready, reassemble the total group.

Coffee Break (10:30 A.M.–10:45 A.M.)

10:45–11:45 A.M. Show film, *The Modern Meaning of Efficiency.*[3] Stop the movie after the clerical record-keeping training sequence. Ask two separate groups to analyze what is wrong with the job and to suggest means of correcting the deficiencies.

Lunch (11:45 A.M.–1:00 P.M.)

1:00–2:15 P.M. Pass out the machine operator case (see pages 315–317). Break into small groups for a 30-minute discussion of what to do in that situation. Reassemble and hear from each group.

[3] Obtainable from BNA Communications, Inc., Division of the Bureau of National Affairs, Inc., 5615 Fishers Lane, Rockville, Md. 20852.

Then pass out the "What Actually Happened" sheet (page 317) and discuss differences in approach.

2:15–3:15 P.M. Show film, *The Factory*[4] (26 minutes), followed by discussion; or substitute some other topic here, such as a discussion of procedures for determining an organization's readiness to undertake a QWL program (e.g., Howard Davis's A VICTORY assessment).

Break (3:15 P.M.–3:30 P.M.)

3:30–4:30 P.M. Ask for questions, conduct a general discussion, and have participants evaluate the workshop. Adjourn.

QUESTIONNAIRE—*QUALITY OF WORK CONCEPTS*[5]

By indicating agreement or disagreement with each statement, you can check your understanding of some basic views regarding programs to improve quality of work and productivity in the process.

Please read each statement carefully and place an "X" on the line which most nearly expresses your beliefs.

Check only one line for each statement.

	AGREE	DISAGREE
1. Some individuals do not want "job enrichment"; they prefer routine tasks they feel they can handle with no strain and low pressure of responsibility.	___	___
2. Motivation is a complex matter. Since what is rewarding to one person may be obnoxious to another, there are no ways to generalize about motivation. Thus, the best way to organize work in a company is to permit everyone to choose the job he would like best.	___	___

[4] Obtainable from Alternatives on Film, 1559 19th Ave., San Francisco, Calif. 94122.

[5] Developed by Human Interaction Research Institute, Los Angeles, Calif.

3. One difference between white-collar and blue-collar workers is that in ratings of aspects of their jobs which are very important to them, white-collar groups tend to rank "interesting work" as #1, whereas the blue-collar groups tend to rank "enough help and equipment to get the job done, job security, and good pay" as their #1 concerns.   _____   _____

4. Management and labor are of necessity in an adversary relationship, and improvements in the quality of work are likely to come only by winning them through collective bargaining.   _____   _____

5. An objective of increasing importance to today's workers is to achieve more meaningful ways of participating in decision making that directly or indirectly affects their welfare.   _____   _____

6. Many people have long experienced discontent and dissatisfaction in their work, but now an increasing percentage seems more likely to express it, and to do so militantly.   _____   _____

7. Most people do not work up to their full productive potential. In fact, a significant proportion of wage earners could, and know they could, accomplish more each day if they tried.   _____   _____

8. Recent college graduates (the 70s) believe that a commitment to a career is not essential. The majority would welcome less emphasis on hard work.   _____   _____

9. When an individual likes his work, understands it, likes at least most of the people he works with, and gets feedback on how well his task group is doing, he and his task group are likely to perform more productively.   _____   _____

AGREE   DISAGREE

10. Nationwide sampling reveals that since the late '60s a growing percentage of persons has expressed dissatisfaction with the work they do.

      ____   ____

11. The true meaning of productivity improvement is to get human beings to work faster and harder so as to reduce costs and increase profits for management.

      ____   ____

12. If workers become more productive through increased efficiency or through better design of the work, this necessarily will lead to a reduction in the workforce.

      ____   ____

13. Workers who feel satisfied with their pay and working conditions will regularly be considerably more productive than workers who find the work itself satisfying but are somewhat unhappy with their pay and working conditions.

      ____   ____

14. To improve the quality of work we need a three-pronged effort: effective motivation of people; appropriate machine and system design (engineering); and an appropriate organizational structure to accomplish the work.

      ____   ____

15. Social scientists suggest that what employees want in order to feel identified with their work is voice in decisions regarding their own jobs. Workers disagree; most say they want less responsibility and fewer decisions to make, not more.

      ____   ____

16. There are really few pitfalls in implementing job enrichment programs. The evidence from case studies of companies that have tried such programs shows that nearly all have met with success over the long run.

      ____   ____

17. Most labor union leaders have expressed enthusiastic support of programs to enrich

jobs and improve the quality of work, but management leaders generally have not been interested in such experiments.

18. The more that young people invest in preparing for work and careers, the higher their expectations and the greater their potential source of dissatisfaction if their goals are not fulfilled.

19. Job enrichment efforts usually end up in failure because their underlying objective is to get workers to take on more responsibilities without opportunity for greater rewards, and eventually workers see through this and rebel.

20. If efforts to improve the quality of work in an organization are to have a good chance of being effective, they generally require the support, understanding, and sustained commitment of top management of the organization, and if the company is unionized, from the union too.

21. Once a decision is made to experiment with efforts to improve the quality of work, the best procedure is to plunge in and start *doing* it, not spend a lot of time talking and planning.

22. The most effective element in an effort to improve the quality of work in an organization is to fire the people who don't produce satisfactorily and find others who will do so.

23. If an organization changes its management style from a more authoritarian work structure to a more participative one, wherein all concerned are given opportunity to have voice in the design and structure of their work, it is important to make clear that decisions still need to be made by whoever has

AGREE   DISAGREE

the responsibility and authority to make them—the essential difference being that under a participative style the decisions are likely to be better informed.

_____   _____

24. The best way to increase workers' motivation to do a good job is to post a clearly spelled-out set of work rules, supervise closely to see that those rules are followed, and promptly discipline anyone who violates them.

_____   _____

25. A key to excellent performance in an organization is to set a model of integrity in behavior and competence in job performance at the top, then give all personnel an opportunity to challenge practices they may regard as inappropriate.

_____   _____

Answer Sheet—Quality of Work Concepts

1. Agree	10. Agree	19. Disagree
2. Disagree	11. Disagree	20. Agree
3. Agree	12. Disagree	21. Disagree
4. Disagree	13. Disagree	22. Disagree
5. Agree	14. Agree	23. Agree
6. Agree	15. Disagree	24. Disagree
7. Agree	16. Disagree	25. Agree
8. Disagree	17. Disagree	
9. Agree	18. Agree	

QUESTIONNAIRE—*Understanding Work Motivation*[6]

Please read each statement carefully and place an "X" to indicate whether you agree or disagree with each.

[6] Revised from and reproduced by permission of Drake-Beam & Associates. Copies (of nonrevised form) obtainable from Drake-Beam & Associates, 277 Park Avenue, New York, N.Y. 10017.

Please check only *one* answer for each statement.

AGREE   DISAGREE

1. Work that an employee considers interesting is an important source of motivation.

2. The opportunity to experience achievement
on the job is an absolute necessity if a person is to be motivated at work.

3. To be a good supervisor, it is more important to be able to organize and structure the
work effectively than to concentrate on
bringing about happy human relations.

4. Shorter hours of work (for example, the
four-day week) are one good tool to stimulate sustained motivational improvement
among employees.

5. Incentive pay plans, if tied directly to individual productivity, are an effective motivational tool and generally work out better
for all concerned than group incentives,
such as cost-savings-sharing plans.

6. Improved two-way communications can
greatly enhance sustained, long-term job
satisfaction of employees even if the work
itself does not provide opportunities for
achievement, recognition, advancement, or
a sense of learning and growth.

7. Plans that push decision-making responsibility down in an organization will be met
with resistance by most employees.

8. Improved working conditions are likely to
create sustained motivation for people to
invest themselves wholeheartedly in their
jobs.

9. Excessive absenteeism may be due to poor
supervision, inadequate pay, or boring
work, among other things.

AGREE   DISAGREE

10. Elimination of the sources of job dissatisfaction, whatever they may be, will result in improved job satisfaction and favorable motivation.
_____ _____

11. One of the most important responsibilities of supervisors and managers is to supervise closely, catch any mistakes, and promptly review all errors with whoever made them.
_____ _____

12. In most cases, extending more decision making to employees involves more risk than gain.
_____ _____

13. One effective way to reduce employee dissatisfaction is to see that people are informed about the reasons for decisions that affect them.
_____ _____

14. Employees on routine or repetitive jobs are likely to become well-motivated and job-satisfied if they understand how their work contributes to the overall company goals and objectives.
_____ _____

15. One of the most common sources of dissatisfaction at work is personality clashes and disagreements. If these conflicts can be minimized, job dissatisfaction will be reduced, but employee motivation and interest in the work will probably not improve.
_____ _____

16. A key aspect of a supervisor's or manager's task is that of providing his people with opportunities for achievement and recognition for that achievement, so they will become motivated.
_____ _____

17. Most employees would prefer to have their supervisors take over the more complex and difficult tasks in their jobs, so long as their pay would not be reduced.
_____ _____

18. Boring, uninteresting work may make some employees more demanding about such

things as pay, working conditions, holidays, etc.   ____   ____

19. Most employee groups would prefer not to receive feedback on their group performance, even if the supervisor has constructive intentions in providing such information, because they do not want to risk receiving unfavorable criticism.   ____   ____

20. Indicators of status and/or seniority—such as well-furnished offices, privileges of various kinds, and service awards—are very important to some employees and strongly contribute to sustaining a high level of motivation and job satisfaction.   ____   ____

Answer Sheet—Understanding Work Motivation

Your answers to the foregoing questionnaire will indicate which of two basic points of view about work motivation and job satisfaction is closest to your own beliefs. The two points of view are represented by the two columns of answers below.

	MOTIVATION-HYGIENE ORIENTATION	TRADITIONAL ORIENTATION
1.	Agree	Disagree
2.	Agree	Disagree
3.	Agree	Disagree
4.	Disagree	Agree
5.	Disagree	Agree
6.	Disagree	Agree
7.	Disagree	Agree
8.	Disagree	Agree
9.	Agree	Disagree
10.	Disagree	Agree
11.	Disagree	Agree
12.	Disagree	Agree
13.	Agree	Disagree
14.	Disagree	Agree
15.	Agree	Disagree

16.	Agree	Disagree
17.	Disagree	Agree
18.	Agree	Disagree
19.	Disagree	Agree
20.	Disagree	Agree

ELECTRONICS ASSEMBLY CASE

A company that manufactures and sells an electronic product (think of an oscilloscope or a television set) had its work structure arranged as follows:

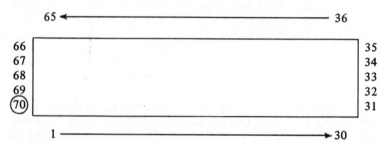

The chassis for the assembly was placed in front of the woman in the #1 position. She installed and soldered the red wires, a repetitive task that a person can be trained to perform in about half an hour. The chassis then moved (on a conveyor belt) to the next woman, and she (#2) installed the white wires. And so to each woman in turn, who installed a wire, or tube, or condenser, or some other part that needed to be added to the assembly.

The seventieth woman, the department manager, was a technician-inspector. She had a B.A. in electrical engineering and a good deal of relevant experience. Her job was to plug the set in and see if it would work properly. If it did not, she would run appropriate diagnostic tests, determine what was wrong, and send it back for correction to the work station(s) responsible for the defect. The department manager had four subsupervisors, or foreladies, to help her and to help and supervise the 69 women on the production line.

The plant was plagued with labor grievances, friction, poor morale, low productivity, a large amount of rework, and an overall decline in share of the market due seemingly to undependable quality and high cost of production. Unless this situation could be improved materially, the company might lose this portion of its total business.

Assume that you are invited in by the president of this company as a consultant to study the problem and make recommendations for improvement. How would you proceed? What are the steps you would take (list sequentially), and for each step, why? (Keep in mind Frederick Herzberg's theory of job context "hygiene" factors and job content "motivators.")

STEPS IN IMPROVING A JOB[7]

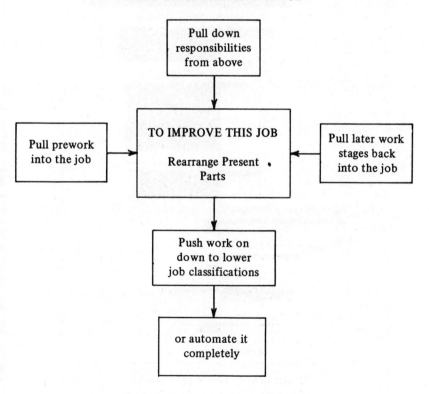

[7] Adapted from R. N. Ford, "Job Enrichment Lessons from AT&T," *Harvard Business Review,* January–February 1973. Used with permission.

Factors which appear as . . .

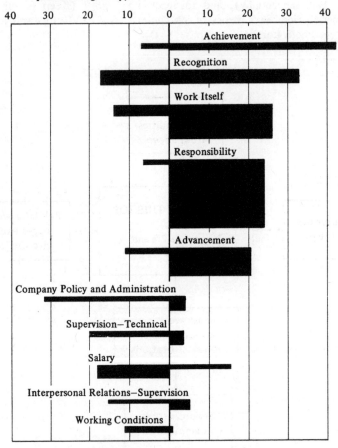

Length of Bar — Percentage Frequency
Width of Bar — Duration of Attitude Change

[8] Adapted from F. Herzberg, B. Mausner, & B. Snyderman, *The Motivation to Work* (New York: John Wiley & Sons, Inc., 1959). Used with permission of the publisher.

MACHINE OPERATOR CASE[9]

Job Objective

To operate a bagmaking machine that manufactures plastic and saran bags for use in food packaging.

Current Situation

This is a three-shift operation with six bag machines in use on each shift. The manning requirements at present are: one operator and two inspector-packers for each pair of machines. The operators load the rolls of plastic tubing on the machines, start the machines running, get the supervisor's approval after a short check run, and then, while running the machine, make the necessary minor adjustments. The operators inform the supervisor if maintenance of a more involved nature is required. The machine automatically cuts the tubing into appropriate lengths for bags and then seals one end of the bag and ejects the bag onto a conveyor. The inspector-packers then pack the bags into cartons, inspecting them for flaws as they do so. Inspector-packers currently move from one machine to another, depending on load requirements.

Symptoms

1. Unacceptable reject rates
2. Excessive downtime
3. High amounts of overtime
4. Marginal productivity figures

Proposed Changes

On this page are listed some of the proposed changes that the management group suggested for improving the situation in the department. Your task is to read over the list and decide which changes you feel would be enriching and which would not be, and then to decide in what order you would implement those changes which you feel are enriching.

---

[9] Reproduced by permission of Drake-Beam & Associates. Copies obtainable from Drake-Beam & Associates, 277 Park Avenue, New York, N.Y. 10017.

	WOULD	WOULD NOT	RANK ORDER

1. For minor maintenance, let operators call maintenance men themselves rather than having supervisors do so. — — —

2. Let operators participate in setting productivity and quality standards for the department. — — —

3. Establish a one-person, one-machine manning setup to allow each person to manufacture, inspect, and pack his own bags. — — —

4. Allow operators to schedule their own orders. — — —

5. Establish incentive pay system to tie operators' pay rates to productivity end or quality. — — —

6. Allow operators to perform quality control function, including the right to reject incoming material and to make final "ship or don't ship" decision. — — —

7. Give operators training in maintenance of their machines and allow them to do all maintenance other than major machine overhaul. — — —

8. Form teams made up of one operator and two inspector-packers and make teams responsible for quality and productivity performance. — — —

9. Cross-train operators on jobs in other departments that send work to the bag machines—for example, the extrusion and printing operations. — — —

10. Give operators supervisory responsibility over inspector-packers. ____ ____ ____

11. Train inspector-packers to do operator's job. ____ ____ ____

12. Assign operators responsibility for end-user accounts so that (when possible) the orders from those accounts come to the same operator each time. ____ ____ ____

13. Allow operator to decide when to start up and shut down the machine, either for production runs or for maintenance needs. ____ ____ ____

14. Allow operator to write own work requests for major overhauls. ____ ____ ____

15. Let operators decide which machines they will run. ____ ____ ____

16. Allow operators to do own machine setup and approve own test runs. ____ ____ ____

17. Give opportunities for operators to take visitors on tours of the bagmaking facilities. ____ ____ ____

18. Give an entire order to a single operator instead of dividing it up among several operators. ____ ____ ____

What Actually Happened

Items 11, 3, 7, 14, 18, 6, 13, 16, 12, and 4 were implemented in that order.

Productivity improved dramatically—as much as 30 percent in some cases. Quality figures improved also, and both downtime and overtime dropped significantly.

B. Appendix
Job-Related Change Options[1]

- Job redesign
- Job expansion
- Capital redesign
- Work simplification
- Self-evaluation of performance
- Peer-group evaluation
- Job allocation
- Work redistribution
- Self-pacing
- Goal setting
- Process layout
- Scrap reduction
- Quality control

- Work-area budgeting
- Production flow
- Materials handling
- Automation
- Initiation of technological change
- Delivery scheduling
- Job reallocation
- Human-resource management
- Job rotation
- "Busy work" vs. contribution
- Task combination
- Work performance feedback

[1] From *Statement of Intent, The Quality of Work Program, 1974–1975,* National Quality of Work Center, 3049 Normanstone Terrace, N.W., Washington, D.C. 20008.

- Ordering supplies
- Ordering maintenance
- Flexible job descriptions

WORK TIME

- Establishing flexible hour system
- Revision of scheduled overtime practices
- Vacation schedules
- Self-scheduling

AUTHORITY SHIFTS

- Reduced supervision
- Autonomous work teams
- Team/group problem solving
- Raising of approval limits

WORK-RULE CHANGES

- Clothing/uniform regulations
- Performance standards
- Flexible job specifications

RECRUITING

- Setting criteria
- Worker involvement in job descriptions
- Job assignments

MOBILITY

- Revision of bidding practices
- Promotion training
- Job posting

TRAINING

- Job-related skill improvement
- Company-time training
- Skill extension
- Worker/union control of training
- Industrial engineering training
- After-hours courses

systems
- Task advancement
- Client/customer relationship

- Elimination of time clocks
- Shift assignments
- Mandatory overtime
- Reduced workweek
- Optional overtime

- Team structure
- Decentralized decision making
- Peer discipline
- Absorbing staff specialties

- Rules of personal conduct
- Crossing craft lines

- Worker involvement in selection
- Worker involvement in hiring
- Internal search

- Revision of job rotation
- Promotion practices

- Intellectual (high school/college) improvement
- Career planning
- Material/cost accounting training
- Self-training/experimentation
- Tuition aid
- Programmed instruction

COMMUNICATIONS

- Employee publication
- Upward communication system
- Open forum
- Ombudsmen

- Suggestion program
- Greater flow of corporate information

ENVIRONMENTAL OPTIONS

SAFETY

- Clothing and equipment
- Noise control
- Workplace medical services
- Improved lighting
- Fire security
- Catwalk rails

- Smoke/fume control
- Machinery/process redesign
- Plant/office/store security
- Rotation on dangerous jobs
- Non-slip flooring
- Safety committees

WORKPLACE IMPROVEMENT

- Lighting
- Seating
- Ventilation/heating/air conditioning
- Restrooms
- Piped-in music

- Noise
- Floors
- Color
- Lockers
- Lunchrooms, cafeterias

OFF-HOUR RECREATIONAL ACTIVITIES

- Bowling leagues
- Basketball leagues
- Anniversary celebrations
- Hobby clubs

- Softball leagues
- Travel clubs
- Gifts to employees

ENVIRONMENTAL IMPROVEMENT

- Parking lot/access roads
- Green space
- Community involvement

- Day care centers
- Air/water pollution
- Company-provided transportation

MONETARY OPTIONS

INCENTIVE PLANS

- Individual incentives
- Group incentives
  Scanlon plan
  Tonnage plan
  Dollar-sales plan
  Rucker plan
  Kaiser plan
- Entrepreneurial participation

PROFIT SHARING

- Stock options
- Immediate distribution sharing
- Keogh plan

- Stock purchase plans
- Deferred sharing

SECURITY EXTENSIONS

- Guaranteed employment
- Guaranteed relocation/
  retraining

- Guaranteed annual wage

COMPENSATION CHANGES

- Annual salary
- Retirement program
- Paid vacations
- Discounts/free meals
- Disability benefits
- Tax consultation

- Health insurance
- Paid sick leave
- Discounts on goods/services
- Death benefits
- Option on increases (annual
  vs. weekly or monthly)

ALLOCATION GAINS

- Standard hour system
- Halsey plan (split time savings)

- Rowan plan (bonus on time
  saved)
- Gantt plan (low guarantee plus
  bonus)

C. Appendix
Civil Service Clearinghouse
Taxonomy

The Civil Service Clearinghouse on Productivity and Organizational Effectiveness has developed a taxonomy, or classification system, for listing studies bearing on quality of worklife and productivity. The reader may find this system useful as a format for organizing the various types of interventions and descriptors relating to the subject.

15. INTERVENTION OR EXPERIMENTAL PROGRAM

RED

JOB CONTENT
- 00 Job redesign
- 01 Job enlargement
- 02 Job enrichment
- 03 Job rotation
- Industrial engineering
- 04 Time and motion study
- 05 Work simplification
- 06 Work measurement
- 07 Part-time work
- 08 Improved work methods
- 09
- 10
- 11

RED

JOB RELATIONSHIPS
- 24 Climate change
- 25 Transactional analysis
- 26 Change agent team
- 27
- 28
- 29
- 30

JOB ENVIRONMENT
- 31 Physical changes
- 32 Office landscaping
- 33
- 34
- 35

RED

Training
- 51 Training
- 52 Laboratory training
- 53 Workshops
- 54 Understudies
- 55 Lecture
- 56 Management training and development
- 57 Apprenticeship
- 58 OJT (on-job training)
- 59
- 60
- 61
- 62
- 63 Cooperative education
- 64 Work-study program
- 65 Tuition-aid plans
- 66 Career planning and counseling
- 67 Personal development and self-aids
- 68
- 69
- 70
- 71
- 72

RED

- 75 Management system improvement
- 76 Progressive budgeting and PPBS
- 77 Personnel management evaluation system
- 78 Systems analysis
- 79 Operations research
- 80 PERT
- 81 Manpower information system
- 82 Cost benefit and cost effectiveness analysis
- 83 Technological improvement and capital investments
- 84 Human resources accounting
- 85 Manpower planning

15. *INTERVENTION* OR EXPERIMENTAL PROGRAM

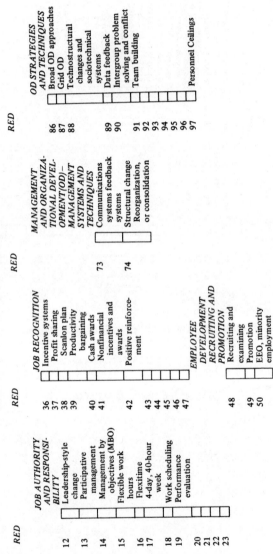

RED

JOB AUTHORITY AND RESPONSI-BILITY

12 Leadership-style change
13 Participative management
14 Management by objectives (MBO)
15 Flexible work hours
16 Flexitime
17 4-day, 40-hour week
18 Work scheduling
19 Performance evaluation
20
21
22
23

RED

JOB RECOGNITION

36 Incentive systems
37 Profit sharing
38 Scanlon plan
39 Productivity bargaining
40 Cash awards
41 Nonfinancial incentives and awards
42 Positive reinforce-ment
43
44
45
46
47

EMPLOYEE DEVELOPMENT RECRUITING AND PROMOTION

48 Recruiting and examining
49 Promotion
50 EEO, minority employment

RED

MANAGEMENT AND ORGANIZA-TIONAL DEVEL-OPMENT (OD)–MANAGEMENT SYSTEMS AND TECHNIQUES

73 Communications systems feedback systems
74 Structural change Reorganization, or consolidation

RED

OD STRATEGIES AND TECHNIQUES

86 Broad OD approaches
87 Grid OD
88 Technostructural changes and sociotechnical systems
89 Data feedback
90 Intergroup problem solving and conflict
91 Team building
92
93
94
95
96
97 Personnel Ceilings

17. DESCRIPTORS

BLUE

00	Antecedent conditions
01	Appeals
03	Audiovisual aids
04	Capital investments
05	Change agent
06	Civil service and merit systems
07	Committees
08	Collective bargaining
09	Communication systems
10	Communication techniques
11	Competition
12	Computerized information system
13	Conduct
14	Consensus
15	Consultants
16	Cost control
17	Creative thinking
18	Decision making
19	Delegation
20	Discipline
21	Employee attitudes
22	Employee conduct
23	Employee handbooks
24	Employee performance
25	Enforcement
26	EEO
27	Expectations
28	Facilities
29	Fatigue
30	Feedback
31	Feelings
32	Forecasting

BLUE

33	Functional specialization
34	Grievances
35	Goal setting
36	Group dynamics
37	Group problem solving
38	Handicapped
39	Human relations
40	Informal organization
41	Internship
42	Job satisfaction
43	Job security
44	Joint efforts
45	Labor-management relations
46	Leadership
47	Long-range planning
48	Mental health
49	Meetings and conferences
50	Minority groups
51	Morale
52	Motivation
53	Motivational factors
54	Negotiations
55	Norms
56	Objectives
57	Older workers
58	Office equipment
59	Office worker
60	Organizational climate and culture
61	Organizational conflict
62	Organizational efficiency
63	Organizational efficiency

BLUE

64	Organizational efficiency
65	Organizational performance
66	Organizational psychology
67	Organizational socialization
68	Organizational structure
69	Orientation
70	Overtime
71	Pay
72	Perception
73	Personality
74	Personnel management
75	Placement
76	Planning
77	Position management and class
78	Power (influence)
79	Problem solving
80	Project management
81	Promotion
82	Psychological stress
83	Qualifications
84	Quality control
85	Race relations
86	Records
87	Regulations
88	Reports
89	Resistance to change
90	Responsibility
91	Rest periods
92	Rewards
93	Rights and privileges
94	Risk-taking

PURPLE

95	Role
96	Safety
97	Shift work
98	Span of control
99	Staffing

PURPLE

00	Standards
01	Strikes
02	Suggestions
03	Superior-subordinate relationship
04	Supervision
05	Supervisors
06	Teamwork
07	Technological change
08	Tests
09	Time management
10	Tools and equipment
11	Traits
12	Transfer
13	Trends
14	Unions
15	Vacations
16	Women
17	Work experience
18	Work groups
19	Work measurement
20	Work standards
21	Working conditions

Bibliography

Included in this bibliography are the sources cited in this book plus some additional, relevant material not specifically referred to in the text. For a very complete annotated bibliography of books, journal articles, and reports on the subject of worklife and productivity, see *The Quality of Working Life, 1957–1972,* an 837-page bibliography prepared by UCLA's Center for Organizational Studies at the Graduate School of Management under a contract with the U.S. Department of Labor, Manpower Administration. The UCLA group has also published a companion piece to the above report: James C. Taylor's *Concepts and Problems in Studies of the Quality of Working Life,* prepared for the Manpower Administration, Department of Labor, Research and Development Contract #81-06-72-09, Washington, D.C., December 1973.

Allport, G. W., "The Psychology of Participation," *Psychological Review,* 1945, *52,* 117–132.

Beer, M., & Huse, E., *Improving Organizational Effectiveness Through*

Planned Change and Development. Unpublished study, August 1970.

Bernstein, H., "Workers Given Chance—and Output Soars." © January 26, 1973, *Los Angeles Times.*

Bluestone, J., *Worker Participation in Decision Making.* Paper presented at the Conference on Strategy, Programs and Problems of an Alternative Political Economy, Institute for Policy Studies, Washington, D.C., March 24, 1973.

Blumberg, P., *Industrial Democracy* (London: Constable, 1968).

Brief, A. P., & Aldag, R. J. "Employee Reactions to Job Characteristics: A Constructive Replication," *Journal of Applied Psychology,* 1975, *60,* 182–86.

Brower, M., *Relations Between Work Redesign, Worker Participation, Productivity, and the Quality of Working Life.* Paper presented at a meeting of the American Psychological Association, New Orleans, August 1974.

Business International S. A., *Industrial Democracy in Europe: The Challenge and Management Responses.* (Geneva, Switz.: the author, 1975.)

Carmichael, J., "Worker Participation in the U.S.," *Harvard Trade Union Program,* December 1974.

Clack, G., *Job Safety and Health* (Washington, D.C.: U.S. Department of Labor, Occupational Safety and Health Administration, July 1974).

Cummings, T. G., *Intervention Studies for Improving Productivity and the Quality of Worklife.* Paper presented at a meeting of the American Psychological Association, New Orleans, August 1974.

Cummings, T. G., Molloy, E. S., & Glen, R. H., "Intervention Strategies for Improving Productivity and the Quality of Work Life," *Organizational Dynamics* (Summer 1975) *4,* 1, 52–68 (introd. 49–51).

Cvlic, C., "Yugoslavia," *The Economist,* August 21, 1971, v–xlii.

Davis, H. R., & Salasin, S. E., "The Utilization of Evaluation." In B. Struening & M. Guttentag (Eds.), *Handbook of Evaluation Research,* Vol. I (Beverly Hills, Calif.: Sage Publications, 1975).

Davis, L. E., *The Design of Jobs* (Reprint No. 163) (Los Angeles, Calif.: UCLA, Institute of Industrial Relations, 1966).

Davis, L. E., & Cherns, A. B. (Eds.), *Quality of Working Life* (New York: Free Press, 1975).

Davis, L. E., & Taylor, J. C. (Eds.), *Design of Jobs* (Baltimore, Md.: Penguin Books, 1972).

Fairfield, R. P. (Ed.), *Humanizing the Workplace* (Buffalo, N.Y.: Prometheus Books, 1974).

Fein, M., "Job Enrichment: A Reevaluation," *Sloan Management Review*, Winter 1974, *15*, 2, 86–87.

Fitzgerald, T. H., "Why Motivation Theory Doesn't Work," *Harvard Business Review*, July–August 1971, 37–44.

Flanagan, R. J., Strauss, G., & Ulman, L., *Worker Discontent and Work Place Behavior* (Reprint No. 338) (Berkeley: University of California Institute of Industrial Relations, 1974).

Ford, R. N., *Motivation Through the Work Itself* (New York: American Management Association, 1969).

———, "Job Enrichment Lessons from AT&T," *Harvard Business Review*, January–February 1973, 96–106.

Frame, R. M., *Organizational Redesign: A Study in Transition*. Prepared for McGraw-Hill, April 1973.

Frank, L. L., & Hackman, J. R., *A Failure of Job Enrichment: The Case of the Change That Wasn't* (Tech. Report No. 8) (New Haven, Conn.: Yale University School of Organization and Management, March 1975).

Frost, C. F., Wakeley, J. H., & Rug, R. A., *The Scanlon Plan for Organization Development: Identity, Participation and Equity* (East Lansing, Mich.: Michigan State University Press, 1974).

Garson, B., *All the Livelong Day: The Meaning and Demeaning of Routine Work* (New York: Doubleday & Co., 1975.)

Ginzberg, E., *The Manpower Connection: Education and Work* (Cambridge, Mass.: Harvard University Press, 1975).

Glaser, E. M., *Improving the Quality of Worklife . . . And in the Process, Improving Productivity* (Washington, D.C.: U.S. Department of Labor, Manpower Administration, April 1974).

Glaser, E. M., & Marks, J., *The Meaning of Work . . . To Five Different Categories of Young Men* (Washington, D.C.: Department of Health, Education and Welfare, National Institute of Mental Health, May 1972).

Glaser, E. M., & Ross, H., *Productive Employment of the Disadvantaged: Guidelines for Action* (Washington, D.C.: U.S. Department of Labor, Manpower Administration, February 1973).

Glueck, W., & Kavran, D., "The Yugoslav Management System," *Management International Review*, 1971–1972, 3–17.

———, "Worker Management in Yugoslavia," *Business Horizons*, February 1972, 31–39.

Goldmann, R. B., *Work Values: Six Americans in a Swedish Plant* (New York: Ford Foundation, March 1975).

Gomberg, W. "Job Satisfaction: Sorting Out the Nonsense," *AFL-CIO American Federationist,* June 1973, 14–19.

Hackman, J. R., "Is Job Enrichment Just a Fad?" *Harvard Business Review,* September–October 1975, pp. 129–38.

———, "On the Coming Demise of Job Enrichment." In *Man and Work in Society* (New York: Van Nostrand-Reinhold, in press).

Hackman, J. R., & Lawler, E. E., "Employee Reactions to Job Characteristics," *Journal of Applied Psychology* Monograph, 1971, *55,* 3.

Hackman, J. R., & Oldham, G. R., *Motivation Through the Design of Work: Test of a Theory* (Tech. Report No. 6) (New Haven, Conn.: Yale University, Department of Administrative Sciences, December 1974).

Hackman, J. R., Oldham, G. R., Janson, R., & Purdy, K., *A New Strategy for Job Enrichment* (Tech. Report No. 3) (New Haven, Conn.: Yale University, Department of Administrative Sciences, December 1974).

Harriman, B., "Up and Down the Communication Ladder," *Harvard Business Review,* September–October 1974, 133–151.

Herrick, N., & Maccoby, M., "Humanizing Work: A Priority Goal of the 1970s." In L. E. Davis & A. B. Cherns (Eds.), *Quality of Working Life* (New York: Free Press, 1975).

Herzberg, F., *Work and the Nature of Man* (Cleveland, Ohio: World Publishing, 1966).

———, "One More Time: How Do You Motivate Employees?" *Harvard Business Review,* January–February 1968, 53–62.

Herzberg, F., Mausner, B., & Snyderman, B., *The Motivation to Work* (New York: John Wiley & Sons, 1959).

Hill, P., *Towards a New Philosophy of Management* (New York: Barnes & Noble, 1972).

Horvat, B., "Yugoslav Economic Policy in the Post-War Period: Problems, Ideals, Institutional Development," *American Economic Review,* 1969, 71–169.

"How Workers Can Get Eight-Hours Pay for Five," *Business Week,* May 19, 1975, 52v ff.

Hoxie, R. F., *Scientific Management and Labor* (New York: Appleton, 1920).

Hulin, C. L., & Blood, M. R., "Job Enlargement, Individual Difference and Worker Responses," *Psychological Bulletin,* 1968, *69,* 41–55.

Janson, R., *Job Enrichment Trial—Data Processing Department Analysis and Results in an Insurance Organization.* Paper presented at the International Conference on the Quality of Working Life, Arden House, Harriman. New York, September 1972.

Jenkins, D., *Job Power—Blue and White Collar Democracy* (New York: Doubleday, 1973).

Juran, J. M., "QC Circles in Japan," *Industrial Quality Control,* January 1967, 329–336.

Kahn, R. L., "The Meaning of Work: Interpretation and Proposals for Measurement." In A. A. Campbell & P. E. Converse (Eds.), *The Human Meaning of Social Change* (New York: Basic Books, 1972).

Katzell, R., *Structural Approaches to Increasing Both Job Satisfaction and Productivity.* Paper presented at a meeting of the American Psychological Association, New Orleans, August 1974.

Katzell, R. A., Yankelovich, D., *et al., An Evaluation of Policy Related Research on Relations between Industrial Organization, Job Satisfaction and Productivity* (Washington, D.C.: National Science Foundation, 1975).

Katzell, R. A., & Yankelovich, D., *et al., Work, Productivity, and Job Satisfaction* (New York: The Psychological Corporation, 1975).

Ketchum, L. D., *Humanizing of Work.* Paper presented at the American Association for the Advancement of Science symposium, Philadelphia, December 1972.

Kochan, T. A., Lipsky, D. B., & Dyer, L., "Collective Bargaining and the Quality of Work: The Views of Local Union Activists," *Industrial Relations Research Association 27th Annual Winter Proceedings* (Madison, Wisc.: IRRA, December 1974), 159–162.

Kristol, J., "Job Satisfaction: Daydream or Alienation?" *The Federationist,* February 1973, 11–12.

Lawler, E. E., *What Do Employees Really Want?* Paper presented at the American Psychological Association Convention, Montreal, 1973.

———, *Pay Participation and Organizational Change.* Paper presented at the Symposium on the Hawthorne Studies, Chicago, November 1974.

Lawler, E. E., & Hackman, J. R., "Impact of Employee Participation in the Development of Pay Incentive Plans," *Journal of Applied Psychology,* 1969, *53,* 6, 467–471.

Lesieur, F. G., & Puckett, E. S., "The Scanlon Plan Has Proved Itself," *Harvard Business Review,* September–October 1969, 109.

Levitan, S., & Johnson, W., "Job Design, Reform, Enrichment: Exploring the Limitations," *Monthly Labor Review,* 1973, *96,* 35–41.

Likert, R., *The Human Organization: Its Management and Value* (New York: McGraw-Hill, 1967).

Lindholm, R., *Job Reform in Sweden: Conclusions from 500 Shop Floor Projects,* D. Jenkins (Ed. and Trans.) (Stockholm: Swedish Employers' Confederation, 1975).

Lupton, T., "Efficiency and the Quality of Worklife: The Technology of Reconciliation," *Organizational Dynamics,* 1975, *4,* 2, 68–80.

Lytle, W., "Obstacles to Job and Organization Design: A Case." In *Quality of Working Life,* L. E. Davis & A. B. Cherns (Eds.) (New York: Free Press, 1975).

Marrow, A. (Ed.), *The Failure of Success* (New York: AMACOM, 1972).

Mire, J., "Improving Working Life—The Role of European Unions," *Monthly Labor Review,* September 1974.

Moore, B., *A Plant-Wide Productivity Plan in Action: Three Years of Experience with the Scanlon Plan* (Washington, D.C.: National Commission on Productivity and Work Quality, May 1975).

Myers, M. S., *Every Employee a Manager* (New York: McGraw-Hill, 1971).

Oldham, G. R., "Job Characteristics and Internal Motivation: The Moderating Effect of Interpersonal and Individual Variables," *Human Relations,* in press.

Oldham, G. R., Hackman, J. R., & Pearce, J. L., *Conditions Under Which Employees Respond Positively to Enriched Work* (Tech. Report No. 4) (New Haven, Conn.: Yale University, September 1975.)

Paul, W., Robertson, K., & Herzberg, F., "Job Enrichment Pays Off," *Harvard Business Review,* March–April 1969, 61.

Price, C. R., *New Directions in the World of Work.* A Conference Report. (Kalamazoo, Mich.: W. E. Upjohn Institute for Employment Research, 1971).

Quinn, R. P., Levitin, T., & Eden, D., *The Multi-Million Dollar Misunderstanding: An Attempt to Reduce Turnover Among Disadvantaged Workers* (Ann Arbor: University of Michigan, Survey Research Center, 1971).

Quinn, R. P., Staines, G. L., & McCullough, M. R., *Job Satisfaction: Is There a Trend?* (Research Monograph No. 30) (Washington, D.C.: U.S. Department of Labor, Manpower Administration, 1974).

Reif, W. E., & Evans, R. J., "The Current Status of Job Enrichment in Insurance Companies," *Best's Review,* October 1973, 82ff.

Reif, W. E., Ferrazzi, D. N., & Evans, R. J., Jr., "Job Enrichment: Who Uses It and Why," *Business Horizons,* February 1974.

Reif, W. E., & Luthans, F., "Does Job Enrichment Really Pay Off?" *California Management Review,* 1972, *15*, 1, 30–37.

————, "Job Enrichment: Long on Theory, Short on Practice," *Organizational Dynamics,* 1974, *2*, 3, 30–38.

Reif, W. E., & Monczka, R. M., "Job Redesign: A Contingency Approach to Implementation," *Personnel,* May–June 1974.

Report on Activities to the President and Congress, National Commission on Productivity and Work Quality, July 1974.

Report on Federal Productivity (Vols. I and II), Joint Financial Management Improvement Program, June 1974.

Report to National Commission on Productivity re: Diagnostic/Job Enrichment Study in Social Security Administration, David Sirota Associates, June 1974.

Roche, W., & MacKinnon, N., "Motivating People with Meaningful Work," *Harvard Business Review,* May–June 1970, 97–110.

Rosow, J. M. (Ed.), *The Worker and the Job: Coping with Change* (Englewood Cliffs, N.J.: Prentice-Hall, 1974).

Rush, H. M., *Behavioral Science: Concepts and Management Applications* (New York: The Conference Board, 1969).

————, *Job Design for Motivation* (New York: The Conference Board, 1971).

Sheppard, H. L., & Herrick, N. Q., *Where Have All the Robots Gone?* (New York: Free Press, 1972).

Sherman, G., "The Quality of Work Troika in Perspective," *Personnel Administrator,* May 1975.

Sirota, D., & Wolfson, A., "Job Enrichment: What Are the Obstacles?" *Personnel,* May–June 1972.

Steere, D. V., & Brown, T. W., *Work and Contemplation* (New York: Harper, 1957).

Strauss, G., & Rosenstein, E., "Workers' Participation: A Critical View," *Industrial Relations,* 1970, *9*, 197–213.

Survey Research Center, University of Michigan, *Survey of Working Conditions* (Washington, D.C.: U.S. Department of Labor, Employment Standards Administration, August 1971).

Taylor, J. C., *Concepts and Problems in Studies of the Quality of Working Life* (Los Angeles: UCLA, Graduate School of Management, December 1973).

————, *Experiments in Work System Design: Economic and Human Results* (Los Angeles: UCLA, Center for Quality of Working Life, June 1975).

Terkel, S., *Working: People Talk About What They Do All Day and How They Feel About What They Do* (New York: Pantheon, 1974).

Trist, E. L., Higgings, G., Murray H., & Pollack, A. G., *Organizational Choice* (London: Tavistock Publications, 1965).

U.S. Department of Health, Education and Welfare, *Work in America* (Cambridge, Mass.: MIT Press, 1972).

Vanek, J., *The Participatory Economy: An Evolutionary Hypothesis and a Developmental Study.* Unpublished study, Cornell University, 1972.

Vough, C., *Tapping the Human Resource* (New York: AMACOM, 1975).

Vroom, V. H., "Industrial Social Psychology." In G. Lindzey & E. Aronson (Eds.), *The Handbook of Social Psychology* (2nd edition, Vol. 5) (Reading, Mass.: Addison-Wesley, 1969).

Walton, R. E., "The Diffusion of New Work Structures: Explaining Why Success Didn't Take," *Organizational Dynamics,* Winter 1975, *3,* 3–22.

————, "How to Counter Alienation in the Plant," *Harvard Business Review,* November–December 1972.

————, "Improving the Quality of Work Life," *Harvard Business Review,* May–June 1974, 12ff.

————, "Innovative Restructuring of Work." In J. M. Rosow (Ed.), *The Worker and the Job: Coping with Change* (Englewood Cliffs, N.J.: Prentice-Hall, 1974).

Wanous, J. P., "Individual Differences and Reactions to Job Characteristics," *Journal of Applied Psychology,* 1974, *59,* 616–22.

Watson, G., & Glaser, E., "What We Have Learned About Planning for Change," *Management Review,* November 1965, *54,* 34–46.

Weinberg, A., *A Worker Exchange Program at Saab-Scania* (New

York: Cornell University, School of Industrial and Labor Relations, 1975).

Whitsett, D., "Where Are Your Unenriched Jobs?" *Harvard Business Review,* January–February 1975, 74–80.

Winpisinger, W., "Job Satisfaction: A Union Response," *The Federationist,* February 1973, 8–10.

Wolf, M. G., "The Relationship of Content and Context Factors to Attitudes Toward Company and Job," *Personnel Psychology,* 1967, *20,* 121–132.

Wood, M. T., Rasmussen, J. E., & Lawler, E. E., *Federally Sponsored Research on the Quality of Working Life: Planning, Support, and Products.* (Washington, D.C.: Department of Labor, 1975).

Yankelovich, D., *The Changing Values on Campus* (New York: Washington Square Press, March 1972).

———, "The Meaning of Work." In J. M. Rosow (Ed.), *The Worker and the Job: Coping with Change* (Englewood Cliffs, N.J.: Prentice-Hall, 1974).

Index